Marriage on the Border

Marriage on the Border

Love, Mutuality, and Divorce in the Upper South during the Civil War

Allison Dorothy Fredette

UNIVERSITY PRESS OF KENTUCKY

Scholarly publisher for the Commonwealth,
serving Bellarmine University, Berea College, Centre
College of Kentucky, Eastern Kentucky University,
The Filson Historical Society, Georgetown College,
Kentucky Historical Society, Kentucky State University,
Morehead State University, Murray State University,
Northern Kentucky University, Transylvania University,
University of Kentucky, University of Louisville,
and Western Kentucky University.

Editorial and Sales Offices: The University Press of Kentucky
663 South Limestone Street, Lexington, Kentucky 40508-4008
www.kentuckypress.com

Maps by Carly Everhart. All GIS data retrieved from: Steven Manson,
Jonathan Schroeder, David Van Riper, and Steven Ruggles.
IPUMS National Historical Geographic Information System: Version 13.0 [Database].
Minneapolis: University of Minnesota, 2018. http://doi.org/10.18128/D050.V13.0.

Cataloging-in-Publication data is available from the Library of Congress.

ISBN 978-0-8131-7915-5 (hardcover : alk. paper)
ISBN 978-0-8131-7918-6 (epub)
ISBN 978-0-8131-7917-9 (pdf)

This book is printed on acid-free paper meeting
the requirements of the American National Standard
for Permanence in Paper for Printed Library Materials.

Manufactured in the United States of America.

Member of the Association
of University Presses

To William, my partner in all things

Contents

Introduction

A Blended Family

Amanda Sterling was born on the western edge of the Ohio River in the early 1830s. Her small township of Pease, Ohio, lay across the river from the industrial city of Wheeling, Virginia, and her early life reflected the fluidity of this watery boundary between two states. By her late teens, she had worked as a hired girl in homes from Bridgeport and Martins Ferry, Ohio, to Wheeling.[1] By various accounts, Sterling was a hard worker with a moral reputation to match her name. According to one of her former employers, she was as "fine" and "modest" a girl "as we ever had about our house." During a time when the United States was experiencing a series of religious revivals, she regularly attended Sunday school and the local church.[2]

Sometime in the late 1850s, Amanda Sterling crossed the Ohio River and settled in Wheeling, the community in which she would remain until her death. There she met Ephraim Trimble, a widower and father of three young children, who began courting her. To Amanda, Ephraim probably seemed like an excellent choice for a potential husband. A few years older than she, Ephraim was a property owner and an engineer on one of the many steamboats that traveled to and from the river city. His occupation may have seemed both exciting and lucrative, since the river was in many ways the backbone of the community. It is not surprising then that in the early months of 1861, Amanda Sterling and Ephraim Trimble married at her brother's home in Ohio.[3] The pair quickly returned to Wheeling to begin their lives together, settling next door to his mother and sister in the sixth ward of the city.

Within a year, Amanda gave birth to their first child—a girl named Alice. Another daughter, Ida, arrived two years later.[4] As the Civil War broke out and tore apart the nation around them, Amanda and Ephraim Trimble's life carried on without much disruption from the growing crisis.

While Ephraim was listed as "Class I" and subject to military duty, he never served in the war, although occasionally the Union government commissioned into service the steamboats on which he worked.[5] Still, even if the Trimbles largely avoided the military conflict that consumed so many others, they could not avoid the domestic conflict that increasingly consumed their marriage.

According to accounts from friends of the husband and wife, the Trimbles had an abusive relationship—perhaps on both sides. Amanda claimed that Ephraim had physically assaulted her on multiple occasions but denied responding in kind. Ephraim made no secret of his treatment of his wife. At friends' homes and in local stores, he bragged about his actions to other men. When Ephraim complained that his wife had failed to properly care for his children, some curious neighbors and family members dropped in on Amanda to verify or refute the gossip, most finding little evidence of a problem.[6]

As his frustration with his marriage grew, Ephraim made his intention to leave Amanda known throughout their community. On one occasion, when walking with his sister-in-law, Elizabeth Trimble, he pointed up to a nearby house and declared that if he could get the occupant, Eliza Hoffman, to run away with him, he would "go the next day, by God." Emphatically, Ephraim told Elizabeth that he loved Eliza's "little finger better than he did his wife's whole body." Ephraim also used his position as an engineer to woo Hoffman, sending her fresh butter and eggs from the steamboats, as well as valentines. As far as neighbors could tell, however, Hoffman rebuffed his advances.[7]

In mid-1864, however, he began wooing another woman—Nancy Sherman, a chambermaid on a steamboat.[8] Perhaps under the influence of this new relationship, in August 1864 Ephraim finally made good on his threats and abandoned Amanda and their two children. Nearly universally, neighbors reported that Amanda had been left in a "destitute" condition. Charlotte Rogers, Caroline Mooney, and many others provided the family with clothing, food, and money. Her condition was so bad that Amanda's neighbors went to the overseer of the poor, John Goudy, and begged him to assist her. For months, family members and friends searched the towns along the Ohio River before they located Ephraim Trimble and Nancy Sherman in Zanesville, Ohio, posing as a married couple with four children.[9] At this point, Amanda began to consider whether or not to divorce her unfaithful husband.

She waited two years to file for divorce. During that time, Ephraim continued to float (literally) in and out of Wheeling, leaving for months to travel on and across the Ohio River. When he stayed in town, he lived with his mother and sister on the same lot—and in the same building—as his estranged wife. Finally, in February 1867, Amanda filed her formal petition for divorce, citing Ephraim's adultery with Nancy and his failure to support his family. She asked for a divorce, as well as custody and alimony.[10] Within a week, the court granted part of her request, requiring Ephraim to support his wife and her suit at the rate of fifty dollars a month. Their legal battle, however, had just begun.

For the next three years, the couple broadcast the most intimate details of their relationship before the court and the local community. Dozens of neighbors testified on either side, and court scribes spilled ink over hundreds of pages of documents describing their case. Ephraim accused Amanda of being lazy and violent, of being a bad wife and mother, of committing incest with her nineteen-year-old nephew, and of having an abortion in her days as a servant. Amanda denied all of his salacious charges and, in turn, highlighted his adulterous ways and his new family across the river. As residents from up and down German Street appeared in court to testify, they opened a window onto this industrial community—its shops, workplaces, and streets. As they recounted details of this relationship, they spoke in German-inflected English and with Yankee lilts in their speech and sometimes with southern drawls. They spoke of factory life, of serving as domestics in wealthy urban homes, and even hinted at the presence of free black residents in Wheeling, just at the edges of these white working-class lives. Their stories are just a few from this conflicted region that was struggling to assert a collective identity in the face of remarkable diversity.

At times, the enormous case threatened to swallow up its two central participants—Amanda and Ephraim Trimble. And yet, in early 1870, the court reviewed all of the depositions and arguments and made a ruling. Amanda received her divorce. She and her two daughters remained in Wheeling for the rest of their lives, seemingly separate from Ephraim. Only death would reunite them, as both found themselves buried alongside their many nosy neighbors in the city's Peninsula Cemetery.

In some respects, every person's story is unique. We are all individuals with our own complex motivations, thought processes, and memories. Amanda Sterling Trimble and Ephraim Trimble are no exception. Complicated and messy people, their impact on the historical record boils down to one divorce case in the Ohio County Circuit Court, disappointing those who want to learn more about their lives. True, their case itself is voluminous compared to many others available to historians. Their acrimony led to dozens of pages of testimony from friends, relatives, and neighbors, and both spouses swore out statements themselves, giving us an unusually rich portrait of this marriage. Yet, these documents, a few census records, and their own tombstones are nearly all that remain of the vibrant, albeit violent, Trimbles.

In other ways, however, we are all products of our communities, living reflections of the attitudes, beliefs, and behaviors that our society values at a particular time and place. Amanda and Ephraim Trimble, in that regard, are representatives of their specific environment—the nineteenth-century border South. Their story and choices represent the culture in which they lived for decades. Amanda Sterling came of age in the 1850s, traveling back and forth across the Ohio River into various homes and communities. As a steamboat engineer, Ephraim Trimble would have spent most of his adult life on this river, a route that also served as his outlet from a problematic marriage. For the Trimbles, the river represented opportunity, income, and escape, an obviously potent combination during an era when the Ohio River literally was the path to freedom for so many enslaved on southern plantations. For those living in the Ohio River Valley, the waterway served as both a border and a marker of their blended communities, places that saw themselves as neither southern nor northern, eastern nor western, but as a middle ground in a rapidly dividing nation.[11]

During the mid-nineteenth century, residents of the nation's middle border fashioned and maintained their own particular regional identity. This identity set them apart, in their own minds and in reality, from the quickly dividing northern and southern regions of the United States. Border men—and women—inhabited a fluid, blended world. The river that lay in their midst brought together multiple geographic zones and also provided an excellent mode of transportation both into and within the region. These migrants into the border brought with them their own cultural sensibilities and fused them into a new regional identity. Fluid borders shaped the political, religious, and economic attitudes of their citizens, directly influencing the path of secession, the conduct of the Civil War, and the fraught reconciliation process. Yet, as Amanda and Ephraim's story reveals, an important element of this story has not been thoroughly examined: the impact of regional identity on the inner and intimate lives of those living along the border. An area from roughly Missouri to Maryland that encompassed Kentucky and the westernmost sections of Virginia, the border South's geographic centrality tied together disparate sections of the country, and its residents came from unusually diverse economic and cultural backgrounds. Ultimately, the level of cross-regional contact in the border South—sometimes called "the crossroads of America"—created what Aaron Astor terms a "heterogeneous border culture," one that very much affected residents' understanding of marriage and marital roles.[12]

This book contributes to a growing conversation about the nineteenth-century border and its unique culture.[13] Specifically, this book addresses the impact this identity had upon the formation of marriages and the marital roles of white border southerners living in Kentucky and West Virginia before, during, and after the Civil War. How did border southerners' hybrid culture shape their household identities and roles? How did these views differ from those of their neighbors in other parts of the South, such as Virginia? And finally, did the Civil War, that vast and devastating conflict, reshape or challenge their views? Using sources such as divorce records, personal diaries, correspondence, and prescriptive literature, this book paints a vivid portrait of border South marriages built on a fascinating blend of mutuality, individualism, and contractualism. These tendencies sat uneasily alongside a hierarchically racialized society, one founded on slavery. This contradiction would not have been possible in a more homogenous and less adaptive region. Border southerners' stories complicate our understanding of southern life in the mid-nineteenth century. It is vital that we continue to explore the concept of "many Souths," as well as how these variations created particular moments of opportunity to expand and remake the gendered assumptions and behaviors of residents.

Marriage on the Border makes five central claims: that white border southerners in Kentucky and West Virginia drew upon newly popular ideals of mutuality and individualism in their marriages; that these philosophies, although found in other southern homes in this era, led to differing behaviors in border southerners, namely, higher rates of divorce than in other eastern or southern communities; that these somewhat progressive attitudes toward divorce and marriage did not mean that border southerners erased all vestiges of hierarchy in their homes, especially since these remained societies with slaves until the end of the Civil War; that residents' border attitudes and identity created fertile ground for such household adaptability and fusion; and that their ability to balance these two seemingly contradictory ideals in their antebellum households allowed them to maintain their understandings of divorce despite postwar threats to their racial system.

This book places particular emphasis on the role of mutuality and contractualism in the construction of household roles and the use of divorce. While previous scholars have touched on these themes, none have explored how the regional identity of the border allowed for their greater use in southern communities, usually portrayed as more regressive and hierarchical than other American regions. In an era when patriarchy still reigned supreme, mutuality did not imply equality. In households built on mutuality, men and women sought balance in their relationships; they valued one another's contributions and gendered characteristics, while also asserting the value of women's education and domestic authority. Mutuality recognized women as competent, whole individuals within the household, even if it still denied them the same access to legal and political rights as men. Despite this, it was nonetheless a pivotal step forward in the long walk toward full equality in marriage. This is not to suggest that some small sense of mutuality did not exist in other parts of the South. Certainly, the ethic of companionate marriage, which often featured a sense of mutuality at its core, pervaded the entire Atlantic world during the early nineteenth century. However, this book reveals the striking and unique ways in which border southerners acted upon that philosophy.

Similarly, border southerners viewed their relationships through the lens of contractualism, meaning that they saw marriage as potentially impermanent—under the right circumstances.[14] Whereas some Americans viewed marriage as permanent because of its sacramental nature and others believed that allowing household members to dissolve their relationship would provide a dangerous precedent in a slaveholding society, border southerners put legal measures in place or manipulated a restrictive legal code in such a way as to allow both husbands and wives to end their marriage contract, sometimes surprisingly easily. Most scholarly attention has fallen on so-called divorce havens, such as Indiana and Nevada, but Kentucky provided its own flexible divorce statutes. Additionally, the story of West Virginia and Appalachian Virginia demonstrates the ways in which residents could fulfill their contractualist ideals, even if the law itself restricted their actions. This pointed use of contractualism would not have been possible if border southerners had not lived in a society that embraced the full implications of mutuality and individualism.

Mid-nineteenth-century border South men and women received a myriad of recommendations about proper attitudes toward marriage, gender roles within the household, and divorce. Living in a region with a greater degree of cultural and geographic diversity, border South residents had more cognitive flexibility when shaping their own marital roles and households. They could choose to follow social patterns from numerous sources and even combine them to form a new system. While the growth in popularity of mutuality and contractualism in the border South paralleled the acceptance of these philosophies in other parts of the United States, their integration into relationships was more pronounced in the border South than in other regions. Even if border southerners were not alone in deploying the language of companionship in their marriages, they chose to employ it differently from their eastern neighbors in Virginia, for example. Specifically, their divorce laws and their manipulation of that law proved their fealty to these ideals more than the empty platitudes of lovers in other parts of the United States. Ultimately, their hybrid border culture allowed citizens of this region to establish and maintain relationships built on mutuality, contractualism, and individualism, alongside a hierarchical slave system. Their adaptability also affected their post–Civil War experience. Because of their mixed border identity and pre–Civil War use of this household structure, many border South residents maintained this marital behavior in the postwar years, despite the social and racial disruption of emancipation.

This book analyzes the construction of white marriages and marital roles in the mid-nineteenth-century border South, specifically portions of Kentucky, West Virginia, and Appalachian Virginia, from the late antebellum period through the early years of Reconstruction.[15] During this era, Kentucky, West Virginia, and Appalachian Virginia residents lived along an increasingly contentious border between the northern and southern regions of the country. At the same time, as Americans spilled into the western frontier, the Ohio River Valley transitioned from a former frontier environment into a jumping-off point for these migrants. Yet the borders that, in many ways, defined their identities were not merely geographic and, soon, political. Much like other international and intranational borders, the region's role as a place of contact and exchange, as well as its mixture of economic, political, social, racial, and ethnic differences, helped create its uniquely blended culture and influenced residents' marital attitudes.[16]

Border South residents embraced their multifaceted identities, contrasting themselves with those "up north," "down south," or "in the west."

They were something all their own—set apart, and yet very much made up of those other regions.[17] Americans crisscrossed the growing nation through the border South, moving west and south, back and forth. In addition, in the border South, slavery coexisted with a burgeoning industrial economy, and immigrants worked alongside free blacks and hired enslaved people. Kinship ties extended from border South citizens throughout the North, Midwest, and South. Furthermore, having once been the edge of the early republic, the border South still retained many of its frontier ways, even as it matured into established states.[18] Border South citizens glorified heroes like Henry Clay, whose penchant for moderation and compromise was legendary, and turned away from the strong "isms" of the rest of the nineteenth-century United States.[19] Perhaps only naturally they also embraced fusion within their own homes, forming marriages based on mutuality in a state that still featured a hierarchical slave system. It was their decreased (though still firm) attachment to this slave system and their strong understanding of their identity as border residents that allowed them to combine these two ideals.[20]

Although a few black couples, both free and enslaved, make their way into these pages, their stories are not the focus of this book. Enslaved couples could not marry in any of these three states in the antebellum era, although they would legalize their relationships by the thousands in the early years following the war.[21] This opportunity and the sometimes less-studied opportunity to legally end their marriages changed freedpeople's lives and their relationship with the law. Certainly, this change created a reaction in white southerners, causing some to cling ever tighter to the restrictions of patriarchal marriages, and the second half of this book explores that reaction. However, an examination of how regional differences shaped black southerners' relationships deserves its own work.

The Kentucky, West Virginia, and Appalachian Virginia marriages described in these pages were characterized by mutuality, love, and respect.[22] Whereas previous generations of men and women relied on familial approval to make an economically beneficial match, nineteenth-century lovers began to turn inward, demanding decision-making power over the selection of their future spouses and seeking marriages of affection and devotion.[23] The distribution and deployment of these ideals throughout the United States was complex, however. Although many southern relationships were fully companionate and loving as early as the late eighteenth century, white southerners still had a strong conception of patriarchal authority and hierarchy within the home.[24] While not all southern marriages were strictly patriarchal during the mid-nineteenth century, some regional variation did exist, at least in the ideal.[25] Nina Silber, for example, argues, "Northerners really did believe that there were certain ways to be 'men' and 'women' and that southerners had a pretty poor grasp on what they were." Southerners, not surprisingly, felt the reverse.[26] In practice, this meant that divorce was often much harder to obtain in the nineteenth-century South than in parts of New England. While courting couples, even in the South, might profess themselves to be future partners and loving companions, the recognition and rights given to aggrieved spouses, especially wives, differed. The belief in many parts of the South, Victoria Bynum has argued, was that "if slavery . . . were to remain stable, so must the family."[27] In the border South, however, changes in the familial structure did not lead to the dissolution of slavery, and in the postwar years, an attempt to return to their antebellum southern ways did not necessarily lead to a return to patriarchy and hierarchy in all areas of the household.[28] In the case of border southerners, to use a cliché, actions spoke louder than words. By writing laws that granted divorce in a broad range of cases or by manipulating the law to get a desired separation, Kentuckians, West Virginians, and Appalachian Virginians demonstrated that a belief in individualism (recognition of the rights of both spouses) and contractualism (recognition of the impermanence of social bonds) was not just an ideal but a lived reality.

However, divorce law in the United States was not distinguished simply by northern and southern divisions. If differences in divorce law by state merely reflected a state's position above or below the Mason–Dixon Line, then the stories in this book could be explained away exclusively by each place's connection with the South or even slavery, rather than their border identity. And yet, New York had the dubious honor of having one of the most stringent divorce laws in the nineteenth-century United States. As Norma Basch has shown, scores of New Yorkers made the trek from their eastern home to the relative wilds of Indiana to obtain a "quickie" divorce (this was a decidedly slower process than it would be for twentieth-century Americans who traveled to Nevada for the same purpose).[29] During the antebellum era, as new states entered the Union and the country's borders were pushed westward, these new states slowly began to liberalize their divorce statutes, leaving unhappily married New Yorkers in the strange position of sharing some of the same legal frustrations as frustrated spouses in coastal southern states.

During this period, western states also expanded access to the vote (at least for white men). In places like the former Northwest Territory, residents viewed themselves as more democratic than eastern elites, and rejected their established hierarchies. The West became known as a land of (white) opportunity and social mobility. Increasingly this drew a diverse group of migrants, including German and Irish immigrants. However, there was a darker side to this ideology, and midwesterners often displayed a racism no more benign than that of their southern counterparts. By the 1840s and 1850s, some embraced the "Free Soil" philosophy, which argued that the region's lack of slavery enabled an equality of labor and greater social mobility in the region. However, they denied these advantages to formerly enslaved people, arguing that this was the only way to achieve true equality for white men. States like Indiana and Illinois repealed voting laws that gave black men access to the polls and even passed laws banning new black residents from entering the state. Many midwesterners saw their region as a white man's paradise.[30] Midwesterners' antihierarchical attitudes trickled down into their family law. The Ohio River Valley, including the border South states of Kentucky and West Virginia, absorbed much of this mentality. Just as border residents in midwestern states both expanded and restricted access to the polls, border southerners chipped away at some household hierarchies, while maintaining their racialized system.

In the field of border scholarship, debate continues over the proper name and dimensions of this region. Christopher Phillips uses the terms "middle border" and "West" interchangeably and includes those states "bordering the Ohio and Missouri Rivers west of the Appalachian Mountains and south and east of present-day Nebraska, Iowa, Wisconsin, and Michigan." He argues persuasively for the inclusion of both free and slave states in this definition, as these borders were never as distinct as they seem in hindsight. Bridget Ford analyzes the "imagined bonds" that tenuously held the region together, using the term "Ohio-Kentucky borderland" for her study. Others, like Aaron Astor and Diane Mutti Burke, focus on one or two states and use the terms "border" and "border states" interchangeably throughout their work.[31]

For this book, I have chosen to focus on Kentucky, as well as the area including and bordering the eventual state of West Virginia. First, I wanted to analyze states in which border flexibility would be tested and demonstrated to its fullest dimension, namely, states where the slave system still existed by the time of the Civil War. For this reason, I chose states in the southern part of this region and also use the term "border South" for my particular area of study. Additionally, Kentucky, West Virginia, and Virginia (which serves as a useful comparison) also shared familial and legal ties, Kentucky and West Virginia having been carved out of the original eighteenth-century boundaries of Virginia. Because of its ties to Virginia and its distinction as a relatively older Ohio River Valley state (having been founded in 1792), Kentucky has often been labeled as more conservative or less radical than its western border counterparts, such as Missouri. However, Kentuckians drew upon their western, as much as their southern, identity and saw themselves as distinct from the eastern slaveholding Upper South states. Second, choosing border *South* states also allowed me to analyze the transition in these states from slavery to emancipation and its impact on white household roles. Kentucky never formally seceded, declaring itself neutral at the war's outset. West Virginians famously created their state during the Civil War, breaking away from Confederate Virginia. Despite their resistance to the Confederacy, however, many in these states still hoped to keep slavery intact. Black emancipation was no simpler—and in fact, could be decidedly more complex—in states that did not secede. This pattern, which complicated the impact of black freedom on white household roles, is addressed in this book.

By the mid-nineteenth century, Kentucky, western Virginia, and Appalachian Virginia displayed traits that were common in what Ira Berlin has labeled "societies with slaves."[32] Slaveholdings were smaller than in other regions of the South, and the line between slave and free grew increasingly fluid in the late antebellum era. However, slavery still affected social relationships throughout the region, and as the boundary between free and slave became blurred, many found the boundary between white and black that much more important. Additionally, although most residents of these counties, and many individuals mentioned in this study, did not own slaves, the presence of slavery in the state and its connection with the local economy had an impact on the entire culture, including individuals who themselves were not slaveholders. Nonetheless, being a society with slaves, rather than a traditional slave society, was part of the border culture that allowed ideas of mutuality and contractualism to flourish.

As stated, a comparison with Kentucky and West Virginia's eastern neighbor, Virginia, suggests how these more strongly self-identified "border" regions differed. Specifically, residents of Kentucky and West Virginia differed from their Virginia neighbors in the extent to which they sought mutuality in their relationships and the degree to which they accepted divorce, through an embrace of contractualism. Virginia was an example of the eastern mentality toward hierarchy and order, as well as a southern state more strongly committed to the institution of slavery. Unlike Kentucky and West Virginia, Virginians ultimately joined the Confederacy, a southern nation formed to protect the institution of slavery. While some Virginians formed passionately loving relationships featuring mutual respect and affection, marriages in Virginia tended to be built on a structure of patriarchy and female obedience. Virginia courts allowed fewer divorces and created harsher requirements to obtain legal separations than did courts in Kentucky and West Virginia. Virginians also fought more strongly to maintain the "traditional" structure of marriage in the face of Confederate defeat and emancipation than did Kentuckians and West Virginians. Letters and court documents from Virginians reveal how they interpreted and acted on the philosophy of mutuality and contractualism differently from their border neighbors. The fluid border culture of Kentucky and West Virginia helped shape citizens' attitudes toward marriage and their postwar experiences. Because of their central location, devotion to moderation, semidiversified economy, migration and kinship patterns, and particular wartime experience, Kentucky and West Virginia make excellent case studies for an examination of marriage on the border, before, during, and after a wrenching civil war. Appalachian Virginia, lying in between these two groups, reveals a region torn between its border neighbors and its eastern Virginia counterparts.

Uncovering the innermost thoughts of lovers and spouses is a daunting task for a historian. Most of us rarely know our own gender biases and assumptions, let alone commit these sentiments to paper. Historians have to read between the lines, pull out snippets of text here and there, and weave together a portrait of a society based on fragmentary evidence. Especially in the midst of courtship, people often disguise their true selves, saying what they believe another person wants to hear, rather than what they really think. In many ways, sources on courtship and marriage should be read as more aspirational than factual. Because of this, I use a broad range of sources, including manuscripts and legal sources. Diaries, correspondence, prescriptive literature, published and unpublished speeches, and essays reveal the complex perspective of middle-class and elite border southerners toward the formation of relationships, as well as the behavior of spouses. They reveal what border southerners believed a marriage should look like and, occasionally, what it was really like. Most importantly, they suggest that border southerners sought to build marriages based upon mutuality and love, even if they often fell short in practice. The language of mutuality was not exclusive to the border, but the border environment allowed men and women to enact the tenets of mutuality and contractualism to a unique extent.

To demonstrate the ways in which border residents applied the philosophies of mutuality and contractualism in their households, I also analyze divorce records from Kentucky, West Virginia, and Virginia from 1850 to 1873. These legal records demonstrate citizens' perceptions and uses of marital law, as well as their marital ideals. As Peter Bardaglio argues, "The laws regulating domestic and sexual relations furnish an entry point . . . for raising fundamental questions about the ideological and social character" of a region and its relationship with the rest of the nation.[33] In Kentucky, West Virginia, and Appalachian Virginia, the growing influence of ideas of contractualism and individualism can be seen in both the law and society even in the 1850s, reflecting the border region's tendencies toward a hybrid culture.[34] Analyzing divorces in these states allows us to learn what spouses expected from one another, what their neighbors deemed acceptable or unacceptable behavior, whether men and women had different expectations for themselves and their partners, and for what reasons the marital contract, once made, could be broken. While not all marriages ended in discord, these court records can provide valuable information about how people expected marriage to work and, therefore, the general gender ideology to which they adhered.[35] These records show the subtle distinctions between these border places and other parts of the nineteenth-century United States. As Yvonne Pitts has argued, "Approaching Kentucky as part of a liminal legal and cultural ground, both embracing and rejecting legal and cultural values from its Northern and Southern neighbors and struggling to assert its own legal identity, offers an opportunity to reconceptualize more broadly the importance of the region as a space where individuals made explicit their ideological commitments because they were contested."[36]

After 1850, both Kentucky and Virginia granted divorces through the court system, rather than by legislative act. Desperate spouses had to first petition their local circuit court, and if the result was unfavorable and they had the resources, they could appeal their decision to the state's supreme court. In order to analyze the broadest selection of cases and to capture the actions of judges at both the local and state level, I have analyzed the appellate records of Kentucky, West Virginia, and Virginia from 1850 to 1873, as well as the cases of six county circuit courts in the same period.[37] Analysis of local records also highlights the voices of a greater number of border southerners, since even the poorer members of society made use of the courts. This book includes the voices and stories of men and women from Franklin and Warren Counties, Kentucky; Ohio County, West Virginia; and Tazewell, Fauquier, and Amelia Counties, Virginia.

A number of factors influenced my sample. West Virginia law still requires that divorce records be permanently sealed, except to people involved in the case. Additionally, because of the cost of storage, the restrictions of the law, and pure neglect, many circuit court records stored in individual counties were destroyed long ago. Luckily, by some twist of fate, Ohio County's divorce records survived. At some point, they ended up in the West Virginia and Regional History Center in Morgantown, where one of the archivists, who also happens to be my father, brought them to my attention. It is to my benefit that this county turns out to have such an important and fascinating story to tell. In order to capture another aspect of West Virginia's story, without having access to the records, I chose rural Tazewell County, just over the border in the mountainous region of southwestern Virginia. It shares many characteristics with its eventual neighbors in West Virginia, and the Virginia General Assembly actually carved the counties of McDowell and Mercer from it, eventually part of the new state.

Within Kentucky, I chose border counties that also had a large enslaved population, in order to test whether these ideals would extend into slaveholding homes. Because of this, I focused on the Bluegrass region, the heart of antebellum slaveholding Kentucky, and ultimately selected Franklin County, home to the state capital, Frankfort. As I began to read wartime diaries and correspondence, I was also drawn to the southern parts of the state, to sample a region where residents' sympathies may have been especially conflicted. For this reason, I chose Warren County, which had a similar proportion of enslaved residents to Franklin County and which served as a southern trade center for the commonwealth. Finally, to compare these border communities with eastern Virginia counties, I chose two counties: Fauquier and Amelia. Fauquier County, located in the northwest, not far from the border itself, still reflected eastern Virginia's economy and culture in its population diversity, commitment to slavery, and connections to Virginia's elite ruling class. For my last county, I wanted to choose the one with the highest proportion of slaves in the state. When that county (Nottoway) proved to have no antebellum divorce cases, I moved down the list until I found a county with cases in both the antebellum and postbellum eras—Amelia County. These six

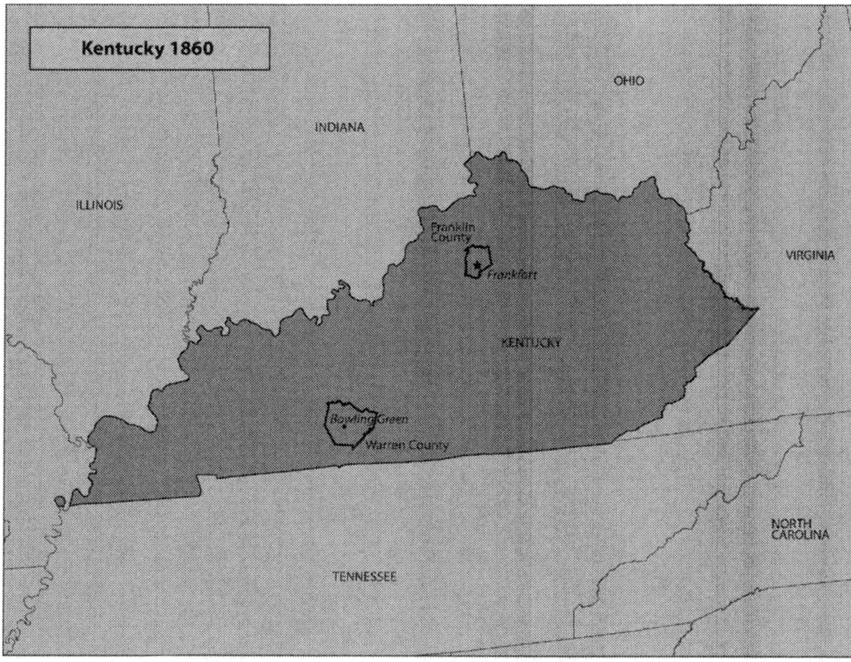

Map of Kentucky, 1860 (counties under examination are outlined).

counties, though not a complete sample, give a compelling portrait of the economic, ethnic, racial, and cultural diversity of the border South, as well as a glimpse into the ways in which residents employed the ethics of mutuality and contractualism in their cases.

When I first visited the Kentucky state archives, located in Franklin County, I was immediately struck by how beautiful the surrounding area was. Rolling green hills surround the roads, marked only by neat wooden fences and the area's trademark black barns. Horses frolic across the Kentucky bluegrass, racing against the evening breeze. Traveling back one hundred and sixty years would reveal a similar landscape that disguised a vastly different society. On those farms and in those barns, a third of the county's population labored as slaves. Franklin and its surrounding counties, in fact, contained the highest percentage of slaves in the state.[38] Though tantalizingly near the Ohio River and freedom, enslaved people in Kentucky experienced many of the same cruelties of slavery as those enslaved in the Deep South. Harriet Beecher Stowe pointedly chose Kentucky as a setting for her 1852 novel, *Uncle Tom's Cabin,* refusing to accept border state slaveowners' arguments about the benevolence of their system. Kentucky slaves may have been more likely than Deep South slaves to work on small farms, sometimes beside their own masters, or to participate in the slave hiring system, but ultimately, their lives were not their own, familial separation was common, and emotional and physical pain were a constant reminder of their status.[39] Residents of Franklin County, like men and women throughout the South, constructed their social ideals in an environment based on racial hierarchy and human bondage.

Many of the county's twelve thousand residents lived in the county seat and state capital, Frankfort.[40] Franklin County residents who took their marital grievances to court often came from Frankfort's working class, whose close quarters bred confrontation and intimate community knowledge of neighbors' relationships. Others lived on rural farms outside the small city and rode in for court days and to conduct business in Frankfort. During the Civil War, the county, like much of Kentucky, experienced internal division and external occupation. Frankfort, in fact, became the only loyal state capital to be occupied by Confederates during the war.[41]

Warren County, Kentucky, located in the southwestern section of Kentucky, is home to Bowling Green, a community that was occupied by both Confederate and Union armies during the Civil War. Created shortly after the commonwealth itself, Warren County served as a commercial and transportation center for the southern part of Kentucky in the antebellum era. In 1838, the Louisville and Nashville turnpike connected the town of Bowling Green to other prosperous areas of the state, as well as to major southern urban centers. With the installation of locks and dams on the local Green and Barren Rivers, the town built a flourishing steamboat trade as well. By 1859, the completion of the Louisville and Nashville Railroad cemented the community's status and trade ties.[42]

Despite its position as a commercial center, Warren County remained largely agricultural. Like Franklin County, a large segment of its population, over 30 percent, was enslaved. Laboring on over 130,000 acres of farms, these enslaved Kentuckians helped produce the county's main crops—corn and tobacco.[43] Shake Rag, a parcel of land donated in 1802 for the use of the town's black population, became the center of a vibrant free community after the Civil War. Many worshiped at the State Street Baptist Church, which had been founded by enslaved men and women in the antebellum era. Eventually, the area would have numerous black-run schools, businesses, and churches.[44]

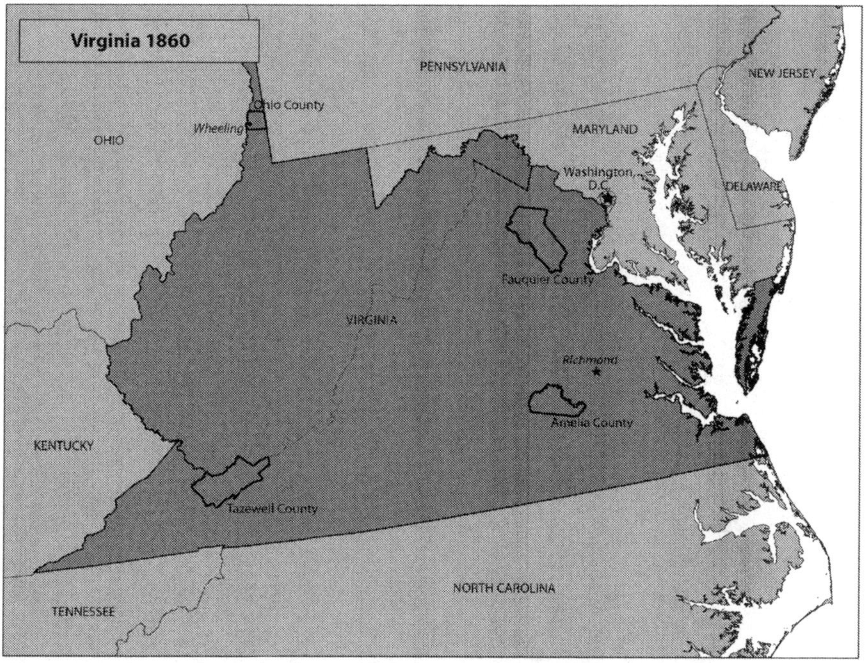

Map of Virginia, 1860 (counties under examination are outlined).

During the Civil War, renegade Kentuckians declared Bowling Green to be the capital of Confederate Kentucky. Despite the fact that the state never formally seceded, the Confederate government welcomed this breakaway Bluegrass band and admitted Kentucky into the Confederate States of America on December 10, 1861. However, the Confederates occupied this new capital for only three months, before they were forced to retreat in February 1862.[45] Bowling Green's position as a trade center ensured that it had an especially tumultuous Civil War experience, as both sides fought to control it.

Not far from Franklin County, the Ohio River winds its way along Kentucky's northern border. From one of its many ports, nineteenth-century Kentuckians could board one of the region's famous riverboats and connect with the Deep South via the Mississippi River or travel upriver to the port of Wheeling, Virginia, county seat of Ohio County. A bustling manufacturing center, by the 1850s, the city's skyline was dotted with factories, many of which employed members of Wheeling's vibrant immigrant community. By 1860, nearly a quarter of Ohio County's population was foreign-born. Many were English or Irish, but among the most prominent groups were Germans, many of whom had fled Europe after the failed revolutions of 1848.[46] Few enslaved people resided in the county, though many free blacks worked in the factories.[47] Wheeling's diversity shaped its religious life as well; no single church dominated the community. In 1860, the county had a Baptist church, two Episcopal churches, one synagogue, a Lutheran church, five Methodist churches, five Presbyterian churches, and one Roman Catholic church.

In 1853, the Baltimore and Ohio Railroad connected Wheeling to Maryland, cementing the city's northern trading and economic ties. Wedged above the Mason–Dixon Line, between Ohio and Pennsylvania, Ohio County had fewer ties to slavery than Franklin and Warren Counties, and its citizens were less conflicted when the Civil War broke out.[48] In fact, the city hosted the first conventions that formed the Restored State of Virginia in 1861 and that laid the foundations for the new state of West Virginia. Wheeling would become the first capital of the state of West Virginia, although it would exchange the honor with Charleston in the decade after the war. Living in a highly urban community nearly twice the size of Franklin County, Ohio County residents knew well how tight quarters, working-class conditions, and a volatile blend of ethnicities and races could shape the construction of marital roles and attitudes.[49]

On the other hand, nestled along the future border of West Virginia and Virginia, Tazewell County, Virginia, was a rural, mountainous county. Still, the county shared many characteristics with its western neighbors over the border. Tazewell County experienced white settlement relatively late for Virginia.[50] Tazewell County's population grew slowly in the antebellum era, and the Virginia General Assembly eventually divided up the sprawling county. In 1837, part of the county became Mercer County, and in 1858, another section formed McDowell County. Both would one day sit on the southern border of West Virginia. Although the formal line between the Virginias would soon run through these mountains, residents of Tazewell County saw the boundary as more fluid, and their family ties and courtships reflected the tight bond between the former neighbors even in the midst of war and secession.

Much of its land was unimproved by the 1860s, and the farms that did cover its rolling hills made money through livestock, rather than the cash crops common to Virginia plantations. Only 12 percent of its population was enslaved.[51] Nonetheless, Tazewell was not the egalitarian, isolated Appalachian mountain paradise envisioned by nineteenth-century travel writers.

Consisting of four central neighborhoods, Tazewell County exhibited a marked diversity of agriculture and wealth. Its oldest community, the Cove, was dominated by large farms and "progressive agriculture." Meanwhile, Abb's Valley, for example, known mostly for a brutal Indian massacre and the capture of local residents, remained largely undeveloped. Tazewell County's main trade connection was through the Virginia and Tennessee Railroad, which reached nearby Wytheville in 1855. While some argue that "the railroad contributed to a commercial revolution in southwestern Virginia . . . that promoted slavery; forged trade links to the Valley of Virginia and the Tidewater; and helped ensure the Southwest's loyalty to Virginia during secession," the railroad was finished only six years before the Civil War. As the later chapters of this book show, the railroad shaped developments in Tazewell County in a slightly different direction from that of its new counterparts in West Virginia, but not until the postbellum period.[52]

Wealthier and more established than Tazewell County, Fauquier County also had a significantly higher enslaved population—about half the county's residents. Founded in 1759, Fauquier County sits about 45 miles from Washington, DC, in the northwestern area of the state.[53] Today, it is known as part of Virginia's horse and wine country, and its topography resembles the rolling hills of Franklin County in many ways. Its county seat, Warrenton, was founded in 1810 at the junction of the Falmouth–Winchester and Alexandria–Culpeper roads. By 1854, the county was connected to other parts of Virginia through the Orange and Alexandria Railroad, which had an extension running directly to Warrenton. From there, Fauquier County residents and their goods could easily travel to Richmond or Alexandria, just outside Washington. However, Warrenton's proximity to these major cities made it a target for both sides during the Civil War, who sought to hold this strategic location between the Blue Ridge and the Union capital. The Warrenton junction was destroyed by Union troops under General William Henry French in October 1863, in one of ten battles fought in the county during the Civil War, and Warrenton itself "changed hands 67 times, a record surpassed only by Winchester."[54]

One former enslaved man recalled his childhood on a Fauquier County plantation as brutal and full of backbreaking labor. He and one hundred other enslaved people worked from sunup to sundown, cultivating tobacco and wheat. He wrote, "This mode of living is no doubt adopted for the express purpose of brutalizing the slaves as much as possible."[55] Although slavery remained a vital part of the county's economy, many slaveholders also began to send their enslaved people "down south" to booming Deep South plantations. Those remaining in Fauquier County lived on farms with about ten to twenty other enslaved people.[56] About 4 percent of the county's population consisted of free blacks. Some of these residents defied Virginia laws that stated that manumitted slaves must leave the state within twelve months or be re-enslaved, and their presence must have been unsettling in a community in which the connection between slavery and race was so vital.[57]

Amelia County lay deep in the heart of Virginia's plantation-filled southern piedmont. Of these six counties, it was the oldest—and the most committed to the peculiar institution. In the late colonial period, the center of slaveholding in Virginia shifted from the state's tidewater region into the piedmont, with the largest number of enslaved Africans in the Chesapeake arriving in Amelia County before the revolution.[58] By 1850, the white members of the community, fewer than three thousand, were vastly outnumbered by almost eight thousand enslaved people. Life on Amelia County's numerous plantations, most of them devoted to tobacco cultivation, was extremely harsh and was strictly divided by race and class.

Like Fauquier County, Amelia County's antebellum farmers could send their crops to market using newly completed railroad lines. The Richmond and Danville Railroad formed a junction with the Southside Railroad at Burkeville in neighboring Nottoway County, and the county's roads and byways soon connected it with this critical hub. As the war approached, Amelia County residents did not waver in their commitment to secession, sending their sons to fight the conflict that soon engulfed the state. As the war came to a close, the battle hit home. As Lee's Army of Northern Virginia fell back from Richmond, they fought one last time against the Union army at Sayler's Creek in Amelia County. Three days later, Robert E. Lee surrendered at nearby Appomattox Court House.[59]

In order to sketch the story of marriage in Kentucky and West Virginia during the mid-nineteenth century, this book explores residents' perceptions as they grew out of the region's complex antebellum society, matured through the Civil War, and solidified in the tumultuous Reconstruction years. Part 1 addresses marriages and divorces in the antebellum era, "before the storm" of the Civil War. Chapter 1 details the growth of a language of domesticity and mutuality in Kentucky, western Virginia, and Appalachian Virginia in the antebellum era. When courting, young border South residents firmly stated their desire to build marriages based on affection, love, and mutual happiness. They embraced all of these characteristics of marriages, despite the dangerous individualism implied by mutuality in marriage. If acted upon, individualism, a remnant of eighteenth-century Enlightenment philosophy, threatened to tear apart the hierarchical household. Yet, in these border communities, mutuality became the ideal for many. Similarly, this chapter explores the impact of discussions of domesticity on masculinity in the region. Part of a transatlantic shift in masculinity, men in the border South reoriented their focus inward, on the family and the private sphere, and embraced a more restrained form of manhood in this era. This chapter also explores how border southerners acted upon these ideals by demanding and receiving divorces when their partners did not live up to these ideals.

Border southerners also made use of contractualism in their divorce petitions, which built upon the language of mutuality and individualism seen in chapter 1. Chapter 2 addresses border southerners' use of contractualism in their divorce petitions during the antebellum era. Contractualism, or the growing view of marriage as not a permanent, sacramental institution but a contractual one with rules, procedures, and escape clauses, allowed more men and women to file for divorce and to use a variety of causes to explain their decision. It was also a dangerous ideal in a society in which so many residents found themselves permanently bound to masters with no legal recourse or escape. Nonetheless, in Kentucky, western Virginia, and Appalachian Virginia, unhappy spouses found an outlet in the local courts and through their use, or manipulation, of legal statutes.

In contrast with the stories in chapter 2, those found in chapter 3 show that eastern Virginians embraced a different understanding of marital breakdowns. In these Virginia counties, few chose to make their spousal grievances public at all, knowing that the courts were unlikely to be sympathetic even if they chose to brave public disapproval. Those few who chose this path shaped their narratives in dramatically different ways from their borderland neighbors, reflecting the differing society in which they petitioned. This chapter focuses especially on the use of rhetoric in these cases, as petitioners framed their cases to present themselves as long-suffering spouses forced to choose this most undesirable option. Their cases also reflected a greater acceptance of gender hierarchy in the home, especially seen in the expectation of wifely obedience.

Part 2, "Weathering the Storm," analyzes how border marriages formed and fractured in the war years and explores how gendered attitudes changed or did not change after the war. Chapter 4 outlines the devastating experience of the Civil War in the border South. The chapter opens with the secession crisis, which gave western Virginians their long-awaited opportunity to break away from their eastern neighbors. A close analysis of the debates and rhetoric in the secession convention, as well as in the later constitutional convention, reveals the impact of the border South's particular form of manhood, detailed in chapter 1. Without this unique understanding of hierarchy, restraint, submission, and emotion, western Virginians may not have ventured down the path to statehood. This section demonstrates the importance of gendered ideals, forged within the walls of the household, to the greater border world. The second half of the chapter explores how the brutal and divided conflict in the border South reinforced the importance of domestic ties and a sense of mutuality within the home. Interestingly, this shift occurred even in eastern Virginia, but it was not strong enough to survive the volatile postwar period, as shown in the next two chapters.

Chapter 5 addresses the collapse of many border South marriages in the years immediately after the war. As in other parts of the United States, the Civil War had a profound impact on the psyche and emotions of the people involved, and years of distance and separation and battlefield trauma led to the breakdown of many relationships. Yet, the situation in Kentucky and West Virginia was exacerbated by two particular circumstances: the establishment of friendlier divorce laws in the antebellum era, built on a greater acceptance of contractualism and separation, and the embrace of domesticity and mutuality before and during the conflict, which ironically led to hastily arranged marriages and higher standards for those marriages themselves. The subsequent increase in the number of divorces in the postwar period is explored in this chapter.

Yet, if ideals of mutuality and contractualism gave residents in Kentucky and West Virginia more freedom to escape unhappy marriages in the postwar period, the situation was different for Virginians. Chapter 6 addresses the impact of emancipation on white marriages in Kentucky, West Virginia, and Virginia during the first eight years following the Civil War, using this comparative approach to argue that black emancipation's effect on white border gender roles was muted by the region's hybrid culture and antebellum experiences. More specifically, in postbellum Kentucky and West Virginia, residents used the same rhetoric and cited the same motivations for separation as in their antebellum cases, reflecting a continued desire for mutuality and individualism in their relationships, while Virginians decried the breakdown of racial mastery, connected this breakdown with potential disruptions to their hierarchical households, and demanded obedience and loyalty from both former slaves and spouses. This chapter demonstrates that understanding the border South's unique antebellum experience is pivotal to explaining its pattern of continuity and change in the postwar era.

Finally, the book concludes with a chapter about those who lived on the borders of the border—the working-class and poor white women of the border South. Their story reveals the potential of border culture—how it gave a voice and agency to women whose stories could be more easily suppressed in a less fluid community. The border created fertile ground for ideas of mutuality and individualism. While this led many to pursue friendship, love, and partnership in their relationships, elite and middle-class husbands and wives of the border South often still adhered to a social ethic that dictated certain gendered behaviors to men and women. As chapter 7 shows, however, in working-class society, these philosophies gave women a greater sense of independence and authority, allowing them to push the boundaries of the household and assert themselves in new ways.

Marriage is at once one of our most fundamental social institutions and one of our most deeply personal institutions. On the one hand, studying marriage enables historians to glimpse the intimate values of those in the past. At the same time, as Laura Edwards argues, marriage "provide[s] the cornerstone for all other social relations, separating the private sphere from the public world, positioning people on either side of that line as either dependents or independent household heads, and then determining their public rights and social obligations."[60] As a lens, marriage allows us to better understand community formation, the construction of social relationships, and regional identity. In the border South, studying marriage at the individual level provides historians with a wealth of sweet love stories and moments of simple devotion and connection. Yet, the study of marriage in a broader fashion also reveals a community's particular worldview, which is connected with attitudes toward race relations, gender, economics, politics, civil rights, and the changing relationship of the individual with the state. Marriage, in this case, serves as a useful tool to demonstrate the impact of border culture on the lives and philosophies of the region's residents.

This analysis of attitudes toward marriage reveals a society in which adaptation and flexibility were common, creating greater mutuality in gender relationships, acceptance of divorce and separation, and continuity in the postwar period. Nonetheless, while the story of marriage in the mid-nineteenth-century border South is one of complexity, fusion, and exchange, ultimately it boils down to the story of men and women meeting, falling in love, and attempting (and sometimes failing) to make a life together in a unique time and place.

Part 1

Before the Storm

1

To Form an Enviable Marriage

In late autumn 1833, Ellen Green of Henderson, Kentucky, wrote a lengthy letter to her fiancé, Hector Green, ruminating on their future together. As their wedding approached, Ellen grew anxious and worked to ensure that her husband-to-be shared her views about domestic tranquility. To make a marriage happy, she wrote, a husband and wife must be those "whom nature formed for each other, who have no divided wish, or thought, and the sanction of one seems all that is desired by the other." A pair such as this, she told Hector, would sustain all kinds of financial, emotional, and familial strain. She had clearly spent many hours envisioning this relationship, even creating a fictionalized couple to stand in for her own aspirations. Lovingly, she described the pair to her future partner. "We see the happy Norman, returning from his toilsome occupation, with a heart overflowing with love for his cherished partner, and the smiles, and endearing fondness of Monimia serve as a compensation for his arduous labours," Ellen told Hector, painting a picture of marital bliss that would strike a chord in many nineteenth-century middle-class homes. "Norman's happiness is in his own domestic circle, where the intelligent converse, and animated countenance of Monimia, serve as his magnet of attraction." This, she stated, was an "enviable" marriage.[1]

Ellen Green's idealized vision of a perfect marriage reflects the rise of a new domestic ideal in early nineteenth-century America. By the 1830s, Americans and their Victorian counterparts in western Europe celebrated and glorified the domestic sphere as a haven, safe from the hectic new world of modern industrialized societies. Similarly, a growing sentimentality showed that romantic love and companionate marriages were becoming common in this transatlantic world. Tucked away on the western border of Kentucky and Indiana, Ellen Green was not isolated from these developments. Influenced by this transatlantic cultural transformation and the growth of a middle-class sentimentality, Ellen, and her fellow residents of Kentucky and western Virginia, were firmly a part of this story, embracing domesticity and mutuality in their lives and in their households.

Kentuckians and western Virginians' relationships reflected these ideals in a variety of ways. When courting, young border South residents firmly stated their desire to build marriages based on affection, love, and mutual happiness. They spent hours pouring their souls into correspondence, as they sought emotional and intellectual compatibility, and when they finally succeeded in securing a mate, they received advice manuals from friends and family members that urged them to build their marriages on the ideal of "mutuality," especially in terms of the household economy.[2] In this, they were not alone. Many other early nineteenth-century couples spoke in a similar language, and companionate marriage was a concept popular throughout the United States. The critical difference in the border South lay in the fact that residents sought divorces if their marriages failed to adhere to these ideals, refusing to stay in relationships without a sense of mutuality. They embraced all these characteristics of marriages, despite the dangerous individualism implied by mutuality in marriage itself. Individualism, a remnant of eighteenth-century Enlightenment philosophy, threatened to tear apart the hierarchical, organic household so central to the white southern way of life. Yet, in these border communities, mutuality became the ideal for many. Young Kentuckians and western Virginians desired and demanded it for themselves, giving power and influence to wives while denying any to their enslaved people. Once again, this border, on the edge of the South and the Midwest, gave birth to both flexibility and rigidity as these couples reshaped one aspect of their households while firmly maintaining another.[3]

The celebration of domesticity in Kentucky and western Virginian was not confined solely to the female members of the white household. Increasingly in the antebellum era, Kentuckians and western Virginians expressed a desire for men to cultivate their domestic side and to become more involved husbands and fathers. Although this rhetoric was not uniquely theirs, white border southerners nonetheless tried to use it to distinguish themselves from other nineteenth-century American men. They explicitly contrasted their masculine ideal with the failures of plantation southerners' manhood, describing planters as violent, unemotional—or too emotional. The particular form of masculinity celebrated in the border South had very real implications for border South families, as well as society. It even influenced the political world, as border South white men defended their decisions during the secession crisis by denigrating the "rash" behavior of other white southern men and celebrating their ability to make calm, rational decisions. Understanding domesticity and mutuality is pivotal to understanding white border South identity in the antebellum era. Differing interpretations of masculinity influenced the ways in which white border South men resisted secession.[4]

Yet, too often, the story of domesticity in the United States has been one centered on the middle-class homes of northern New England. There, the "cult of true womanhood" influenced a generation of white women, who saw its core tenets—piety, purity, submissiveness, and domesticity—as laws structuring their development into housewives.[5] Early women's historians argued that the ideology of separate spheres grew out of industrialization in these communities. As men left the home to earn wages, the home became increasingly "private" and feminized, while the public world became more masculine. As women became increasingly associated with this private sphere, their image took on these "soft" characteristics and they earned a monopoly among the sexes on morality and piety. Increasingly, historians have complicated this portrait of the two spheres, demonstrating that both the public and private worlds were porous and overlapping. Others have revealed that white southern women, whose economic worlds were not nearly as industrialized, still valued these feminine values in the early nineteenth century.[6] The semi-urban communities of the border South provide a middle ground. In the shops and homes of places like Wheeling, Frankfort, and Bowling Green, men and women shared numerous gendered spaces, none of which were purely domestic or economic. This may explain the popularity of mutuality and male domesticity in these places. Even more than in strictly urban, industrial New England homes and large plantations in the Deep South, these homes lent themselves to a more equitable division of labor and a greater appreciation for one's partner.

At the same moment as the domestic sphere began to gain a mythological status in many middle-class Victorian homes on either side of the Atlantic, men and women increasingly began to value romance. Long based on economic and familial concerns, marriage instead became a matter of individual affection. Companionate marriages, or relationships based on mutual affection and compatibility, became increasingly common after the mid-eighteenth century but exploded in the mid-nineteenth century. As American culture celebrated sentimentality, couples began to assert their desire to find partners that were amiable, well-matched, and affectionate—something very similar to the fictionalized Norman and Monimia described by Ellen Green.[7] As more couples sought companionate marriages, a new ideal blossomed into fruition—"mutuality."

Mutuality is a term that sounds almost foreign to twenty-first-century ears. Equality, a modern ideal, makes a lot more sense, both as a concept and as an aspiration for a marriage. Yet, it is anachronistic to look for such traits in most nineteenth-century relationships. Outside of a handful of radical activists, most nineteenth-century spouses could never hope to aspire to equality. Society was not constructed to allow it. Legally and politically, men had all the power. Even men active in the abolitionist or early feminist movements could only gift their wives with the illusion of equality. As Suzanne Lebsock quips, companionate marriages were only as "companionate" as men wanted them to be.[8] Men still ultimately decided whether they wanted to allow their wives to stand on a similar status to them in the household, and even if they chose this, outside the walls of the home, society and the law placed wives below their husbands regardless of their private relationship. Yet, viewed through nineteenth-century eyes, mutuality seems positively progressive.

Courting men and women in the border South increasingly wrote that they sought a relationship based on "mutuality." In practice, this was an ill-defined goal, but often it meant that both partners contributed economically to the household, both had important emotional needs, and both needed to be intellectually compatible. A relationship based on "mutuality" acknowledged the identities and desires of both people, something that the law certainly did not do. In most places in the antebellum United States, when a woman married, she lost her legal identity and became *feme covert.* Her legal identity was literally "covered" by her husband's. Married women could not own property, write a will, sue, or be sued in court.[9] In a relationship with mutuality, women were still often subordinate, but they were nonetheless valued. For example, wives' economic contributions were usually more supportive than contributory. They might build their husbands' fortunes through their maintenance of the household or through their careful budgeting. "Mutuality" was built on and celebrated gendered differences between men and women but did give women an authority based on their particular roles as wives. Like the celebration of female domesticity in the nineteenth century, society's embrace of mutuality could lead to an expansion of women's rights, if not for fully progressive reasons. In New England, for example, many women leveraged their new status as domestic queens to join reform movements, including temperance, abolition, and, eventually, suffrage.

However, in a society structured upon racial slavery, even something as innocuous as "mutuality" could prove threatening. White southerners valued hierarchy throughout society. Clearly, racial hierarchy formed the backbone of plantation society, but households also featured a strict gender hierarchy as well. Men were the masters of these so-called small worlds, dominant over both their slaves and their families.[10] All of these elements of their mastery were intertwined, and chipping away at one endangered the other. Because of this, mutuality in relationships held far less appeal in slaveholding society than in nonslaveholding society. Yet, these slaveholding communities also lay on another, more neglected border—that between East and West. Border southerners' embrace of mutuality reflects their absorption of a streak of antihierarchical sentiment from their midwestern neighbors. Therefore, even in the heart of slaveholding Kentucky and western Virginia, mutuality struck a chord, especially since it applied to the white members of the household.[11] This ideal reflected a hesitant progress and perfectly encapsulates the flexible and contradictory identities of border southerners during this era.

Before marriages could reflect the acceptance of mutuality in the border South, white men and women had to find partners who would fulfill this goal. Although most courting couples spent little time alone to determine their compatibility, many poured their feelings onto the page, shedding light on their new demands and aspirations for a marriage partner. As it was throughout the early United States, courtship in the border South was a ritualized process with fairly strict social norms. Most white men and women who fell in love and married either knew one another through family or childhood friends or met at parties, church socials, and on summer visits throughout the region. Once a proper introduction had been made, they courted under the watchful eye of their parents and community, sometimes escaping for a private walk or buggy ride. Often the only place to find any semblance of social intimacy was in correspondence, though even in letters certain proprieties had to be observed. Especially when men and women lived apart, letters were vital to a relationship and allowed romantic affection to blossom.[12]

In Kentucky and western Virginia, courting men and women sought mutuality in their relationships and spent pages assuring their lovers that they would strive to maintain such a goal in their marriage. In the midsummer months of 1841, Edward Bennett of Louisville, Kentucky, wrote to his fiancée, Judith Bellestine of Philadelphia, Pennsylvania, about his excitement over their upcoming marriage. "I believe fully, my dear Judith, that it will contribute greatly to our mutual happiness," he told her. "I feel abundantly satisfied that my own happiness will be greatly enhanced by the society of my dear friend whom I ardently love." Edward, like many young Kentucky men, believed that his marriage would be a source of happiness for both himself and his wife and sought a friend, rather than a subordinate, to make this possible. He saw his wife as a companion and a partner.[13]

This is not to say that border South men did not consider other characteristics besides love in a future mate, but affection soon came to feature most prominently alongside others in their letters. Young William Johnson wrote to his mother before his 1860 wedding: "I think I am about to marry as noble a lady as I have ever seen, but who will make a gentle, affectionate, sensable, and good wife." Not unconcerned about worldly matters, he admitted that he wished "for her sake" that she had property but concluded that he would marry regardless of her financial background. Ultimately, he told his mother, "I have always desired to marry for happiness, not for money."[14]

Other smitten suitors felt the same way. In a letter to his sister, Phoebe, in August 1836, Will Coburn, a Kentuckian, described his feelings for Sue Ballinger. "Her condition in life I considered on a par with my own," he told his sister. Sue and Will had comparable family and economic backgrounds, as well as similar "dispositions." But most importantly, he wrote, "I had loved Sue from childhood up. It was not a burning impetuous love that I had for her, but unlike any other attack of the kind I have ever had it was ardent, yet cool and reflective."[15] This love made his courtship honorable and worthy and convinced him that Sue was the best possible wife for him. While many other nineteenth-century men may have shared these attitudes, border southern men imagined their beliefs to be unique, a reflection of the way they envisioned their larger relationship with New England, the South, and the Midwest. Will, like many other border South men, emphasized the emotional rationality of his feelings, and especially contrasted his particular love with the economic calculation of wealthy northern elites and the rashness of hot-headed southerners. Will Coburn used a common rhetoric to define a unique regional identity; as with their attitudes toward hierarchy, slavery, and politics, in their minds, border southerners' ideas about masculinity and affection were a symptom of their "moderation."

As men and women of the border South sought greater mutuality in their relationships, they set the bar higher for their own requirements in a partner. This added tremendous stress to the courtship process. Before, although young men and women might have chafed under the restrictions and demands of their families, they had little choice in the matter. Now, men and women expanded their options but put more pressure on themselves to make the right decision. Making a love match in an era in which two lovers spent little time alone was a challenge indeed. Nineteenth-century men and women had additional, gender-specific pressures as well. Men took courtship seriously and sought actively to cement their relationships into marriage. Marriage marked entrance into adulthood (and subsequently, manhood), as well as an end to loneliness for many who had begun lives on their own, and ultimately it brought them companionship.[16] Men teased each other about marriage, but clearly sought the goal themselves. G. B. Miller, of Lexington, Kentucky, insisted to his friend Barnabas Lee that it was "Amen to love matters for me at least." He hoped it would not be so for Barnabas, though, and asked that if "fortune's swift-revolving wheel" threw him upon the bridal altar, he would tell his friends, so they could share in his happiness.[17]

Meanwhile, friends and relatives often cautioned women to be careful in choosing a husband. Marriage held more perils for women, who had fewer options to leave an unhappy relationship and less independence once married. Many women got cold feet at the thought of leaving the comforts of home for the dangers of marrying a relatively unknown person.[18] Kentuckian Susan Bullitt Dixon wrote her sister, Helen, in 1853, after she heard about Helen riding around town in a hack with a man named Patrick. "If [he] courts you," she told Helen, "dont you marry him. *He* could never make up for home, which you have no idea how you will miss till you leave it." Marriage, she warned Helen, was very different than a short visit from home. She stated emphatically, "Dont you ever marry unless you love him better than your own life and the whole world."[19] Both men and women in the border South assumed that marriage, dangerous as it was, would never be formed without love and mutuality as its basis. Ironically, though, the growing emphasis on finding a loving and compatible partner caused greater hesitance for some women, as these ideals were harder to achieve and to uncover in the limiting courtship process.

As relationships became based on common interests and affection, border southerners debated whether a couple should have similar dispositions when they married or whether such compatibility grew over time.[20] Often these debates broke down on generational lines. In 1854, A. C. Williams, attending the Kentucky Military Institute in Frankfort, wrote to his niece, discussing a mutual acquaintance's tumultuous relationship. The woman in question, Louisa, had made a very "unfortunate" marriage, A. C. told his niece, and he quickly diagnosed the problem:

> I don't think it is generally so well for a female to put off marrying till their views or impressions, their notions and youthful finer feelings, their tastes, likes & dislikes, become all warped, dried, steeped, sallied & peppered so that anything out of their old, stereotyped notions & habits would wrinkle their faces to look like a dried gizzard, making all the babies cry, and souring all the milk in the whole neighborhood round.

Instead, he believed women should marry young (and avoid widowers with children, like Louisa's husband). He tempered his harsh words by stating that a young couple would grow together and "adapt themselves to each other" with time.[21] His attitude reflected the growing acceptance that spouses would influence one another in a relationship but showed some hesitancy, as he still put much of the onus on women to adapt. He seemed slightly out of step with his niece, who may have shared younger border southerners' beliefs that compatibility could, and should, be determined before a couple married. Williams may have accepted compatibility but not mutuality, for he certainly believed that women should adapt to their husbands, rather than maintaining their own, though mutual, needs and interests.

The expansion of female education in the first half of the nineteenth century, often leading to new private and public authority for women, became intertwined with a growing acceptance of mutuality in marriage. Border South men valued their wives' opinions and often sought companions whose education and training made them intellectual, as well as emotional, partners.[22] Both in the antebellum North and South, female education expanded to include "more than social graces," and many border South men praised this development.[23] For example, in an address delivered on the second anniversary of Van Doren's Collegiate Institute for Young Ladies in Lexington, Kentucky, Charles Morehead glorified the goals and power of female education. He argued that women in Kentucky enjoyed authority of their own and were not forced to submit to the "tyrannical exercise of power on the part of the husband."[24] He praised female education for transforming women from objects of beauty and attraction into intellectual beings, which gave rise to companionate marriages. Morehead linked female education with the happiness of both partners in marriage and with women's rights themselves.

However, Morehead also expressed an overriding concern for the well-being of men, arguing, "How much more estimable and useful is he like to become with an accomplished female for his companion, than if united to a mere brainless plaything."[25] Advocates such as Charles Morehead may have noted the connection between female education and the benefits to men without fully realizing the ironic consequences for women's rights outside the home.[26] Still, if mutuality was the desired trait of many border South marriages, women's education would have to rise to meet this goal. The South was not an educational wasteland during this era, although northerners liked to think that it was.[27] Still, most southern schools lagged behind northern schools in terms of educational value and their accessibility to women. Border South states like Kentucky and western Virginia led the region in educating their citizens and especially the female ones. Residents' attempts to make their marriages more compatible and equitable fueled the expansion of education in this region.

Kentuckian Sallie Offutt's uncle certainly did not overlook the connections between a good education for women and a better marriage. He rejoiced that she lived in a new era. In this new world, he stated, "Men are beginning to be governed by moral influence . . . and the influence of women is beginning to be felt." Because of this, women had more access to education and "their rights are respected." If she was intelligent and took advantage of these changes, she would be blessed with scores of worthy suitors. If uneducated, a woman, at best, would get a beau who was a "stupid fellow and never will respect her rights."[28] A good education was a valuable asset for a woman who wanted to attract a respectable partner and achieve a marriage based on mutuality. Kentucky women supported this philosophy, too. In a composition for her 1851 examination at the Science Hill Academy in Shelbyville, Albana Carson stated, "God has endowed woman with a mind not inferior to that of man." To defend this, she argued that God created woman to be a "help-meet" and "suitable" for man. "Surely," she reasoned, "there could have been little suitability in an inferior intellect."[29]

Chester D. Hubbard, a western Virginia politician, also advocated for an expanded intellectual and public role for women.[30] Actively involved in various reform movements, Hubbard was a founding member of the Wheeling Female College and an advocate for temperance.[31] Hubbard's wife, Sarah, was also active outside the home, raising money, for example, for a statue of Henry Clay.[32] At a temperance meeting, he gave a speech directly addressing women's role in public life. While he was "no admirer of Mary Wollstoncraft [*sic*]," he told his audience that he admired a "woman who sympathizes with her fellow creatures, and who is neither afraid to be seen nor heard pleading the cause of the sons and daughters of misery and misfortune." Speaking directly to past notions of manhood, he stated that he knew there were many who "lament[ed]" the end of the "age of chivalry," but that women did not. Women, he stated, did not desire to be a "mere toy or plaything" but to take part in life and show their "effect on the destiny of our race."[33]

In many ways, the courtship of Salathiel Voris and Mary Woolridge provides an excellent example of how one border South couple sought to convey and fulfill their desire for mutuality in their relationship. In July 1857, Salathiel Voris, of Franklin County, Kentucky, wrote to nineteen-year-old Mary Woolridge, declaring his love for her. He assured her that "nothing shall be left undone that is in my power to do But what shall be for your happiness." Unfortunately, she did not return his love—at first. In the summer of 1857, Salathiel sent Mary a ring, which she refused.[34] Two months later as he prepared to leave for work on the railroad, he wrote to assure her that the love he had for her was no "youthful passion but sincere and deeper grounded." He begged her to reconsider, as he could not forget her. Over the coming months, he wrote again and again, asking her to become his "partner for life" and to let him become her "kind and affectionate Companion."[35]

Mary wavered in the spring of 1858, asking for his picture; yet by early summer 1858, her letters slowed to a stop. Salathiel wrote in a panic. "I wrote to you as I felt I was sincere," he pleaded. "I asked your permission to correspond with me you gave your permission. have I written or treated you in any way that is not right. then why is it." They patched things up by midsummer, and he visited her parents, drinking a cordial with her mother. His feelings had not "lessened a partickle but have increased." Mary, however, kept him at arm's length, warning that she wanted to make sure the pair were right for each other and that she "met no person [she] liked better."[36]

By the end of the summer, Mary had broken off their relationship again. Salathiel could not believe it. He wrote to Mary: "[I] offered you . . . a strong arm and willing heart, pledged myself to go through this cold world regardless of trials to stand by you in the hour of affliction to console you when in trouble. to be your faithfull supporter in time of need." In

January 1859, she blamed her health for not accepting his proposals. "It seems that you cannot get your consent to Marry Me," Salathiel chided Mary. "I want one that will love me care for me for which I will do the Same regardless of all *obstacles.*" Though she continued to be coy throughout the summer months, by fall he still persisted. He wrote that he hoped she would change her mind.[37] She could guide him, he promised, and would always be an influence on his character. Finally, by early 1860, Salathiel's perseverance paid off, and Mary accepted his proposal. The two wed in Frankfort, Kentucky, in January 1860, at her father's home.

Salathiel's letters to Mary demonstrate the depth of romantic fervor that many Kentucky and western Virginia men exhibited while wooing their potential wives, and his language reflects a strong sense of mutuality. He desired a partner for life, a companion, and a mutual source of comfort. He constantly sought reciprocity of feeling from Mary and assured her that nothing was more necessary to a successful marriage than a loving and sincere heart. His continued use of this rhetoric indicates that he knew Mary ultimately wanted a marriage based on mutuality as well. Mary's hesitation was not uncommon. In an analysis of middle-class New England women, Nancy Cott argues that the "canon of domesticity" actually gave marriage even more importance. Marriage symbolized an important new social role and increased isolation from the world.[38] In addition, female acceptance of the romantic ideal set the bar that much higher in finding a partner. Ultimately though, Mary found his sales pitch appealing enough to overcome her parents' objections, and her own, and married Salathiel.

Once a couple came to an agreement, an engagement and wedding soon followed. For those of the lower classes, engagements were rarely formally announced, and weddings were often quick and simple, whether in a family home or before a justice of the peace. For those of the middle or upper classes, though, engagements and weddings were often more lavish and complex affairs. During the nineteenth century, the engagement evolved into an important transition period between courtship and marriage. In addition, as the century progressed, the beginning of the engagement became increasingly private, involving intimate gestures such as a proposal, rather than symbolizing a public announcement of the couple's intention to marry.[39]

Moving from courtship to marriage, however, brought a true test of the new ideals of mutuality and compatibility. In the nineteenth century, men and women spent very little time with members of the opposite sex. Their worlds revolved around same-sex socialization, usually beginning in their adolescent years.[40] Even elite white women's clothing, which featured expansive and limiting hoop skirts, was designed to isolate them from the masculine world and men themselves. As young men and women courted and fell in love, they may have had a cultural ideal for which to strive, but they often had no real understanding of how to implement these standards. Couples learned quickly whether the passionate declarations from their correspondence would hold up against the day-to-day trials and tribulations of marriage and family life. While some did not, many happily enjoyed long and successful relationships. In order to ensure such happiness, many turned to friends, relatives, and even advice manuals for instructions on the types of marriages that border South residents desired.

Beginning in the 1820s and 1830s, American and European publishers churned out hundreds of books, pamphlets, and novels that demonstrated to men and women the proper ways to behave. In New England, this literature helped shape the creation of domesticity as a feminine ideal during this era and contributed to a strong sense of common womanhood.[41] Advice literature generally focused on a few categories, including parenting, childrearing, women's social roles, female education, and the relationship between men and women.[42] These manuals, usually published in places like London, New York, or Boston, made their way into border South homes by the mid-nineteenth century and influenced the development of these households and their gendered ideals. Although they were certainly also found in the hands of brides and grooms in homes farther south, the border South, with its diverse economy and ties to northern markets and urban centers, made an especially lucrative market for these publications. Reading these slender manuals and sermons, Kentuckians and western Virginians absorbed more deeply the philosophy of mutuality in marriage.

On her wedding day in January 1860, Mary Woolridge's uncle, James Owen, presented her with an advice manual written by a Fall River, Massachusetts, minister. The book, *Bridal Greetings,* outlined the "mutual duties of husband and wife," urging couples to forgo the sentimentality of their courtship days and prepare for the "stern realities of rugged life." The author, Reverend Daniel Wise, warned couples against unreasonably high expectations for married life, reminding them that courtship was often filled with deception as both sought to woo a future spouse. He told couples this not to strike fear into their hearts on their wedding day but to better prepare them for the challenges of a life with a husband or wife with whom one had spent little time before the wedding. Upon discovering these differences, he wrote, "the parties either yield to each other, learn the art of mutual assimilation, and pass life in comparative enjoyment," or they quarrel and "begin a career of domestic misery, ending in separation or death."[43]

According to the Reverend Wise, the first thing many couples should deal with was the transition into each other's families. Happiness in marriage, he wrote, depended upon everyone accommodating to one another and finding their roles. Wise noted, "It is the *right* of the wife to preside as a queen over her household." Not only did Wise advocate the domestic ideal for wives, he also promoted frugality for both spouses, telling the story of a newly married couple whose desire to live in a "genteel" neighborhood led to their insolvency within three years. "By prudent economy in the commencement," they might have lived without such a crisis. In order to avoid bankruptcy, Wise advised husbands and wives to work together to economize.[44]

Most importantly, though, *Bridal Greetings* emphasized mutuality in order to make a marriage happy. Wise told a parable of a husband who asked his wife to pull a line over their roof while he held the opposite end. After she gave up, they both pulled together, and it went over easily. Wise believed that only working together would make a home happy. "I am not a convert to the doctrine . . . 'One quiet, both happy,'" he stated. Labor, pleasure, pain—all must mutually be enjoyed or suffered.[45] Similarly, the advice manual that Noah Cartwright and Julia Frances Rush received on their May 12, 1859, wedding day in Jefferson County, Kentucky, stated that marriage was a union for the "reciprocal benefit of the two persons who agree to form it." Repeatedly, the minister who authored the pamphlet reminded couples that they were two friends, "*fellow travelers* on the road of life," and companions, brought together by "tender attachment." Husbands and wives swore before God to care for and comfort one another. Wives were told to remember the hardships their husbands faced in the workplace, and husbands were asked to remember their wives when making decisions. Reverend James Bean asked, "For though not able to dictate, may she not be capable of advising?"[46] Notably, both *Bridal Greetings* and *The Christian Minister's Affectionate Advice to a Married Couple* were published in New York, indicating the fusion of northern urban sensibilities into border South society.

Peter Van Winkle, a western Virginia politician in the late 1850s, also shared these views in his unpublished essay on social attitudes and household roles for men and women. A New Yorker by birth, he made his home in Parkersburg, Virginia, and eventually served at the convention to form the state of West Virginia and also as a state senator.[47] Van Winkle began work on his domestic treatise during his marriage to Julia Rathbone, and it contained chapters devoted to such subjects as the relations of the household and its members. Van Winkle admitted that there were basic differences between the sexes, referring to women as "timid and retiring," and arguing that a woman made decisions not "so much upon her intellect as upon her emotions." Yet, he did not believe that marriage was a relationship akin to that of master and dependent. Drawing from the Biblical tale of Adam and Eve, he contended that the marital relationship was one based first and foremost on companionship. A good marriage had a mutuality a man could only achieve with another "endowed like himself with those emotional as well as intellectual capabilities." Van Winkle believed that a wife was entitled to a certain amount of power and input in the household, and that any use of a man's power when not to aid the household was "tyrannical." He concluded that the inability of women to cope with the more difficult duties of the household head was the result of socialization, since "where she has been treated as the companion of her husband, her adaptation is as perfect as is that of the man."[48] Although Van Winkle's treatise remained unpublished, it clearly indicates his participation in a new language of mutuality common in the nineteenth century.

Border South ministers incorporated the sentiment of mutuality in their wedding services as well. In the mid-1850s, William Thomas McElroy began performing weddings for free black residents of Kentucky. During the typical ceremony, he reminded the couple that marriage was a religious institution bestowed by God. Thus, certain duties accompanied it, including the cultivation of "mutual love for one another." Both husbands and wives should learn to deal with each other's faults, encourage one another, provide comfort, employ "honesty and industry," and make each other happy. As the pair held hands, he would remind them that their joys, sorrows, and hearts were now one.[49]

In the mid-nineteenth century, the publication of advice manuals, often in New York or London, brought new philosophies of mutuality into all parts of the United States, contributing to a new understanding of marriage. Without a strong publishing industry in the South, many southerners relied on northern publishers for their advice manuals and other literature. However, this did not make them unthinking consumers. The specific advice manuals chosen by these Kentucky and western Virginia families were a reflection of their attitudes. These manuals also echo the language found in courtship letters. Young men and women tried to find partners who shared their desire for a marriage based on mutuality, and when they married, they read advice manuals that reassured them that this goal was achievable in the real world.

In *Bridal Greetings,* Reverend Wise described an ideal relationship as one in which both partners considered each other's feelings and in which they were intellectually and emotionally compatible. Yet, his advice to married couples reflected the harsh realities of marriage. When he used the term "mutuality," he did not merely conceive of it in a romantic sense. He realized that one of the core components of this new ideology would be the economic functioning of the household. Husbands and wives could display their newfound mutuality through their mutual frugality and economy. The ideals laid out in advice manuals were still that—ideals. Not only that, they were not exclusive to this region. However, when marriages failed to live up to the high standards in these manuals, many border South residents took things a step further, airing their grievances in the divorce court.

In the first half of the nineteenth century, household labor and economy formed a critical part of female domestic ideology. In both the antebellum North and South, women assumed they would play a role in maintaining their husbands' economic security and would perform household responsibilities vital to its efficient management.[50] Yet, subtle differences distinguished northern and southern women's domestic work expectations. Contrasting the ideals of the economical northern housewife, the aristocratic southern lady, and the diligent yeoman farmwife, Keith Barton argues that while the three roles featured many common traits, the "individualism and market relations of the northern middle class" distinguished northern women's ideal. According to Barton and other scholars, northern women were considered expert domestic managers. Public figures, such as Catherine Beecher, advocated for the "scientific management of kitchens." Elite southerners, on the other hand, saw women as part of a greater hierarchical structure, "not as members of a separate women's culture whose empire was the home." Likewise, the roles of southern farmwives were less clearly differentiated from those of their husbands, who also labored alongside them.[51]

Additionally, a key component of the growing privatization of the household was the association of the woman's sphere with domesticity and *not* economy. Women worked, certainly. They managed the household affairs and servants, they raised and educated children, and they entertained and socialized with their husband's peers and business associates.

However, increasingly during this era, society viewed these roles as manifestations of a woman's love for her family, rather than as viable economic contributions to the household.[52] To be domestic and feminine was to distance oneself from the market and economic world. Yet, the ways in which authors like Reverend Wise deployed mutuality mark it as distinct from domesticity. They do not demonetize the contributions of wives but rather argue that they are part of a "mutual economy" that benefits all members of the family. It is particularly telling that western Virginians and Kentuckians embraced this understanding of marriage, as based on mutuality rather than pure wifely domesticity. Southern farms and plantations could not become semi-isolated domestic spheres in the same way as some northern homes could. Similarly, as in the greater Ohio River Valley, the semi-urban communities of the border South featured a number of spaces in which market and home overlapped. Once again, their unique combination of upper South and midwestern culture—in this case, economics—shaped their household roles. In the border South, the household was never completely feminized and that led to an assertion of women's contributions in other ways to the running of the home.

Throughout Kentucky and western Virginia, women were expected to be efficient and economical housewives. This behavior was so idealized by some communities that a woman's frugality and industry became a defense of character in divorce cases. Members of the community praised women who worked hard, especially in the face of listless husbands. They stood in support of them when they tried to break ties with their husbands, who had failed to be mutually supportive. John McCarney told the Franklin County Circuit Court that Eliza Glenn deserved a divorce from her "dissipated" husband, Squire, because she was "an industrious, well behaved lady." Eliza worked for McCarney, a tailor, "labour[ing] late and early . . . for the support of her self & children."[53] When Kentuckian Christiana Merritt sued her husband, Richard, for divorce in 1854, she told the court that she had always been a "prudent, industrious and faithful wife." Richard, on the other hand, had become a "habitual drunkard."[54] Thirty-year-old Lutheran Buckley called George Mullins to defend her petition for divorce against her husband, Michael, for cruelty and intemperance. He told the court that he had "never seen any thing amiss in Mrs. Buckley." Moreover, Lutheran was an "industrious neat woman, and that is her general character."[55] In Ohio County, western Virginia, Mary Robinson attributed her husband's successful grocery business to "industry & economy, practiced by both your oratrix & himself."[56] These women used their behavior as a defense, knowing that this ideal might strike a chord with border South judges who subscribed to a sense of mutuality in marriage.

In their divorce cases, border South husbands and wives debated how well each had fulfilled their mutual duty to cultivate a strong household economy. They often disagreed on who was at fault, but nonetheless agreed on the sort of behaviors each expected of the other. In 1852, forty-two-year-old Maria E. English filed for divorce in the Franklin County Circuit Court. Married to her husband, Morris, for about eight years, she stated that she had been forced to flee their home two years earlier because of his cruelty, intemperance, and neglect. He beat her "unmercifully" and, because of his drinking, failed to provide the family with necessary items. Morris denied all her charges, assuring the court he always had plenty of "bacon corn beef & hogs."[57] Instead, Morris criticized Maria's housekeeping and frugality.

When asked by the defense if "there was a lack on the part of Mrs English in not keeping her house as a neat industrious woman would keep her house," their neighbor Thomas B. Johnson admitted that the house was "not kept as I should like my house to be kept." Morris's lawyers pressed further, getting Johnson to testify that Morris had provided Maria with an enslaved woman to aid in sewing and other work and that a woman who exercised the proper amount of industry could have kept a good house with what Morris provided.[58] Morris and Maria's debates demonstrate the roles each expected the other to play. Maria sought a good provider and stable husband, while Morris saw his wife as both a homemaker and an economic assistant. As his case and others show, border South men expected their wives to help cultivate and grow their financial resources through their careful actions.

During their twenty-five years of marriage, Franklin County residents Jane and Henry Vawter constantly vied for control of the household economy. Initially, she and Henry had lived in peace and harmony, raising four children and achieving some financial stability with "the mutual industry and economy of herself and the s. Henry." Such cooperation had helped create an estate containing 140 acres of land (worth about $1,500) and numerous horses, cows, hogs, and other stock. Yet, she charged, Henry constantly prevented her from using these resources to fulfill her domestic duties, locking up plates and cooking utensils when guests arrived to see her and preventing her from selling butter to make extra cash.[59] On the other hand, in his answer, James responded that Jane took his crops without his knowledge, selling them for her own profit, not the family's. The Vawters' case reveals the precarious position of women in the household. Neither the couple nor the neighborhood seemed certain of the role Jane should play in dividing up, selling, or distributing the produce of the farm. Some thought her actions typical of a proper farmwife, whose position allowed for dabbling in small economic side projects; others thought her independent efforts took away from the household and that her role should always be first and foremost to follow and support her husband.[60]

Border South men were also expected to be industrious. Susan Callahan defended Morris English as a "very" industrious man (and incidentally called Maria English a "careless housekeeper"). In William Howard's Warren County divorce case, his neighbors defended his performance as a husband and stated that he had always provided well for his wife, Catherine. Even after she abandoned him, he continued to rent his small farm outside of Bowling Green, cultivating a small crop, although her departure forced him to return to his parents' house for meals. He had upheld his economic and household obligations; Catherine had failed to do so with hers.[61] In 1855, Catharine Lynch charged her husband, John, with abandonment and failing to support her. In his successful cross petition, John Lynch used deponents to show that he had been "an industrious hard working man and provided well for his family."[62] Border South men also touted their industriousness when they wooed their future wives. While wooing his future wife, Salathiel Voris admitted that he was poor but told her that "by industry and perseverance I feel confident that I shall be enabled to accumulate enough to make life pleasant."[63]

When his wife, Sarah, sued him for a divorce, Warren County resident Hiram Boyd enlisted the help of a lawyer to defend his reputation. Former employers, neighbors, and housemates testified that he was a "hard working man." A local farm laborer, Hiram admitted to being poor but adamantly defended his work ethic. Most days his wagon could be seen leaving home before the sun rose and arriving home after it set. Even his drinking did not deter his productivity. One former employer admitted that he got drunk a couple of times on the job but stated that he could still "attend to his business" in that condition. Similarly, Joseph Hays, who often drove with Hiram to work, seemed to think he could drive the wagon quite well after drinking, although after getting a "little too drunk" one day, he did drive the wagon into a ditch. In fact, although multiple deponents brought up his drinking, the court treated both Sarah and Hiram fairly equally in their eventual decree, divorcing each with no subsequent blame.[64]

Wives could successfully obtain a divorce if they showed that their husbands had been poor providers or had forced their wives to work.[65] Border South residents wanted wives to be industrious, efficient household managers, but not to the point of excessive labor. After all, in a society in which enslaved people did much of the visible labor, forcing any white women to work too hard could demean both them and their families. In Martha Hicatt's 1854 divorce petition, she stated that she had been a "prudent industrious" wife for James Hicatt for almost two decades, when he drove her off with threats to her life. Even during their marriage, James had been intemperate and neglectful, forcing her to work to support the couple's five children.[66] Likewise, forty-year-old Patrick Fitzgerald's frequent bouts of drunkenness left his wife, Mary, nearly fifty, without resources. She told the Franklin County Circuit Court that she had nothing to support herself or her children, except that "earned by her daily labor." She, not her husband, paid for her children to go to school.[67] Often, husbands' abandonment forced wives to work, something from which marriage should have protected them. In response to her husband's charge of abandonment, Elizabeth Snelling told the court that he, instead, had abandoned her, a fact that led her "by honest industry to support herself."[68]

Margaret Bole, a forty-seven-year-old New York transplant living in Wheeling, western Virginia, had perhaps the best grounds on which to charge her husband with misappropriating her duty as a household manager. During the early 1850s, William Bole owned a boot and shoe store on Main Street in Wheeling; he, Margaret, and their six children lived in the same building, above the store. Their marriage, detailed in voluminous depositions, was a tumultuous one. Margaret's petition charged him with vicious abuse that ranged from striking her, spitting in her face, and threatening to shoot her. Once, she wrote, he "drew a knife upon her threatening to rip her up." For months prior to their separation, she spent each night locked in the garret of the store building with her children, while he threw dishes at the door and demanded to be let in. Finally, in October 1853, William Bole left Wheeling, supposedly for Zanesville, Ohio. Instead, he made his way to New York City and onto a ship bound for Australia. In a letter to a friend, he wrote that his wife had been "the cause of all this trouble" and that she would "rejoice" over his departure.[69]

Perhaps one reason Margaret might celebrate his absence was his treatment of her economic role within the household. In her petition, Margaret wrote that William "compelled [her] to perform all the menial offices about their household and never permitted her to hire a Servant." In addition, he forced her to do both the housework and the store work, all while cursing and swearing at her in front of their children and neighbors.[70] Northern women hired domestic workers to relieve some of their household work burden even further. Hiring these workers "did not lead to a life of leisure, but it did allow women to differentiate household labor by assigning arduous tasks to servants while reserving for themselves those that required creativity, organization, or experience—responsibilities fit for expert housekeepers."[71] William prevented Margaret from attaining her elevated status as domestic manager by co-opting her labor in the store and by preventing her from hiring assistance.

Living in the most urban of the six counties sampled, Margaret Bole seemed to believe in both the tenets of mutuality and domesticity. She saw her role as purely devoted to her family, not the functioning of her husband's store. Men worked outside the home, while women labored inside at "nonwage activities."[72] Women's role in the domestic sphere gave them a new authority in the household, one that would be diluted if this position was not respected. She was not alone in this belief, but it was more commonly found among the most urban border southerners rather than rural border southerners. Rural border southerners still tended to view the home as an economic sphere for both partners, while urban residents tended to waver between the desire for feminine domesticity and the reality and needs of both partners to be economic contributors. The difference also revealed class divisions in these urban communities. Urban border southerners with greater financial means, like the Boles and the Englishes, strove for a northern middle-class style of domesticity. Margaret Bole used her husband's refusal to hire domestic help and free her for more specialized labor as evidence of his failures. To defend himself against Maria English's charges, Morris English pointed out that he had hired an enslaved woman to relieve her burden in the household.[73] In these cases, husbands wanted wives to be scientific managers, rather than laborers. However, working-class urban border women, like Eliza Glenn, Lutheran Buckley, and Mary Fitzgerald, expected to work and used their industriousness as a defense in divorce cases, calling out their neglectful husbands while lauding their own economic achievements.[74]

In the nineteenth century, new ideals glorified industriousness for both spouses, as advice manuals, sermons, and novels demonstrated that mutual economy would lead to a productive home and happiness for both. Not only did border southerners emphasize their desire to marry for mutual love, they also stressed to their future spouses that, working together, husband and wife would become a success. Ellen Green assured her future husband, Hector, that she did not mind his lack of fortune. "I can assist you in accumulating," she told him. "We may yet get along independent of others."[75] Their misfortunes would only aid the pair in learning frugality together. In western Virginia, Waitman T. Willey's wife, Elizabeth, chided him for lending money so easily and frequently to friends. "You will think that you made your money and have a right to do as you please with it," she wrote, "but I think I have an interest in the matter. I helped to make your money at least took care of it which is the same thing."[76] Using the rhetoric of mutuality, women and men in Kentucky and western Virginia defended their roles as economic partners and attacked the other for failing to live up to their ideals.

In rural Warren County, women not only defended the economic contribution of their labor but also that of the valuable property they brought to the marriage. As married women, they had little legal claim to the property, and many cited this as their very reason for requesting a divorce. Yet clearly, these border South women did not view their identities or their possessions as absorbed completely by their husbands upon marriage. Absorbing Enlightenment ideas about individualism, their language insisted that property brought into the marriage was "my" property; property accumulated or maintained during the marriage was "their" property. Very rarely did their rhetoric give their husbands sole ownership over the household property.

Priscilla Potts, for instance, signed an agreement with her husband, Jonathan, upon their marriage, that forbade him from exerting sole control over her premarital property. However, shortly after their marriage, he sold her most valuable property for a pittance. In this southern society, that property could be only one thing—enslaved men and women. Priscilla claimed that she owned eighteen or twenty enslaved men and women at the time of her marriage. Jonathan had proceeded to sell them without her permission for about $500, despite the fact that another deponent valued these human beings at over $9,000. Although that property was gone by the time she filed for divorce, Priscilla told the court that she wanted to reclaim her right "as an unmarried woman" in order to apply for widow's benefits from the United States government, owed her after a previous husband's death. The court ultimately gave her the divorce, her rights as *feme sole,* although it did not agree that she needed alimony from Jonathan's estate. Priscilla won her property rights back but lost the protections of femininity (alimony) in the process.[77]

Other women brought attention to the ways in which their husbands' marital property rights could hurt wives, refusing to submit to an antiquated legal system that deprived them of legal voice or power. Avery Williams hinted that her husband had only married her for her money. Edwin's abuse began immediately after their wedding and lasted until he had spent all her inheritance. At that point, he left Kentucky for Illinois and married another woman in that state. In another case, in her petition against Edwin Hancock, Polly Hancock stated that "they" owned a few horses, cattle, beds, and a wagon but that at the time of the divorce, her husband had maintained possession of all of these. Worse, he refused to let her see or have access to her children. She pleaded with the court for intervention. Her husband, she believed, would "waste what little estate they have" unless she got an injunction. She also requested immediate custody of her children. The court swiftly granted all of her requests. Another woman, Elizabeth Lancaster, went so far as to demand her premarital property, full custody of her children, and a restoration of her maiden name.[78] Her decision to make this request, not typical in these cases, reflects the attempts of divorcing border South women to reclaim an individual identity of which their husbands had deprived them. When these women married, they wanted a partnership, not a loss of self, and they requested divorces when their marriages did not meet this ideal. These women questioned both the law and the actions of the men in their lives.

During the nineteenth century, the border South developed a reputation for moderation, exemplified in politicians like Henry Clay, as well as in these states' stance on secession and the Civil War. Henry Clay, known as the "Great Compromiser," valued calm negotiation, rather than the perceived "doctrinaire" ideologies of the North and South. As the Civil War approached and this region became a geographical, as well as cultural, middle ground, this belief in the power of moderation intensified, extending to the development of gendered ideals as well. Amy Greenberg describes the development of two regional masculinities in the antebellum era—"restrained manhood" and "martial manhood." Martial men revered physical strength, drinking "to excess," and exerting power over members of both sexes. Greenberg argues that "they were not, in general, supporters of the moral superiority of women and the values of domesticity." On the other hand, "restrained men" centered their lives around their families, their faith, and their business acumen. Because of their fears of drinking and vice, they were also likely to support the temperance movement.[79] Overall, the men in this sample of border southerners adhered to a masculinity akin to the "restrained manhood" described by Greenberg, but their ability to blend this form of masculinity with an authoritative dominance over enslaved people, for instance, demands a modification. In this case, the term "moderate manhood" may better apply to white border South men, who fused elements of both types of manhood to maintain power and love in their homes.

Male domesticity was a crucial element of the new marriage based on mutuality. While often seen as more exclusively part of the public sphere, many nineteenth-century men found the private sphere equally vital to their identity, especially those that subscribed to a restrained or moderate manhood.[80] These antebellum men valued both their wives and their homes, and many new brides were pleased to find their husbands as caring as they had promised in their proposals. As border South men increasingly identified themselves as distinct from other Americans, they argued that their form of masculinity also distinguished the region. Even though their language and rhetoric could easily have been found in the letters of men in these other places, border Southerners perceived their form of masculinity to be unique, and their manner of wielding it in circuit courts and even legislative halls reveals their unique use and understanding of it.

If a marriage of mutuality was the goal, the active participation and devotion of both partners was crucial to its stability and happiness. As James Bean reminded husbands in his advice manual, "Conjugal affection is a delicate plant [that] dies when scarcely any time is spent at home."[81] Husbands, he believed, should devote time and attention to their wives and cultivate a relationship with them, just as they would with the outside world. Devotion to one's family was a worthy trait in public men. Writing to a friend about an 1844 Lexington parade in Henry Clay's honor, G. B. Miller commended Clay for his love of city, friends, home, and wife.[82] At Kentucky judge George Robertson's funeral, the Reverend Robert Christie eulogized: "He also sustained and filled with affectionate assiduity the tenderest relations of domestic life, whether of husband, father, or grandsire."[83] Despite a distinguished career, which took him from circuit-riding lawyer to the United States Congress, Robertson's devotion to home and family garnered specific and pointed praise in speeches and in his son's biography.[84] Other men described their attitudes toward domesticity themselves. George Johnson, the Confederate governor of Kentucky, once wrote his wife a poem describing her place in his life:

> As Home, with joys seem sweetly blest
> Upon the wave-capped sea,
> When seen the last, from the billows crest;
> So then art, Love !! to me.[85]

For the most part, border South husbands still held the upper hand in marital relationships. Both in law and largely in practice husbands had enormous power, and wives often submitted to it.[86] Married women had few legal rights, especially in the first third of the nineteenth century. Under coverture, they actually lost their legal identity upon marriage. Especially compared with acceptable practice in today's society, nineteenth-century border South marriages were largely one-sided. However, many men respected their wives' opinions and positions. Ellen Bodley was shocked when her husband wavered in his plan to stay in Louisville, Kentucky, rather than move to Mississippi because she had expressed a desire to leave. "When I think how much uneasiness I have caused you my dearest husband it makes my heart sick," she wrote to William. She promised to be happy and content, so long as she had "the best husband in the world."[87]

According to the ideology of feminine domesticity, a wife had a duty to create a comforting domestic haven for her husband, a place to escape from the hectic public world. Yet, as domesticity also came to be seen as a masculine ideal, some women expected their husbands to act as comforters as well.[88] Modern medicine was in its infancy in the early nineteenth century, and women spent much of their lives suffering from one ailment or another. Pregnancy was such a dangerous period of one's life that many women wrote informal wills when they discovered their condition. Yet, a marriage based on mutuality demanded that both partners support and care for one another "in sickness and in health." Border South women looked to their husbands to alleviate their physical and emotional pain, and many husbands promised to (and did) care devotedly for their sick wives.

Kentuckian Salathiel Voris told Mary Woolridge that "nothing would afford me more pleasure than to be found trying to comfort one that I love dear." A year later, when she still continued to hesitate to marry him, he swore, "I will Stand by you in the hour of Sickness nurse you add to your comforts try to console you in the hour of Trouble."[89] Failure to provide aid and assistance to a wife was considered problem enough to receive attention in some divorce petitions. Rebecca Robinson argued that her husband, John, abused her, stated that he no longer loved her, and "left her without tea or coffee, & indeed destitute of any comfort when she was sick."[90] In her petition, Sarah Boyd stated that her husband, Hiram, unceremoniously dumped her at a boardinghouse when she grew sickly, while he countered that he had only left her there after hiring a nurse to care for her.[91]

Male domesticity was also intimately entangled with ideas of fatherhood. As society encouraged men to spend more time at home and cultivate their domestic circle, more focus fell on the father–child relationship as part of this equation. With the rise of mutuality, less emphasis lay on male authority in the marital relationship, and this soon spilled over into other areas of the household. Advice manuals encouraged men to raise their children through loving authority, not pure dominance. During this era, men juggled contradictory ideas of patriarchal power and growing individualism, but it is clear that they often sought close and caring relationships with their children.[92] In addition, as nineteenth-century parents began to view childhood as a vital phase in a person's life to be protected and cherished, they devoted more and more time to ensuring their children's happiness. Often, this meant spending considerable time with them.[93] Nineteenth-century men, like those in the border South, expected to cultivate close relationships with all members of their familial sphere.

In late 1854, Kentuckian Mildred Bullitt wrote to her daughter, who had recently given birth. She asked about the baby's health, whose name it would bear, and what kind of father her husband, John, would be. "Does he cultivate a taste for kissing the baby," she asked. "If he doesn't he dont deserve to have a baby."[94] Husbands wrote to their families and friends, gushing over their new children. Kentuckian S. T. January told his mother, "Henry is as well, and more Interesting than when you saw him." He proudly told her that his son had learned to say "papa." Whenever January entered the room, he told his mother, his son would cry or crawl to him. He fretted slightly over the baby's health and weight, but said he hoped it would soon be "fattening."[95]

Border South mothers and fathers encouraged their children to form strong and lasting bonds with their parents. Lucinda Helm, for example, chided her young daughter that she had written to her father only once while he was away in Nashville, Tennessee. "Darling you should answer his letters immediately," she told her. "No man could be more devoted to his family, & you know his love for you was always particularly tender."[96] She recalled how her husband used to carry his daughter to the table and sit her next to him for dinner. Some fathers still maintained their distance, and, tellingly, occasionally referred to their infants as "it." Shawn Johansen argues that this shows that the fathers either did not recognize the child's identity or had not yet developed a strong relationship with the baby.[97] But many, when they spoke of their new babies, used loving and caring language. John Wall told his mother his new daughter was doing wonderfully. "I shall not brag too much upon her beauty," he wrote, "but I will say that it is the sweetest and best little creature in the world."[98] Caring fatherhood became another critical component of mutuality in the nineteenth-century border South.

Whether in their views on the centrality of the home in their lives, the proper role of educated women, or their attitudes toward their children, men in the nineteenth-century border South exhibited many signs of domesticity. Obviously, this does not discount their continued authority over their wives and children, but during this era, this authority began to be softened by a companionate and loving touch. And this belief in a moderate manhood extended beyond the household. As chapter 4 will show, it also influenced their decisions in the political realm, even in their most consequential decision—whether or not to secede from the Union in 1861.

During the 1850s, Kentuckians Susan Scrogin and Henry Haviland corresponded frequently, first as friends and then as lovers. Both courted others before they settled down. Susan met one potential suitor on the train.[99] Henry made the acquaintance of multiple ladies while he attended fairs in Kentucky and Ohio.[100] Yet, by 1861, Henry proposed, confessing to Susan that his feelings toward her had changed. Susan quickly accepted his proposal. When Henry expressed frustration that he was not a wealthier catch, Susan dismissed his fears and told him that love was all she sought. Henry gladly accepted this answer and rejoiced in her happiness, stating that "the extent of my happiness would be governed by yours for I could not be, if *you* should be unhappy."[101]

Henry explained how his feelings had grown slowly from friendship into love, as he came to respect her as a partner and companion. Susan gratefully accepted his offer but warned, "All that I have to offer any Gentleman . . . is my hand and the love of an honest heart." When he responded that he also had little wealth, she soothed him by promising, "That is not what I love for, it is on the qualities of the heart alone that I base my Love, to gain future happiness."[102] The couple eventually married in 1868, had one child (a daughter), and remained together till Susan's death at age seventy-three in 1897. In their correspondence, couples like Susan and Henry emphasized the mutual benefits of their relationship to each other's happiness and emphasized the connections between love, friendship, and partnership.

During the thirty years prior to the Civil War, the ideal of mutuality expanded throughout the nation. Although the border South was not the only region to experience this shift, their unique regional identity and culture allowed this philosophy to flourish to a greater extent than elsewhere in the South. As Bridget Ford has argued, competing ideologies, whether religious, political, or even gendered, created an environment in which adaptability and flexibility reigned supreme.[103] Uniquely positioned on the edge of both a North–South and East–West axis, this region embraced new philosophies toward marriage and, specifically, a new role for both men and women within the relationship. Studying the words and behaviors of couples during courtship, in prescriptive literature, or throughout their married lives reveals that antebellum white border South residents sought mutuality, companionship, domesticity, and industriousness for both partners. As chapter 3 will show, although eastern Virginian couples cared deeply for one another, their correspondence and records indicate that female submissiveness, strict social hierarchy, and male dominance retained a hold on marital relationships. Many Kentuckians and western Virginians were more likely to seek mutuality in their marriages, reflecting their hybrid border identity and weaker attachment to a strictly "southern" identity. More importantly, they acted upon this rhetoric in unusual ways, allowing for a greater number of divorces than in eastern Virginia counties. People seeking divorce deployed the language of mutuality in their cases, to demonstrate their worth as partners and their spouses' failures. They then took this one step further, arguing that marriage itself was a contract between two mutual partners and could, therefore, be undone.

After all, even in marriages based on mutuality, couples disagreed and fought. Especially in a relationship of mutual partners, egos and feelings were often bruised, and couples had to learn to respect and look out for one another. Francis Pierpont, of Fairmont, western Virginia—future governor of the Restored State of Virginia—expressed such sentiments to his wife, Julia. Clearly devoted to her, he valued her opinions, praise, and advice, but the two sometimes disagreed over their marital duties. After an early fight during their marriage, he even contemplated separation if Julia felt unsatisfied by his "ability to appreciate [her] feelings." In the end, he left it to her to decide and "take the responsibility."[104] The Pierponts had a marriage of mutuality, yet the need to balance the feelings of both led to marital conflict and even a contemplated (though not actual) separation. As the next chapter will show, Francis Pierpont was not the only border southerner who considered separation or divorce, nor the only one to accept his wife's ultimate decision in the matter.

2

No More, Together

Sometime in the 1830s, in Garrard County, Kentucky, one couple found themselves "mutually dissatisfied" with their marriage. Although Jesse and Jane Simpson had been married for many years, they now could no longer bear to live together. With little fuss, they agreed upon the terms of their separation, laying them out in a formal separation agreement and abandoning their shared home.[1] At the time of the Simpsons' separation, however, most courts and legislatures in the United States did not recognize "dissatisfaction" as grounds for divorce. Kentucky was no different. Because the Simpsons could not legally obtain a divorce, their separation agreement was more of a customary agreement than a legally recognized one. Jesse and Jane must have known that they could not get a divorce, since they settled on this path. However, Jane's actions after they signed this contract suggest that she did not agree with the limitations on divorce in the state.

In their separation agreement, Jesse and Jane Simpson attempted to divide their property without the intervention of the court. Jesse gave Jane custody of their child, as well as a thirty-dollar note and one enslaved girl. Jane and her child lived peacefully for a few months, at which point Jesse returned, kidnapped the enslaved girl from Jane, and sold her for $150, refusing to give any of the money to his estranged wife. In response, Jane took him to court. The case, *Simpson v. Simpson,* went all the way to the Kentucky Court of Appeals, but Jane did not find the relief she sought. The Court of Appeals rejected her claims. Instead, they argued that under common law, husband and wife were "entirely incapable of contracting directly with each other, and therefore, such a contract [is] considered a nullity." Specifically, the doctrine of coverture subsumed a wife's legal identity to that of her husband upon their marriage. Without an independent legal identity, she had no ability to consent to a contract, thereby rendering the Simpsons' separation agreement void. The Court of Appeals saw the Simpsons' case as indicative of a larger threat to Kentucky marital unity: "If voluntary articles of separation, such as these as are exhibited in the present case, are to be recognized and enforced as valid contracts, in a Court of Chancery, it certainly would be adding, by judicial authority, another, and an almost illimitable ground for partial divorce, which would greatly weaken the sanctions by which the institution of marriage is upheld."[2]

Not all Kentuckians shared the trepidation of the Kentucky justices in 1836. Jesse and (especially) Jane Simpson, for one example, had just established their belief in a couple's right to *agree* to divorce, something that seemed radical to many at the time and especially so in a southern state. And, in fact, many members of the Kentucky legal system would soon shift their attitudes as well. By the 1850s, Kentucky had one of the most generous divorce codes in the growing United States, including a provision that allowed couples to divorce after a mutually agreed-upon separation of five years. Divorcing spouses' ability to do so undercut the power of coverture, so central to the Court of Appeals ruling in 1836. As the Civil War approached, it seems that Kentuckians, and others in the border South, valued the ability to more easily end an unhappy relationship. This shift also reflects residents' evolving beliefs about what marriages should look like. As marriages in the border South became increasingly defined by their mutuality, both emotional and economic, so too did the divorce process increasingly reflect the mutual needs and demands of husband and wife. In Kentucky, by the Civil War, the legal system allowed greater flexibility for unhappy couples, while western and Appalachian Virginians manipulated the restrictive legal code in Virginia to achieve similar results. Both approaches reflected residents' understanding of marriage as contractual by nature.

Specifically, this chapter explores the ways in which border southerners in Kentucky, western Virginia, and Appalachian Virginia embraced an ideology of contractualism in their marriages. Historically, the debate over divorce often revolved around attitudes about the contractual nature of marriage.[3] Under traditional Catholic law, for example, marriage was (and is) considered a sacrament and, therefore, indissoluble. However, during the Protestant Reformation, Martin Luther criticized the number of sacraments in the Catholic Church, instead arguing that the Protestant church should recognize only the three sacraments explicitly found in the Bible. In many Protestant churches, such as that of the Puritans who founded the New England colonies in North America, marriage was not a sacrament but a religiously imbued legal contract. Marriage, like other contracts, relied on the consent of two competent adults. If either of those parties broke the terms of the contract, the other had the right to end that contract. Because of this religious split, the Puritan colonies granted the greatest number of colonial divorces in North American (even more than Great Britain itself). The Church of England, which was the dominant church in the southern colonies, still viewed marriage as a sacrament, restricting the region's divorce law. Before the American Revolution, for example, Virginia's legislature had not granted a single divorce. South Carolina's legislature would not do so before the Civil War.[4]

Supporting a contractual interpretation of marriage did not just reflect regional differences in religious views. It also reflected attitudes about the permanence of all social institutions. With the formation of the new nation in the late eighteenth century, many states began to draw distinctions between their legal systems and that of England. Independence gave states the freedom to challenge many aspects of English law, which had made divorce nearly impossible. Yet, this evolution occurred at a different pace throughout the new country. As the New England states broke from English tradition and moved their divorce cases into the courts in the 1790s, southern states continued to resist judicial divorce. Thomas Buckley has stated that if these adaptations in divorce law amounted to a "true legal revolution," then "the South's revolution was decidedly retarded."[5]

However, divorce laws in the early United States also reveal differences between the original thirteen colonies, now staid eastern states with an established wealthy upper class, and the expanding nation. As new western states entered the union, they challenged the older hierarchies embraced by the eastern elite. Especially as the United States entered the era previously known as the Jacksonian era, western states saw themselves as the bearers of a rejuvenated and expanded American democracy. They adapted, revised, rewrote, and built on the legal codes of the coastal states. Family law was no exception.[6]

Nonetheless, as with so many things in the antebellum era, slavery left an indelible and undeniable impact on family law. In the early antebellum period, dissatisfied couples could obtain a divorce in every state aside from South Carolina.[7] While northern states often adhered to a contractual view of family life, the South rejected this change. There, "race and caste, a rural culture, a hierarchical society, and a pervasive localism" contributed to a particularly southern interpretation of legal matters.[8] Especially in a region in which social hierarchy and mastery were such vital parts of household life, divorce represented a threat to power, control, and the slave system itself.[9] Granting unhappy spouses the right to divorce their partners obviously chipped away at the permanence of marriage itself, but it threatened the South in larger ways as well. As the nineteenth century began, southerners began to defend slavery as a positive good, rather than a necessary evil, and their arguments about its benefits shifted. Specifically, white southerners argued that black southerners were better off than white workers in the North. White southerners touted the supposed "cradle-to-grave security" of the peculiar institution and glorified the southern family, "black and white." What might it lead to if members of this family, even the white members, were allowed to dissolve the bonds that tied them together? This power was even more dangerous when bestowed upon the female members of the family, who were supposed to be deferential and subordinate to their husbands and fathers, as a slave would be to his master.[10] White southerners had very real reasons to fear the growth of divorce in the United States during the nineteenth century.

An acknowledgment of the contractual nature of marriage would also grant some semblance of competency and power to husbands *and* wives in marriage. The growing northern debate over slavery caused many antebellum northerners to reassess the marital relationship and reorient it toward a contractual mold. Married women were emboldened to push for their rights to property and wages. Using the language of contract within marriage opened the door to the notion of marriage as being between two consenting equals.[11] In many ways, it paved the way for more liberal divorce statutes. After all, a contract, once made, could be broken if one party failed to uphold their end of the bargain. Contractualism flew in the face of coverture, as so clearly reflected in the warnings of the Kentucky justices in 1836.

In the decades preceding the Civil War, Americans wrestled with challenges and changes to the family structure that resulted from the Industrial Revolution, the women's rights movement, the spread of slavery, the rise of abolitionism, and the growth of companionate ideals of marriage.[12] They also built upon, referenced, and adapted a century's worth of common law that contributed to their own definition of marital roles. In the seventeenth and eighteenth centuries, the American colonies had adopted English common law. Under such law, a married woman experienced a sort of "civil death" as her legal identity was subsumed into that of her husband. This is still reflected in the traditional wedding ceremony's language: "I now pronounce you man and wife." A man maintained his public identity and his legal power, while a wife was nothing more than that. She could not control her property, make a will, or run a business without her husband's permission. Most important, she could not sue or be sued in her own name. In return, her husband promised protection, support, and dower rights (one third of his property) upon his death, and he could not transfer or sell property without his wife's signature, acknowledging the revocation of her dower rights.[13] To allow married women to sue for divorce, especially in their own name, was to break coverture temporarily and, if the case went her way, permanently. It gave women the power to demand better treatment and status. Elizabeth Cady Stanton realized the power of a woman's right to divorce when she said:

> No words can describe the infinite outrages to which women are subject in compulsory relations for which the law gives no redress. . . . Now, with higher light and knowledge of the true marriage, and all the responsibilities that grow out of it, they begin to feel themselves more degraded by remaining with unworthy and unloved partners than by sundering the holy ties that bind them in such unions.[14]

Divorce could prove a powerful weapon in a previously powerless woman's arsenal.

In his lengthy 1816 treatise expounding on the American legal system, Tapping Reeve devoted seventeen chapters to the relationship between husbands and wives, although he labeled them "baron and feme," a telling distinction.[15] Many early American lawmakers adopted this language exactly when drafting state and local statutes regarding marriage. During the American Revolution, elite white men showed little willingness to challenge the hierarchy of gender, even while they fought the hierarchy of aristocratic political power. Nonetheless, the ties between political equality and the law of "baron and feme" remained, influencing the pattern of divorce into the Jacksonian era.[16] As settlers expanded west, creating new states in their path, the body politic expanded to include all white men, regardless of their propertied status. This change occurred most rapidly in these western states. During this era, a westward trend in liberalization of divorce laws also occurred. Newly created divorce laws in these states reflected a greater acceptance of contractualism, which allowed both men and women to end their relationships for a variety of grounds. Indiana, for example, became an infamous nineteenth-century "divorce haven," a title transferred to Nevada by the twentieth century. Unhappy residents of staid eastern states like New

York sometimes took a lengthy train ride to the Hoosier State to file a semi-quickie divorce against their spouse.[17] These western states rejected some aspects of the political and the gender hierarchy of their eastern counterparts. (Some of the hierarchical traditions, but not all—most of these western states also enacted racially restrictive laws, even barring black residents altogether in some places.) Still, these newly created western states showed a frontier willingness to challenge authority in multiple areas of their lives.

Border southerners' acceptance and use of contractualism in their divorce proceedings reflect a combination of these influences.[18] By and large, settlers in these states were members of various Protestant denominations, including the Baptist, Methodist, Lutheran, and Episcopal churches. Virginia law reflected more of the Episcopal tradition, whereas Kentucky law reflected the same frontier beliefs that led this region to be a center of early nineteenth-century religious revivals and new American denominations such as Methodism. Border southerners also had a fraught relationship with slavery. While border southerners certainly accepted slavery and especially its accompanying racial hierarchy, these states also harbored residents whose complex attitudes toward the peculiar institution frustrated other southerners. Kentucky, home to the antislavery politician Cassius Clay and the radical college of Berea, had one of the most prominent abolition movements in the South. Western Virginians struggled to assert their rights in a state run by a slave-owning aristocracy. While western Virginians were certainly not Garrisonian in their attitudes toward racial equality, they vilified the southern aristocracy and their reliance on the institution of slavery. Like other border southerners, these western Virginians challenged the accepted political hierarchy of the eastern elite, and some also attacked the gender-based hierarchy of the household.

American divorce law reflected a strong belief in the value of marriage as the foundation of civil society. Throughout the colonial era and into the nineteenth century, the law often discouraged divorce as a reprehensible and avoidable act and usually forbade remarriage. Because of this, most unhappy couples during this era never chose the path of divorce. Instead, many likely lived in quiet misery, refusing to risk social shame. Others may have chosen an "informal divorce," running away from their partner and never legalizing the separation. The actual cases in this chapter reflect only a small percentage of border South residents, since most couples never filed for divorce. Even in a "divorce haven" such as Indiana, the number of divorces filed pales in comparison with our own twenty-first-century statistics. However, the beliefs at the core of these couples' complaints and demands were shared by many beyond the few who chose this option. The statements in these divorce bills built on broadly held conceptions about what a marriage should look like and how each partner should behave. The couples in these cases would not have filed using these charges if they had not expected to find some support for their use. They would never have found relief if the legal code (in the case of Kentucky) and the legal system (in western and Appalachian Virginia) did not accept their desire for a way to dissolve their marriages.

Border southerners' conceptions of divorce were dramatically different from those of their counterparts in eastern Virginia. In Kentucky and western and Appalachian Virginia, unhappy couples showed few qualms about demanding a divorce for a variety of reasons. Like the Simpsons, they may even have agreed upon this course of action. They believed they had the right to end a marriage that was unhappy, dangerous, or effectively over. To them, marriage was a contract, something that existed at the discretion of both parties. They also had an inherently individualistic and personal belief about the contractual nature of marriage. They did not extend their understanding of the marriage contract to all social contracts. The case was different in Virginia, where both litigants and lawmakers invoked the threat to society at large posed by personal divorce cases. Unsurprisingly, Virginia resisted the changes in divorce law that occurred after the Civil War more strenuously than either Kentucky or West Virginia; attitudes in the latter states made it possible for them to separate divorce law from larger social changes such as emancipation. Even as border South households remained firmly ensconced in regional societies of slaves, they accepted a contractual understanding of marriage and the divorce process, as demonstrated by their acceptance of collusion and mutual separation and their purposeful use of the law itself.

In antebellum Kentucky, western Virginia, and Appalachian Virginia, changes in both the law and social perceptions of marriage allowed divorce petitioners to achieve success by such controversial practices as collusion and mutual separation, while decreasing their reliance on emotionally laden descriptions of their relationships. While many of their southern neighbors continued to resist reforms in divorce laws and fostered social conventions that frowned upon separation, border South courts displayed more flexibility and a greater acceptance of the ideals of contractualism and individualism in marriage, and petitioners took advantage of this. Divorce, both in law and practice, evolved in particular ways in the border South. While some historians argue that antebellum southern elites opposed divorce as a threat to household unity and structure, the reality of life in the upper South during the decade preceding the Civil War challenges the blanket application of such a statement. In central Kentucky and the western mountains and cities of Virginia, cracks emerged in southern patriarchy, racial and gender subordination, and household hierarchy.

This chapter explores the content of the law and its application by the citizens of Kentucky and Virginia.[19] Law is both a creation of and a reflection of society, and therefore, we must understand the law itself, as well as how it was interpreted, shaped, and manipulated by the people. In this case, what was the content of the statutes under which residents sued for divorce during the antebellum era, and what does this demonstrate about a larger discourse on marital roles and rights? Under state law during the nineteenth century, complainants could sue for divorce on various grounds, including abuse, desertion, abandonment, neglect, impotence, and adultery. Subtle differences in state statutes and their application reflect varying social and legal perceptions of divorce. The content of these state statutes, the causes that were most often used by residents, and differences in rates of success all demonstrate how divorce law and practice changed in Kentucky and western Virginia during these years. Most notably, Kentucky law provided its citizens with a wide range of options when they petitioned for divorce, including mutual separation, a fact that revealed a strong belief in contractualism.

Yet, Virginia's divorce code lagged behind Kentucky's, restricting unhappy couples' options in that state. However, not all areas of the state supported the stringent application of this law. Looking closely at local cases reveals that residents of western and Appalachian Virginia manipulated their state's laws in order to achieve a remarkably high rate of success in their divorce petitions, especially when compared with the use of the law in eastern Virginia. In the nineteenth century, most courts frowned upon the appearance of collusion in divorce cases, preferring a strictly fault-based interpretation of the law. Yet, the cases of Ohio and Tazewell Counties, Virginia, hint at collusion below the surface of these cryptic filings.

How did Kentucky, western Virginia, and eastern Virginia each respond to cases of collusion and mutual separation? In Kentucky, the legal system progressed more quickly, and the evidence from court cases shows that petitioners took advantage of the many possible causes for absolute divorce. In fact, state statute allowed couples to divorce one another almost without cause, an unusual occurrence in any state during this era. Yet, in Virginia, in order to achieve comparable results, Ohio and Tazewell County petitioners had to produce very particular narratives to fit the narrower range of possible causes. While Kentucky couples were able to admit overtly their mutual desires for divorce, western Virginians hid these truths beneath the veneer of the law. In Ohio and Tazewell Counties, petitioners wielded the charge of adultery to successfully end their relationships. In many cases, this was a conscious decision, suggesting a societal acceptance of divorce that had advanced past the position of the law. Ultimately, the actions of western and Appalachian Virginians, as well as Kentuckians, reflect their stronger belief in contractualism compared to eastern Virginia petitioners.

To obtain a divorce, interested parties had to navigate a tricky legal process, following the guidelines and requirements in the statutes and legal code of Kentucky and Virginia. First, the wronged party filed a bill of complaint with the local chancery court. Bills of complaint usually stated when the couple had "intermarried," how long one or both had been residents of the county in question, and the reason for the complaint. The plaintiff concluded the bills of complaint by pleading that he or she was "without remedy in the premises, except in a Court of Equity" and by asking that the plaintiff's spouse be made defendant, requesting divorce, custody (if applicable), and in rare cases, the stipulation that the spouse not be allowed to remarry.[20]

After the plaintiff filed a bill of complaint, the court issued a summons to the defendant to answer the bill and to witnesses to appear for their depositions. If the defendant no longer lived in the county (and therefore lay beyond the reach of the court's summons), the plaintiff had to publish notice of such a fact, as well as the date for depositions in a local newspaper. In Virginia, such notices ordered that rogue spouses "appear here within one month after due publication of this order, and do what may be necessary to protect [their] interests herein."[21] In Kentucky, the court often appointed an attorney to serve as defendant in place of absent spouses. This attorney usually wrote to inform the defendant of the divorce suit, if his or her whereabouts were known.

At this time, a defendant might file an answer, responding to the claims of the plaintiff in the bill of complaint. Though one might expect more objections to the salacious claims many petitioners made about their former spouses, numerous defendants did not file answers. Many had already left the county; perhaps others found the truth, ugly though it was, hard to contest. If a defendant chose not to answer, the court accepted the bill as confessed. Witnessed and notarized by a justice of the peace or a notary public, depositions, the next step, were often given at a local attorney's office. There, officials swore in witnesses and recorded their answers to a series of direct questions. These depositions then became part of the larger court record in the case. Depositions often focused on the character of the defendant and plaintiff, and how each had or had not lived up to his or her "proper" role as husband or wife. In sensational cases and especially when one spouse was charged with adultery, witnesses might be called to account for the reputation of the deponents themselves.[22] After the bill of complaint had been filed, the summonses delivered, the answer (if given) noted, and the depositions for one or both parties taken, the court issued a decree, declaring whether or not the divorce was granted and who should pay the costs of the suit (usually the major legal punishment to befall the spouse considered "at fault"). Not all cases reached the decree stage, however. Courts sometimes dismissed cases for lack of cause or proper payment; some complainants withdrew their suit upon reconciling with their spouses; and other cases never reached a conclusion, without any recorded explanation.

In some ways, it is difficult to draw conclusions from divorce records, a notoriously biased source. Courts were wary of any signs of collusion between couples seeking divorce. For this reason, blame would be assigned to one spouse, while the divorce petition painted the other spouse as devoted and loving. Often, divorces went uncontested not because only one partner was at fault, but so that unhappy couples could more quickly and smoothly obtain relief. Either way, as other scholars have shown, divorce bills and depositions were constructed narratives, designed "to persuade."[23] Petitioners often adopted the language of the statutes verbatim, charging their spouses with having "an outrageous, ungovernable temper" or treating them in an "inhuman manner as to indicate a settled aversion to her, and to destroy permanently her peace and happiness."[24]

Though much of this practice went unacknowledged, some spouses drew attention to the constructed nature of divorce petitions, whether to object to a divorce or turn the court's opinion in their favor. In his answer to his wife's 1854 bill charging him with being cruel, intemperate, and neglectful before finally abandoning her, Banks Menefee wrote, "Great pains have been taken by the getters up of this suit to make out a case for divorce and many expedients to accomplish this end proposed have been resorted to as will fully appear to the Court."[25] Still, even if litigants skewed reality in order to curry favor, their choice of grounds under which to sue can be revealing. In other words, their choice of narrative and their method of constructing that narrative tell as much about their attitudes as about their actual marital experience.[26]

Petitioners constructed their narratives around existing state law regarding divorce and separation. In the 1850s, Kentucky's divorce law was surprisingly progressive.[27] As in most states, a spouse's imprisonment, concealment of a "loathsome disease," or force or fraud in the arrangement of marriage allowed the wronged partner to receive a divorce. Statute allowed divorce for either party in case of impotency and separation for five years or more, though the statute did not specify that such separation must be an abandonment. Only three states in the entire country allowed divorce for mutual dissatisfaction. Kentucky, a border South state, was one of them. The innocent party could obtain a divorce after their spouse had abandoned them for only one year, a very brief time in American divorce laws. If this were not quick enough, proving adultery, in addition to abandonment, would allow a wronged spouse to receive a divorce in only six months.[28]

Kentucky state statute also delineated causes specifically for wives and husbands to receive divorce. Wives, when not at fault, got a divorce if the husband had been a "confirmed drunkard" for more than a year and had "wasted" his estate. The law also protected wives if their husbands displayed cruelty toward them, mental or physical, for no less than six months. Husbands received a divorce if their wives were pregnant with another man's child at the time of marriage and they had no prior knowledge of such a fact. In addition, a wife's adultery or "lewd, lascivious behavior," even without a specific adulterous act, could result in a husband's successful divorce suit.[29]

Besides allowing divorce for numerous reasons, Kentucky's statutes were unusual in that all of these requirements applied to absolute divorce, not divorce *a mensa et thoro,* or divorce from bed and board. Common in the antebellum United States, a divorce from bed and board equated to a legal separation.[30] Neither spouse could remarry during the other's lifetime, but the court freed both from financial and social obligations to one another. Especially for women, the opportunity to live and contract as a *feme sole* once again could be valuable. Most states gave primacy to this type of case, but in Kentucky divorce *a mensa et thoro* was relegated to one brief section, which stated that "decree for separation or divorce from bed and board may also be rendered for any of the causes which allow divorce, or for such other cause as the court in its discretion may deem sufficient." In other words, the law gave judges wide latitude in determining the causes of separation.[31]

During the same era, Virginia's divorce statutes were much stricter. Petitioners could obtain an absolute divorce, or divorce *a vinculo matrimonii,* only when their partner committed adultery, had "natural or incurable impotency of body existing at the time of the matrimonial contract," or was imprisoned for seven or more years. In cases of adultery, the offending party could not remarry, ever. Unlike Kentucky, Virginia law stipulated that charges of cruelty, or "reasonable apprehension of bodily hurt," and abandonment or desertion would result in merely a divorce from bed and board.[32]

Even before Kentucky allowed judicial divorce, some in the state felt that the legislature allowed too many separations. In 1848, for example, James Ann Pearce, a resident of Frankfort, Kentucky, wrote to a friend, "I do hope that the Legislature will grant no divorces. The facility with which divorces are obtained is a disgrace to Kentucky."[33] What spurred Kentucky legislators to grant these divorces? What influenced their decision to write laws that gave so many options for frustrated spouses? Certainly, they appear, in some superficial ways, to be no different from the legislators in Virginia who drafted much stricter laws. A sample of both legislatures reveals that about nine out of ten lawmakers owned slaves, regardless of which state they lived in.[34] Clearly, slaveholding was necessary to obtain wealth and political power in both of these states, but it did not necessarily directly shape these lawmakers' decisions on divorce law.

Further analysis of Kentucky lawmakers' votes, either on individual divorces or on the decision to allow the judicial branch to begin processing divorce cases, reveals that slaveholders and nonslaveholders in the legislature voted evenly for and against these measures. For example, the 1849 Kentucky House of Representatives voted to give Thomas A. Lovelace a divorce from his wife, Eliza Ann Lovelace. Of those who voted in favor of this divorce 94.1 percent were slaveholders, whereas only 84 percent of those who voted against it were. In other words, nonslaveholders made up a *larger* share of those who voted against this divorce. Two months later, the legislature passed a bill to allow for judicial divorce, a measure that increased the number of divorces granted in the state. In that case, slaveholders were slightly more likely to vote against it, but about 90 percent of both the yeas and nays were slaveholders.[35] Clearly, slaveholding was not the deciding factor that separated Kentucky's divorce law and practice from that of Virginia.

Virginia lawmakers resisted the liberalization of divorce law in the pre–Civil War era, continuing to uphold their stringent statutes, despite various constitutional conventions and legal changes in the jurisdiction of these cases. Kentucky lawmakers, on the other hand, allowed their citizens greater flexibility in ending their marriages, despite the potential danger this decision would pose to the social structure of their slave society. Perhaps a close proximity to Indiana, infamous as a "divorce mill" in the antebellum period, influenced the construction and interpretation of Kentucky's laws.[36] Living in a newer state, and one at the border to the west, Kentuckians looked to a future in which the marriage contract, once made, could be broken without damaging society in a fundamental way.[37] Used to balancing slave and free, Kentuckians could reconcile the impermanence of marriage and the permanence of slavery. More deeply entrenched in the slave system and deeply imbued with an eastern community's fondness for hierarchy and tradition, Virginia's lawmakers showed continued resistance to such an idea.

Yet not all Virginians concurred with these values. Those in the northern panhandle and the Appalachian region of the state divorced at a greater rate than their fellow Virginians in Fauquier County, outside Washington, DC, or Amelia County, deep in the heart of the state's plantation region. This was in spite of the fact that the courts in all four of these counties used the same legal code. Amelia County residents, for example, filed for only two divorces in the ten years before the Civil War, while residents of Tazewell County, in the mountains of southwestern Virginia, filed for twenty-one. The success rate of these petitioners is also striking. Over 80 percent of petitioners in Ohio and Tazewell Counties received their requested divorces, versus only about 13 percent of petitioners in Fauquier County. Amelia County's success rate was the highest, 100 percent, but the number is skewed by the fact that only two people filed for divorce in the decade before the Civil War. In addition, in Fauquier County, the vast majority of petitioners either filed for or received divorce from bed and board, in line with the stringent Virginia statute.

On the other hand, in Ohio County, residents either asked for or received an absolute divorce three-quarters of the time during the decade prior to the war. Even more striking, in Tazewell County, not a single petitioner asked for a bed and board divorce during this period. These numbers

Table 2.1. Petitioners Filing for Absolute Divorce by County, 1850–1861

	Franklin County (KY)	Warren County (KY)	Ohio County (VA)	Tazewell County (VA)	Fauquier County (VA)	Amelia County (VA)
Absolute Divorce	93.7% (45)	95.5% (21)	69.2% (9)	100% (21)	37.5% (3)	100% (2)
Divorce from Bed and Board	6.3% (3)	4.5% (1)	30.8% (4)	0% (0)	62.5% (5)	0% (0)

Note: These data are derived from all cases encompassing these years found at the Library of Virginia, accessed through the online Chancery Court Records Index; in circuit court cases on microfilm at the West Virginia and Regional History Center, Morgantown, West Virginia; and original copies of the circuit court records at the Kentucky Department for Libraries and Archives, Frankfort, Kentucky. All statistics reflect the number of cases found, since numerous natural and man-made disasters may account for cases missing or destroyed. While an absolute divorce returned two people to their unmarried status, a divorce from bed and board was a legal separation, and neither could remarry.

indicate a greater acceptance of divorce in Ohio and Tazewell Counties, among circuit court judges and among the citizenry itself. In this way, the attitudes of residents of Ohio and Tazewell Counties aligned more closely with those of their Kentucky neighbors, with a similarly high rate of successful divorce as well as absolute divorce. Over 90 percent of Kentucky petitioners, for example, asked for or received a divorce *a vinculo matrimonii.*

However, Kentucky law enabled its citizens to employ numerous explanations for their marriage's demise, ranging from cruelty to abandonment, and the state's statutes granted absolute divorces for many of those causes. How did western and Appalachian Virginians, constrained by Virginia's more restrictive statutes and limited in their methods, obtain so many absolute divorces? Breaking down all six counties' divorce records during the ten years prior to the war reveals how petitioners constructed their narratives according to each state's statutes and their own desires and demands.

In Ohio and Tazewell Counties, where absolute divorce was more commonly obtained, adultery was the most frequent charge. On the other hand, in Fauquier County, where litigants usually asked for or settled for divorce from bed and board, intemperance and cruelty were more common charges. Although the two divorce petitioners in Amelia County both cited adultery as a charge, the details of their cases prove their exceptionality. One wife accused her husband of fathering a child with a free black woman living in

Table 2.2. Divorce Status by County, 1850–1861

	Franklin County (KY)	Warren County (KY)	Ohio County (VA)	Tazewell County (VA)	Fauquier County (VA)	Amelia County (VA)
Granted	56.6% (27)	54.5% (12)	76.9% (10)	80.9% (17)	12.5% (1)	100% (2)
Not Granted	43.4% (21)	45.5% (10)	23.1% (3)	19.0% (4)	87.5% (7)	0% (0)

Note: These data are derived from all cases encompassing these years found at the Library of Virginia, accessed through the online Chancery Court Records Index; in circuit court cases on microfilm at the West Virginia and Regional History Center, Morgantown, West Virginia; and original copies of the circuit court records at the Kentucky Department for Libraries and Archives, Frankfort, Kentucky. All statistics reflect the number of cases found, since numerous natural and man-made disasters may account for cases missing or destroyed.

the neighborhood, and, more threatening to the social order, accepting that child as his own. Another wife charged her husband with cruelty, neglect, abandonment, adultery, and imprisonment, a laundry list of charges that certainly suggests the uphill battle petitioners faced in eastern Virginia. Finally, in Franklin County, where numerous charges could result in a petitioner's divorce, adultery was among the least common charges a petitioner made. In Warren County, adultery proved less popular than desertion and equally popular with cruelty.[38] While this breakdown could reflect the real variation in marital crises across these two states, the differences among the six counties also reveal the way citizens in each felt about divorce and separation. Eastern Virginians appeared more content to meet their state's stringent requirements, while western and Appalachian Virginians pushed the envelope in favor of a greater divorce rate.

Kentuckians had no need to make such allowances. They could divorce for a range of reasons, reflecting their more flexible laws. There, the influence of ideas of contractualism and individualism can be seen in both the law and society, reflecting the state's border tendencies toward a more moderate hybrid culture. Of the six counties sampled, Franklin County residents initiated the highest number of divorce cases, forty-eight, from 1850 to 1861. Warren County, Kentucky, residents filed for twenty-two divorces, the next highest number.[39] In Fauquier County, litigants may have feared a loss of social approval if they filed for full divorce. If so, they may have chosen to

Table 2.3. Causes for Divorce by County, 1850–1861

	Franklin County (KY)	Warren County (KY)	Ohio County (VA)	Tazewell County (VA)	Fauquier County (VA)	Amelia County (VA)
Adultery	22.9% (11)	31.8% (7)	61.5% (8)	95.2% (20)	37.5% (3)	100% (2)
Abandonment	41.7% (20)	54.5% (12)	46.2% (6)	57.1% (12)	50.0% (4)	100% (2)
Separation	2.1% (1)	9.1% (2)	0.0% (0)	0.0% (0)	0.0% (0)	0.0% (0)
Cruelty	41.7% (20)	27.3% (6)	23.1% (3)	0.0% (0)	62.5% (5)	50.0% (1)
Intemperance	43.8% (21)	9.1% (2)	15.4% (2)	0.0% (0)	62.5% (5)	0.0% (0)
Imprisonment	2.1% (1)	0.0% (0)	15.4% (2)	0.0% (0)	0.0% (0)	50.0% (1)
Other	0.0% (0)	13.6% (3)	0.0% (0)	0.0% (0)	12.5% (1)	0.0% (0)

Note: These data are derived from all cases encompassing these years found at the Library of Virginia, accessed through the online Chancery Court Records Index; in circuit court cases on microfilm at the West Virginia and Regional History Center, Morgantown, West Virginia; and original copies of the circuit court records at the Kentucky Department for Libraries and Archives, Frankfort, Kentucky. All statistics reflect the number of cases found, since numerous natural and man-made disasters may account for cases missing or destroyed. Many divorce cases have multiple charges. This chart reflects the number of times someone accused their spouse of a charge, which means the total number of charges is more than the number of cases filed.

raise smaller issues and accept legal separations, rather than bring more dramatic charges and receive full divorce. In Amelia County, it would appear that most residents did not file for divorce at all. Balanced on the edge of the North, Ohio County was in many ways more a reflection of its two neighbors, Ohio and Pennsylvania, than of its own state's ideals. Similarly, living along the border of the future state of West Virginia, residents of Tazewell County may have shared their future neighbors' attitudes about contractualism, or at least they refused to let elites in Richmond or the East dictate their lives. Tazewell residents, who may have chafed under the strict limitations of the Virginia statutes, charged adultery more frequently, in a manipulation of the statutes they disliked to achieve goals more amenable to their ideals.

While the differences in these six counties' rates of divorce are more striking, gender differences between the cases in Ohio, Tazewell, Franklin, and Fauquier are subtler. Historians have shown that divorce laws in the South were often less favorable to women than men.[40] In some states, such as Louisiana, for example, a husband could obtain a divorce (from bed and board) for a wife's adultery, but a wife had to prove both her husband's adultery and the fact that he kept his "concubine" in a dwelling.[41] Nonetheless, in many places, including Kentucky and Virginia, women were more likely than men to pursue a divorce in the first place.

In four of the six counties, almost three-quarters of the petitioners were women.[42] As previously stated, married women were considered *feme covert* and could not contract in their own names, conduct business, buy or sell land, or earn wages. Especially when a husband failed to support his wife financially, whether through neglect, intemperance, or worse, abandonment, married women found themselves in a vulnerable position. Without their husbands, they became the primary breadwinners and were often forced to work to support their children or themselves. Yet, as still-married women, they did not legally have the right to earn this money in their own name or to control what funds or property they now possessed. Thus, when a separation occurred, women were more likely to seek a legal divorce to recoup their legal status, while husbands observed no difference in their legal and political standing. Many sought a divorce only in order to remarry; many did not do it even then. As Norma Basch has shown, divorce in the nineteenth century was, in many ways, a "woman's remedy."[43] For the most part, this was a common trend in both border South and southern states. For many women, divorce seemed like a promising route through which to obtain their old *feme sole* status.

That said, despite the similar rate at which women petitioned in Fauquier, Amelia, Franklin, and Ohio Counties, their success rates varied, as not all counties were equally willing to grant petitioning wives their financial, physical, or emotional freedom. In Fauquier County, no woman received a divorce in the ten years prior to the Civil War, while men met with a fifty-fifty chance of success. On the other hand, in both Franklin and Ohio Counties, women found more success than not, although in neither case were women more successful than men. In all three counties, male petitioners met with more sympathy from the judges or chose narratives more pleasing to the ruling elite.[44] Once again, Amelia proved the exception, although the two wives there had to prove extreme cases to obtain relief.

Table 2.4. Divorce Status by County and Gender of Filer, 1850–1861

	Divorce Status	Husband Filed	Wife Filed
Franklin County (KY)	Granted	66.7% (8)	52.8% (19)*
	Not Granted	33.3% (4)	47.2% (17)
Warren County (KY)	Granted	50% (6)*	62.5% (5)
	Not Granted	50% (6)	37.5% (3)
Ohio County (VA)	Granted	100% (4)	66.7% (6)
	Not Granted	0% (0)	33.3% (3)
Tazewell County (VA)	Granted	78.9% (15)	100% (2)
	Not Granted	21.1% (4)	0% (0)
Fauquier County (VA)	Granted	50% (1)	0% (0)
	Not Granted	50% (1)	100% (6)
Amelia County (VA)	Granted	0% (0)	100% (2)
	Not Granted	0% (0)	0% (0)

* In one case, a husband or wife filed, but the other spouse, who filed a cross petition, was successful in getting the divorce.

Note: These data are derived from all cases encompassing these years found at the Library of Virginia, accessed through the online Chancery Court Records Index; in circuit court cases on microfilm at the West Virginia and Regional History Center, Morgantown, West Virginia; and original copies of the circuit court records at the Kentucky Department for Libraries and Archives, Frankfort, Kentucky. All statistics reflect the number of cases found, since numerous natural and manmade disasters may account for cases missing or destroyed.

Petitioners often successfully obtained divorces when they used the law to their advantage. Although judges in Kentucky and Virginia may have personally decried the practice of divorce, the law did allow for such action in certain circumstances, and if one could demonstrate those circumstances, there would be little reason to deny the separation. Often, a successful divorce suit came down to a choice of narrative and a partner's response. In Kentucky, though, things grew less complicated as the antebellum years waned. Some petitioners began to employ mutual separation as a cause for divorce, despite legal fears about collusion. In western and Appalachian Virginia, couples used adultery charges in a subtle form of collusion, although this was outside the law. Both methods, though, reflect the growing acceptance of contractualism in these border regions.

Nineteenth-century courts frowned upon collusion between divorcing couples, preferring to fault one party over the other in the dissolution of marriage. According to Hendrik Hartog, "If a husband and wife agreed to divorce because they, as private individuals, wanted a divorce, their agreement, all by itself, was reason enough to deny the divorce." Even when suing for abandonment in the antebellum era, men and women usually had to prove that they had not driven their spouses away.[45] Couples without the financial or legal means to divorce often resorted to separation agreements, but unfortunately, without a trustee, such an action was technically against the law.[46] Under coverture, husband and wife were one; therefore, he would only be transferring property and making arrangements with himself, which he could undo at any time. To many lawmakers, voluntary separation and separation agreements threatened marital unity because of the individual authority they bestowed upon wives through the act of making contracts. Such authority threatened the stability of the marital relationship and threw into question all elements of the household hierarchy. Especially in the South, justices tried to prevent women from becoming "contractually capable actor[s]," and many believed that divorce should be granted only to relieve one partner's extreme duress and should never be allowed to threaten the underlying power structure of society.[47] Collusion and contractual agreements both appeared to do so.

In some ways, collusion represented a threat to the traditional hierarchical and structured nature of marriage, and, therefore, many courts resisted divorce in these circumstances. However, after 1850 in Kentucky, justices seemed willing to allow mutually dissatisfied couples to legally go their own ways. In addition, Kentucky's requirements for divorce due to abandonment or desertion were less stringent than those in other states. Kentucky required abandonment for only a year in order for wronged spouses to file for divorce. Oftentimes, courts waived such requirements in cases of adultery or cruelty.[48] In western and Appalachian Virginia, collusion may have played a role in the higher divorce rate, but through more subtle means. In Ohio and Tazewell Counties, respondents employed the charge of adultery to great effect and, although we cannot know for certain, may have done so in consultation with their unhappy spouses.

Such flexibility was not always the rule in the border South. Looking at legislative divorces and informal separations in Kentucky during the years of the early republic, Honor Sachs argues that courts were unwilling to allow separations in cases where wives abandoned husbands and that both litigants and legislators manipulated cases to reflect an accepted gender narrative of marriage and divorce.[49] Even with such deceptions, divorce was not widely obtainable in frontier Kentucky. Hesitation remained common in the early antebellum years. In refusing to divorce Jane and Jesse Simpson, despite their separation agreement, the 1836 Kentucky Supreme Court stated that "the well-being of a society, as well as the policy of the law and the objects and duties of the marital contract require, that those who are united in marriage should live together."[50] Yet, legal requirements and understandings of marriage and separation evolved quickly in this booming border state. Just six years later, the Franklin County Circuit Court quickly divorced Simeon and Mahala Carrall, even though she clearly agreed to his desire for such an outcome.[51]

In April 1842, Simeon filed for divorce after five years of marriage to Mahala. The couple had lived together only three months after their marriage, when "greatly to the surprise and mortification" of Simeon, she left their home and refused to return. Despite Simeon's repeated requests for her return, through word of mouth and a formal letter, she continued to live apart from her husband. She responded firmly to his pleas, "You nead never to make any calculations of my living with you agane I never intend two so long as I draw the breath of life."[52] Left with no other choice, Simeon pleaded with the court for a full divorce.

In response to Simeon's petition, Mahala readily admitted that she had voluntarily abandoned her marital home and refused to return. Mahala told Simeon and the Franklin County Circuit Court that he could get a divorce whenever he wished. "I grant you the priveilege of sodoing I never have objected to it from the beginning," she assured him. She would not explain to the court her reasons for leaving her husband but stated that "they were sufficient in her judgement to induce her to take the steps which she has done." She repeatedly insisted that she had no objections to the court giving Simeon his divorce. Yet, while this seems to be a clear case of collusion and agreement between the parties to divorce, the Franklin County Circuit Court agreed within two months to divorce the couple.[53]

Two factors may explain the difference between the Carralls' case and the Simpsons' case. First, the Kentucky Court of Appeals, not the local chancery court, made the final ruling in the Simpson case. As was often the case, local courts in Kentucky adapted more quickly to the needs of their citizens and may have taken into consideration community issues of little concern to the higher court.[54] Second, the variations in the two cases reflect the slow legal evolution experienced nationwide throughout the antebellum period. The Carralls' case was not an anomaly in Kentucky but the beginning of a trend, one that became more apparent as the 1850s wore on.

As collusion gained acceptance in the 1850s, some Kentucky couples found it unnecessary to employ the value-laden terminology of previous petitions. In his 1856 petition for divorce, George McKee did not accuse his wife, Susan, of abandonment or desertion. Instead, he wrote that the couple had lived together for "some years" and then "seperated, and have been living seperate and apart without any cohabitation for the space of five consecutive years last past, with no intention of living together again."[55] George McKee was no legal novice. In fact, he was a judge in Garrard County and a lawmaker when many of the divorce statutes had been written. Thus, he would have been well versed in the legal requirements for divorce. His willingness to admit to mutual separation reflects a larger acceptance in the Kentucky legal community of collusion, as the antebellum era came to a close.

Such willingness did not result in total social acceptance of divorce in antebellum Kentucky, however. Sarah's response to Judge McKee's divorce bill demonstrates that divorce was still seen as a failure on the part of one, or both, individuals. She agreed that they had lived together until 1849, at which time "they seperated and have since lived seperate." She paused before closing, though, to defend her character. She felt obligated, she wrote, to state that the separation was "occasioned by no misconduct on her part," and she defended her behavior as a wife, her fidelity, and her efforts to promote the couple's happiness.[56] Yet, unlike other wives, she did not then place the blame on her husband. Sarah knew that society would likely assume that one person was at fault, and since she had actually left their home, blame was likely to fall on her shoulders. However, she did not find it necessary to turn against her husband, which indicates her belief that society might be willing to accept a separation where neither party was at fault. Their gamble paid off; six months later, the Franklin County Circuit Court granted the couple a divorce but did not place the burden of responsibility on either party.

James P. Smith of Warren County, Kentucky, refused to state the cause of his separation, claiming it was "not necessary to relate." He then proceeded to state that the couple had not lived together for the requisite amount of time (five years or more). Because of this, Kentucky law made him eligible for a formal divorce. Of course, he also added, almost as an afterthought, this was "especially" true as his former wife had moved to Missouri and remarried in that state. Bigamy would easily be grounds for divorce, but it is striking that this was not the main cause for which James

Smith chose to file. Instead, he suggested that, regardless of his wife's current living situation, their decision to part, whatever the reason, should be enough to satisfy the court.[57]

Though most couples still chose not to cite "mutual separation" as the reason for their divorce, its mere presence in the legal code and in a small handful of cases suggests the shifts occurring in the border South during the late antebellum period, as views of mutuality, individualism, and contractualism gained traction alongside the extant slave system. On the edge of the South and the Midwest, Kentucky soon became the forefront of a slow legal evolution in divorce law, an unexpected development in a southern state. In western and Appalachian Virginia, petitioners displayed some of the same desires for absolute divorce as their western neighbors, but they were hampered by the legal system. Yet, the extent to which they relied on adultery charges suggests a deliberate manipulation of the legal system to obtain a more favorable result.

Christina Wells of Wheeling, Virginia, received her ultimate goal—a full divorce—when she charged her husband, Levi, with adultery in 1857. For Christina, her divorce, which fully severed her finances from her husband and bestowed her maiden name upon her once more, gave her control over her successful millinery business in Wheeling. Levi made no objection to her charges, in part because they were true, but also because he wanted the divorce as much as Christina did. In a letter to his mistress, Annie, Levi told her that his love for her was true and promised to marry her soon. "I will Have a divorce . . . soon," he assured her, though he remained cryptic about how he would obtain it.[58] For some western Virginians, an adultery charge proved to be the one most likely to gain the sympathy of judges and to fit with the stringent divorce laws in place in their state. Their decision to spin these narratives reflects their desire for more flexible divorce laws and their more fluid notion of marital permanence. In the Wells's case, Christina wielded the charge of adultery, and Levi acknowledged the divorce case but did not respond to her accusations. Both received the goal they sought—divorce.

In 1859, Leah Charles told the Tazewell County Court that her husband, George, had become dissatisfied with their relationship shortly after their 1851 marriage. Dissatisfaction being insufficient to obtain a divorce in Virginia, he got one instead, she stated, "by intrigue & corruption." In his 1853 petition for divorce, George had accused Leah of abandonment and, ultimately, adultery. However, Leah knew that George was filing for divorce in 1853; she herself had signed the court summons sent to her. She did not respond or object to his accusations. Even more striking, Leah wrote the 1859 letter to the Tazewell Circuit Court for a revealing reason: George and Leah wanted to remarry, something prohibited to Leah under the original decree. The court swiftly granted the couple's request. The couple remained together until George's death as a Union prisoner of war four years later.[59]

Of course, the high number of adultery accusations could indicate a particularly promiscuous population. However, while Ohio and Tazewell County petitioners had the highest rate of adultery charges, they were also among the least likely to respond to the charges laid against them by their spouses.[60] Respondents charged with the ultimate marital crime—infidelity—chose to remain silent; this showed an acceptance of their crime, a disregard for their reputations, an increased ability to become anonymous, or a tacit agreement by the parties to use the adultery charge to achieve divorce in an unfriendly legal environment. Generally, uncontested bills met with a higher rate of success than contested bills.[61] In fact, Ohio and Tazewell countians' use of more salacious charges such as adultery seems to have been effective; these two communities had the highest rate of divorce of the six counties.[62] Eight of Ohio County's thirteen divorce suits and seventeen of Tazewell County's twenty-one cases were successful, giving petitioners in each county a success rate of about 80 percent.

In Tazewell County, court records reveal how this pattern could have developed. In case after case, the same names appear, serving in different capacities. Simeon Payne, for instance, was a constable in Tazewell County, charged with serving summonses on spouses and witnesses, but he also served as a witness in multiple litigants' depositions. Tazewell County seems to have been a close-knit community. George W. Payne was the Justice of the Peace, and Nancy, David, and James Payne also served as deponents in various cases. Simeon himself used the information he gleaned from participating in multiple divorce cases to file his own bill against his wife, Jane, in 1859, accusing her of adultery and fornication. She quickly responded that his bill was a lie and that he had even tried to hire people to seduce her in order to make his case stick. Specifically, she knew of one man whom he had offered "ten dollars if he would seduce respondent & be a witness against her."[63] Simeon was one of only two Tazewell litigants in the prewar era who did not succeed in getting a divorce. Although he obviously wanted to manipulate the legal system as he may have seen others do before him, his wife refused to cooperate, foiling his plan. The fact that his failure could

Table 2.5. Response to Petition by County, 1850–1861

	Franklin County (KY)	Warren County (KY)	Ohio County (VA)	Tazewell County (VA)	Fauquier County (VA)	Amelia County (VA)
Response	41.7% (20)	18.2% (4)	23.1% (3)	4.8% (1)	37.5% (3)	50% (1)
No Response	58.3% (28)	81.8% (18)	76.9% (10)	95.2% (20)	62.5% (4)	50% (1)

Note: Courts asked accused spouses to file answers to their accusers, though not all chose to do so or could be found. These data are derived from all cases encompassing these years found at the Library of Virginia, accessed through the online Chancery Court Records Index; in circuit court cases on microfilm at the West Virginia and Regional History Center, Morgantown, West Virginia; and original copies of the circuit court records at the Kentucky Department for Libraries and Archives, Frankfort, Kentucky. All statistics reflect the number of cases found, since numerous natural and man-made disasters may account for cases missing or destroyed.

be attributed to her resistance suggests that collusion between spouses was pivotal to the success enjoyed by other petitioners.

In Warren County, Kentucky, petitioners did not need to use adultery charges to obtain a divorce, but they still might work surreptitiously behind the scenes to manipulate their partner or the legal system. When Sarah Boyd accused her husband of being abusive, he flatly denied her charges and assured the court that he only wished to live together once more. Yet, a fellow boarder in their home stated that Hiram often spoke of his desire to get a "disverse," to use his own word. In fact, he tried to bribe Sarah to file for divorce, stating that if she would give him her most valuable slave and a "*plum, clear, & clean disverse,*" he would leave her alone forever.[64]

Franklin County respondents also reflected the social attitudes of their communities. When spouses filed a divorce petition, the courts summoned their partners to answer for their alleged marital crimes. Most chose not to do so, but a large number, nearly 40 percent, did in Franklin County. Rather than indicating spousal conflicts, these answers often demonstrate agreement; respondents made their answers in cross petitions, uniting in the original petitioner's request for a divorce.[65] Nonetheless, these cross petitions still utilized the language of fault, nudging toward collusion while maintaining the illusion of blame. In an 1853 cross petition, Squire Grant Glenn denied his wife Eliza's allegations of abandonment and neglect and charged her with abandoning their Paris, Kentucky, home. He stated that "as plt [plaintiff] prays for a divorce and refuses to live with him again," he would also like a divorce. Eliza quickly changed her charge to intemperance, and the court granted her the divorce. Similarly, in 1853, after Henry Snelling accused his wife, Elizabeth, of abandonment without cause, she filed a cross bill accusing him of abandonment. The court quickly granted the divorce, in his favor. In an 1853 Warren County case, Jonathan Morgan charged his wife, Nancy, with lewd and lascivious conduct with men in the neighborhood. She denied his charges, simply stating that the couple had not lived together for five years. She wrote that she was "perfectly willing for the court to grant complainants prayer for a divorce." Finally, not only was Warren County resident Margaret Martin not ashamed or upset when her husband, Joshua, filed a petition for divorce, she assured the court that she was "*greatly* gratified" that he had done so since it gave her the chance to file a successful cross petition against him for cruelty, neglect, and intemperance.[66] In all four cases, the petitioners tried to paint one another as guilty, but each also agreed to the ultimate outcome and demonstrated that to the court. While these cases reflect subtle changes, cases of separation demonstrate even larger shifts.

Western and Appalachian Virginians may have hidden their true intent, assuming that the legal system would flag their cases or find cause to deny them if they revealed their goals. However, in Kentucky, residents' rhetoric of contractualism reflects their understanding of marriage as based in a mutual sense of love, affection, and even sensuality. By this standard, failure to satisfy one of these would naturally create a breakdown in the relationship, something the court should understand and accept. For example, when John Kinslow and some of his neighbors confronted Eliza Jane Kinslow over her marital infidelity she "reckoned it was not worth while to deny it." As for the cause, she simply reasoned that she did not love her husband more than anyone else and therefore should probably not live with him as his wife.[67]

Even the court employed rhetorical flourishes that celebrated the benefits of divorce. After granting Melinda Frances Wilkinson a divorce from her neglectful and absent husband, the Warren County Circuit Court issued a decree that read, "She is hereby divorced from her husband, Thomas Edward Wilkinson the defendant in this cause and is restored to all the rights and privilidges of an unmarried woman and be as free as the birds in the open air." Sometime later, someone crossed out the final words, but clearly at the time, a poetic judge or court scribe had found them appropriate to the case.

In the contentious battle between Sarah and Hiram Boyd, in which she accused him of cruelty and he accused her of abandonment, the court decided to divorce them from one another, and neither gained the upper hand in the decision. She would get all her prior property, but Hiram would be able to enjoy "a life of single blessedness."[68] The court's use of this phrase demonstrates a belief that ending an acrimonious marriage was preferable to forcing two unhappy people to remain together for any social or religious reason.

In Fauquier County, Virginia, couples did not employ the charge of mutual separation or charge their partners with adultery as frequently as did residents of the border South. Some did attempt to make separation agreements, which had a tenuous legality. These separation agreements provided mutually dissatisfied couples with a source of relief from the problems of an unhappy marriage, but eastern Virginia residents and courts displayed ambivalent feelings about the viability or legality of such action. The court's reaction to these agreements demonstrates its hesitation to accept concepts of contractualism and individualism during this period.

Before their ultimately unsuccessful divorce proceedings in 1854, Banks and Susan Menefee signed a separation agreement. Married in 1839, Banks and Susan lived together in Warrenton, Fauquier County, Virginia, until late 1852, when Banks moved out of their home into a local hotel. Within a year and a half, Susan took him to court, charging desertion and abandonment, on top of physical and mental cruelty.[69] Before she took her case to the courts, though, Susan's friends convinced her that a more private separation agreement would suit her needs. She agreed "at once . . . preferring a pecuniary sacrifice, rather then have these delicate affairs dragged before a court of justice." A month after Banks's departure, Susan stated, her attorney drew up an agreement, one which, in her view, was overly generous toward her husband. The couple agreed "to live separate and apart from each other," and her husband agreed to provide his wife with maintenance and support. Yet, when Susan began to hire out her slaves in January 1853, Banks refused her right to do so and claimed them as his own. Interestingly, Susan did not ask the court to uphold the agreement, admitting that she knew full well that it would not do so, but stated that she included the information about the agreement in her divorce case only to "show the cause of the delay in instituting this suit."[70]

Banks's answer to Susan's divorce petition told a slightly different story. Though he agreed with his wife that he sought to avoid public scrutiny, he differed over the timeline of events. He argued that he had never voluntarily abandoned her but had "made every effort to dissuade Plff from a separation." Banks told the court that he had not signed the agreement, wary of its legal validity. Warned by counsel, he stated that such an action was "against the policy of the law." He also noted (perhaps revealing the real reason for his hesitation) that while Susan might control the slaves, he could not enforce her agreement to unite with him in conveying his land.[71] Each attributed some value to the separation agreement, especially social, but they both seemed to doubt the likelihood of a court upholding these agreements. In Fauquier County, where far fewer divorces in general were given out, couples may have also found that separation agreements, which they continued to make despite this legal climate, would have to remain outside the walls of the court. For the Menefees, a separation agreement would be their only source of relief. Their case was dismissed in September 1853 by mutual agreement, with both parties promising to pay half the costs.

In the border communities of Franklin and Warren Counties, Kentucky, and Ohio and Tazewell Counties, Virginia, divorce cases reflected a growing absorption of new attitudes toward marriage and divorce. Couples were less likely to hide their desire for a separation, from either the community or the court. Kentuckians took advantage of their flexible divorce statutes and filed the highest number of cases, while western and Appalachian Virginians' use of adultery gave them the most success in their cases. Either way, the language of these two counties' residents indicates a greater desire to end their relationships when either or both partners were unhappy and also a begrudging agreement on the part of the courts to do so. In the 1850s, Fauquier and Amelia Counties, and their residents, resisted the pull of contractualism, which allowed couples to agree to break the bond that bound them.[72] In their estimation, marriage was not something easily deserted or abandoned, and one's reward for doing so should not be divorce.

Analysis of state statutes and local court cases reveals that border residents manipulated, adopted, and challenged the legal system, reflecting their own understandings of marriage. During the 1850s, the marital attitudes of residents in such areas of the border South as western and Appalachian Virginia and Kentucky were in flux. On the precipice of war and on the dividing line of the nation, residents in the two states experienced a legal evolution as the decade wore on, due to the advancement of time and the growing influence of various economic, political, and social ideologies. When Kentucky and western Virginia couples chose to end their relationships in this era, the wide range of tools they used reflected these influences. Ending one's marriage was a controversial choice in any region during the 1850s. Yet, this process was complicated in the border South by residents' use of multiple and often contradictory strands of gender ideology. Neither the legal nor the nonlegal community was widely accepting of divorce in Kentucky or western and Appalachian Virginia, but in both states men and women found ways to break the bonds between them in ways that made their choice seem more palatable to those around them. Their ability to do so, while using a variety of narratives, reflects the fluid, mosaic nature of border South society.

In Kentucky, as well as in western and Appalachian Virginia, ideas of contractualism influenced the breakdown of marriage, allowing mutually consenting couples to separate and requiring divorce applicants to defend their character less vigorously than in the past. In Kentucky, the legal system gave couples the opportunity to employ a range of charges against their spouses; partners could even admit outright that they both sought an end to their marriage for no other reason than their own prerogative. In western and Appalachian Virginia, many spouses filed divorce petitions using the charge of adultery and received favorable results. Without a change in the law, they could do little else to obtain the divorces they sought. In all of these cases, litigants' actions reflected a growing belief in the contractual nature of marriage, which gave them the ability to end a relationship that did not reflect their ideals.

The immense variation within the upper South demonstrates its border qualities and sheds new light on the influence of regional identity on marital roles. In Ohio, Tazewell, Warren, and Franklin, those counties further to the west and with weaker ties to slavery, couples asked for and received divorce, even absolute divorce, more frequently. They were less likely to structure their homes in a hierarchical fashion that required unwavering obedience to the household head. These counties showed some acceptance of the dissolvability of the marriage contract. In eastern Fauquier and Amelia Counties, which had higher slave populations and larger farms, mastery remained vital to the structure of society. Acknowledging the contractual nature of marriage threatened to empower wives, and as the next chapter will show, eastern Virginians resisted this change as the Civil War, which would tear their state in two, approached.

3

To Honor and Obey

On the eve of the Civil War, Lucinda Deaton reluctantly filed a bill with her local circuit court. Her story was straightforward and not uncommon. Now in her mid-forties, she had married her husband, Alfred, at around the age of seventeen. Within a few years, she gave birth to the couple's first child, Elinor. Five more children soon followed. However, in 1847, Alfred left, refusing to support his wife or children in any way. Lucinda was forced to move in with their grown son. She pleaded with the court that she was penniless and that her whole family would suffer because of it. Although her husband owned a large property and also made money through his mercantile business, she had seen nothing from it. He also reportedly told the local merchants not to sell her any goods. "Without some aid," she warned, "[I] must come to beggary."[1]

Lucinda lived in Amelia County, Virginia, just west of Richmond. In this rural county, over 70 percent of the county's population was enslaved, which left about three thousand free residents. Other than neighboring Nottoway County, it had the highest proportion of enslaved people in the commonwealth.[2] It was not a place where a divorce bill was likely to find a warm reception from the community or legal system. Lucinda probably knew this. This may have been in the back of her mind when she assured the court that she did not "desire a divorce from the bonds of matrimony." Instead of filing for a divorce, even a divorce from bed and board, she asked only that the court compel her husband to support his estranged wife financially. Yet, even setting the bar a little lower, Lucinda was unsuccessful. She revoked her request within a year, after little movement in the case.[3]

Why did Lucinda end her bid for alimony? The reason may have been simple—she reconciled with her husband. In fact, census records complicate the story laid out in her bill. From these, it appears that Lucinda and Alfred lived together in both 1850 and 1860, meaning that he had not been "living apart from her" since 1847, as she stated. Also, they had either resumed or were continuing their cohabitation around the time she asked the court to dismiss her petition.[4] Perhaps Lucinda's petition was nothing more than legal pressure, a way to force her husband either to allow her to return home or to support her. However, even with these changes to the story, Lucinda's case reflects the "harsh legal culture" of Amelia County, Virginia, which was further symptomatic of the plantation region of the state.[5] Lucinda may have dropped her case because she realized it would not go in her favor.

Even though Lucinda balked at asking the court for a divorce, she was more assertive than many others in central and eastern Virginia. She still chose to air her personal grievances and travails before the court, alerting the community and the justices to the broken state of her marriage. In a sample of five counties in this region, few divorce cases can be found. In Nottoway County (with about 73 percent of its population enslaved) and Caroline County (with almost 60 percent of its population enslaved), not a single person filed for a divorce or a separation during the decade before the Civil War. Only two people filed for divorce in Amelia County during that same period.[6] Clearly, Lucinda's decision to file for alimony, rather than divorce, reflected the community and legal system's negative attitudes toward separation. These communities did not share Kentucky and western Virginians' beliefs about the contractual nature of marriage. In eastern Virginia, it was truly "'til death do us part."

Lucinda's story, at least as she constructed it for the Amelia County Circuit Court, also reflected white eastern Virginians' beliefs about divorce in other ways. According to her petition, her husband left her in 1847, but she did not file for another twelve years. This was common in eastern Virginia divorce cases. Petitioners knew that in a climate unreceptive to divorce, they had to work harder to prove the necessity of their case. Petitioners also had to show that this was not a hasty or careless decision but a last resort. Like Lucinda, most petitioners who filed in counties like Amelia or Fauquier waited years after their spouse had committed an offense worthy of divorce. Others featured a long list of grievances. Just two years before Lucinda filed her petition, Frances Cole complained to the Amelia County Court that during their lengthy marriage, her husband had beaten her, whipped her, abandoned her, refused to support her, been imprisoned, and finally, begun living with another woman. The court granted Frances a rare divorce, but she had to use nearly every possible cause for divorce to obtain it.[7]

While in Kentucky and western and Appalachian Virginia, many relationships began to reflect a belief in mutuality and contractualism before the Civil War, marriages in eastern Virginia evolved along a different path. In those sections of the state that featured a strongly developed slave system and sat further to the east, white residents valued a sense of hierarchy in their homes, between master and slave and between man and wife. Divorce threatened to destabilize the racial hierarchy and general structure of society. Bonds in Virginia, whether literal or figurative, were permanent.

Patriarchy and its broader counterpart, hierarchy, filled the pages of Virginians' letters, books, and court cases. Here, a white man's mastery depended on his ability to control his dependents and exact deference from them. Virginia's divorce records and laws reveal a weak commitment to mutuality, which would acknowledge the individual needs, wants, and, at its extremes, the rights of wives. Certainly, Virginians did use the language of love with their lovers and spouses. There is no denying that they, too, were influenced by the transatlantic expansion of companionate marriage. However, courting Virginians emphasized the patriarchal bargain of marriage to a greater extent than did courting border southerners. Women offered obedience and submission to their husbands, in return for protection and privilege. It was a bargain that many white southern women said they desired for themselves, but it left little room for women to be independent of or equal with their husbands. White southern men argued that white southern women were idolized and elevated above the status of their northern sisters. The presence of slavery, in this defense, freed them from the drudgeries of the household. They had no need to look outside the home for reform. Their husbands could protect and speak for them. It was a patronizing chivalry that gave women a pedestal to stand on but refused to let them budge off of it.

Eastern Virginia marriages reflected a weak commitment to marital mutuality and to contractualism. Specifically, variations can be seen in the extent to which residents emphasized marital obedience for women. This variation reflects a number of geographic, economic, and cultural differences but most specifically the border identity of Kentucky and of western and Appalachian Virginia. There, white household relationships were built on the larger culture's adaptability and fusion, and they brought together ideas of individualism despite the presence of a hierarchical slave system. In eastern Virginia, on the other hand, flexibility had no place in the cultural understanding of residents. Without such a blueprint, any chip in the armor of household hierarchy threatened to destroy the entire social structure. Especially in counties like Fauquier and Amelia, with half or three-quarters of the population trapped in slavery, this could prove devastating to the economy, social relationships, and the traditional southern "way of life."[8] This affected white women's ability to file for and, especially, to receive divorces. In eastern Virginia, married women shared the same status, that of *feme covert,* as western and Appalachian Virginia women. Yet, in western and Appalachian Virginia, women chose to file using their own name more often than eastern Virginia women. There, married women were not granted a similar sense of individualism.

As Lucinda Deaton's case demonstrates, unhappily married Virginians fought an uphill battle to effectively separate from or divorce their spouses. Although western, Appalachian, and eastern Virginians in the antebellum era operated under the same legal code, petitioners employed this code in different ways. In western and Appalachian Virginia, petitions were straightforward and usually relied on the charge of adultery. Because of this, they were also largely successful. In eastern Virginia, where divorce was granted only in extreme circumstances, to saintly petitioners who had exhausted all other options, petitioners piled on charge after charge against their spouse, describing in emotional language a tale of domestic woe. Eastern Virginians also waited longer and were, nevertheless, less successful than their Kentucky or western and Appalachian Virginia counterparts.

Just as with Kentuckians' newfound desire for mutuality in marriage, eastern Virginians' commitment to hierarchical relationships found its way into the advice manuals given to brides and grooms on their wedding day. The Louthan family of eastern Virginia, for example, owned *The Etiquette of Courtship and Matrimony.* In it, men (the instigators of relationships) were told to investigate a potential love interest's family status and arrange for a meeting through a friend. Women should obey their parents' advice at all times, and a man must get their consent before writing to a woman. While courting, men should be respectful, sober, ambitious, and "ever ready to honour [womanhood's] virtues and defend its weakness." Women should be dutiful, respectful, neat, pious, kind, forbearing, cheerful, domestic, humble, and charitable. Once engaged, it was the duty and privilege of the fiancé to "give advice to the fair one who now implicitly confides in him." If he found fault with or flaws in his intended wife "which he would wish removed or amended," he should inform her immediately, before they married.[9] This would prepare both for their roles of advisor and advisee in marriage. In this Virginia family, men and women had definitive roles to play, with the man playing the superior one. While *The Etiquette of Courtship and Matrimony* warned a husband that he should conceal nothing from his wife as "their interests are mutual," the authors urged the wife to "pay some court" to her husband. When her husband arrived home from a long day of work, she should soothe him and make him happy, and he should "be free from the care of having to satisfy the caprices of a petted wife."[10] In these authors' views, mutuality, if it existed at all in a relationship, benefited the husband, not the wife. She was a caregiver, not a companion.

If she did not need to be a full companion to her husband, a woman would also not need the same level of education. Although many eastern Virginians embraced education, especially an ornamental one, for their daughters, some balked at an education that challenged a woman's traditional role. One relative informed Virginian Maria Curtis that he was astonished by the "impruden[t]" habit of women taking public examinations at boarding schools and female colleges. He objected for a number of reasons. First, he stated, men needed an education because they actually "exer[t] an influence upon Society," while women did not. Women belonged in the home, he insisted, and education need only prepare her for that role. Women who believed in public examinations and commencements as part of their education acted like they "wear the breeches" and are in "full Bloomer costume." He was proud that "Virginia is yet free from this pollution."[11] To these men, female education threatened social hierarchy and order and the subordinate position of women within the patriarchal world.

Virginia households retained many facets of their hierarchical structure, and female and black dependence were integrally tied together to construct masculinity and male authority.[12] Suzanne Lebsock, in her study of Petersburg, Virginia, argues that "men retained the upper hand in almost every aspect of marriage; mixed with the new ideal of mutual affection and respect were substantial elements of male dominance and coercion."[13] Household dominance was a delicate game for Virginia men. Most husbands were not directly confrontational or aggressive with their wives, considering such behavior to be ungentlemanly. In this, they also revealed the influence of the rhetoric of mutuality and domesticity. Instead they "cultivated an air of polite condescension" toward their wives, as seen in the communication between Alice and Carter Harrison, of Williamsburg and Richmond.[14] The couple had a loving relationship, but at times their correspondence reveals a tension over Carter's authority that sheds light upon Virginia marriages.

Even before their marriage, Carter's excitement about their wedding revolved around his ultimate happiness. He could not wait for Alice to be "mine exclusively and *forever*" and he complimented her sense and virtue "which must be possessed to make a man happy."[15] Carter's desire for dominance may have come, in part, from their age difference, as he was a good bit older than she. In his correspondence, he called Alice "my precious" and "my dear child," terms that diminished her power. "It is one of my greatest pleasures to 'spoil' you," he told her.[16] Once married, the couple began to quarrel, and Carter told Alice he believed that some time apart would be good for them. When first married, he had not believed it was possible to "have a cross word or bad feeling" toward his wife, but tranquility had given way to human nature.[17]

Carter worried that he had made Alice "less good tempered and complying" than when they met. His criticisms, he assured her, were part of his duty as household head to correct her housekeeping or parenting behavior. "I was always accustomed to seeing my mother yield to my father's judgment and wishes," he explained.[18] Carter struggled with his desire for her obedience and his wish to earn Alice's love. A devoutly religious man, he turned to God to give him patience but also kindness and love for his wife.[19] Like many other white southern men, Carter Harrison seemed to both love his wife and resent her for how weak his love made him feel; his instinct was to blame her and ask her to restore his dominance. Marriages of mutuality did not come naturally to the southern elite.

Especially in more rural areas, such as Fauquier County, Virginia, divorce cases also show evidence of husbands' displeasure at their wives' perceived disobedience, betrayal, and defiance, reflecting their marital ideals. These attitudes were in contrast with the growing demand for mutuality in nineteenth-century America. In a society much more firmly linked with the institution of slavery, the breakdown of a marriage reflected deeper cracks in the foundation of all social relations. In his study of California from 1850 to 1880, Robert Griswold finds little mention of obedience or submission as a laudable goal for women. Instead, he argues, "What emerges from the divorce evidence is not a picture of submissive women at the beck and call of their husbands but rather one in line with the assumptions of domesticity and the companionate ideal."[20] Yet, the same was not true in eastern Virginia. Raised in a slave society, Virginia men learned their role as masters at a young age. Violence and dominance, so much a part of slavery itself, became part of everyday life. Honor and white southern masculinity depended upon the authority they earned from their household dependents, both white and black. While many also sought elements of mutuality in their marriages, their relationships were complicated by a larger social attachment to hierarchy and patriarchy.[21]

In 1854, in Fauquier County, Susan Menefee charged her husband with abandonment and assured the court that up until the time of his desertion, Banks, her husband, had been "to all intents and purposes . . . master" of their home.[22] Using similar language, in response to the petition of his wife, Elizabeth, for divorce in 1848, John Jackson denied that his wife could not return home to him because of his behavior but warned that "it would doubtless be impossible for her to return to her duty as long as she indulges the feelings of hate and the spirit of disobedience which she has imbibed."[23]

The Elizabeth and John Jackson divorce provides an excellent example of one eastern Virginia couple's struggle to define the role of women in the household. In late 1848, Elizabeth sued her husband, John, for divorce with the aid of their son, William. Though the case was eventually dismissed on the technicality that plaintiffs could not initiate a case in a county in which they did not live (Elizabeth was then living with William in Washington, DC), the rhetoric of John's answer shows that he saw Elizabeth's divorce suit as a threat to male power.[24] Elizabeth told the court she left John in the mid-1840s because he not only treated her with "a degree of cruelty which seldom marks the conduct of one human being to another" but also committed adultery. John Jackson vehemently denied all her accusations, including cruelty and adultery, and maintained that she could return at any time, so long as she "behave[d] herself as becomes a wife sensible of the obligations which her marriage vows impose upon her."[25] In fact, John insisted he was the picture of a southern husband, "devot[ing] the supreme of his life to providing for the support and education of his children and for the comfort and welfare of his wife and family." While only a small farmer, John had managed to utilize his few resources to allow his family to live in comfort, at least for their social position. In fact, John argued that Elizabeth had been quite happy with their life until the intervention of the couple's son.[26]

John's formal response contained repeated references to Elizabeth's failures as an obedient wife and his disappointment at his son's role in the affair. John charged William with making Elizabeth forget the "duty" she owed in exchange for John's protection and support. In a hierarchical household, all dependents owed allegiance to the head, and William was taking critical aim at this structure. In fact, at times it is difficult to determine whether John was more upset with his wife or his son for defying him.

In court, John called William's actions an example of "filial disobedience" and "vengeful hate." He linked the pair in his mind; William's act of disobedience, after all, had been to gain influence over his mother (thereby usurping his father's role) and convince her to publicly denounce her husband as an unfaithful and cruel partner. John believed that William had convinced his mother that she could obtain half her husband's property and live in "affluence" with William in Washington, DC. Unsure of whose disobedience threatened his authority more, John charged his son with aiding his mother in "wantonly abandoning and forsaking her husband."[27]

William and Elizabeth's joint defiance of John's authority was even more threatening to the patriarchal household because of its place in a slave society. While men in other regions certainly did not countenance all cases of wifely and filial disagreement, in the South, male household power retained a fragility not found elsewhere and could not be questioned without a dangerous recognition of the precarious role of authority in slavery. In John's case, he directly argued that his wife and son's actions were a threat to his control over his slaves. In his statement, he charged Elizabeth and William with "induc[ing]" his slaves "to run off from him" and into their home, forcing John to give up his farm and rent out his land. This threatened not only his livelihood but also his standing in the community and his position as a white southern man. Knowing all this, John warned the court of the potential crisis that would occur if they ruled in Elizabeth's favor. He pleaded with them to maintain their position as bulwarks against the dissolution of the home, stating that he hoped "the laws of his country will not be made the engine of his oppression or the means of encouraging either the disobedience of his wife or his son."[28]

John Jackson was not the only Virginia man to claim that his wife was under the influence of another person when she wanted to divorce him. Men saw the "next friends," who united with their wives in legal cases due to their *feme covert* status, whether a son, a father-in-law, or a friend, as pollutants in their otherwise happy marriages.[29] Many, like Banks Menefee, argued that "if left to herself," his wife Susan never would have made the accusations against him and that the charges owed their "existence to the selfishness of him who figures as her next friend." In his case, the "next friend" was Susan's brother-in-law, John T. Branaugh, whom Banks believed was scheming to get control over his property. Banks echoed John Jackson, stating that he would be perfectly willing to accept Susan back into his home and to support and provide for her, "if she were willing to accept it and [behave] herself in a manner at all approaching what is due from a wife to a husband."[30]

Beyond Virginians' disapproval of possibly manipulative "next friends," the continued use of this legal technicality speaks volumes about the place of women in this society. In the nineteenth century, women sued with the help of their next friend because of their legal incapacity as *femes covert.* Courts obligated minors, "idiots," or others unable to act for themselves to sue with a next friend. In Virginia during the antebellum era, this category still included married women. In Franklin and Warren Counties, Kentucky, evidence shows that courts and citizens no longer observed this outdated concept.[31] Virginia's retention of "next friends," and their suspicion of those persons, reflects a general unwillingness to believe that women could be legal actors on their own, or further, rational, decision-making partners in marriage.[32]

In some domestic violence cases, eastern Virginia husbands defended their actions as part of their duty as masters. After all, as the rulers of their home, they were obligated to regulate dependents, and in many places the common law allowed husbands to chastise their wives with a stick no bigger than their thumbs.[33] For example, when Mary Jane Ramey sued her husband Isaac for divorce in 1852 on the grounds of cruelty, he denied all charges of excessive violence. Instead, he wrote that he considered her behavior "indelicate," which "imposed on him, as the guardian of her house, as well as of his own, the painful duty of admonition, remonstrance, and repremand."[34] Wives who stepped out of line or exhibited too much independence needed to be checked. This attitude was not uncommon in the antebellum South. For instance, in North Carolina, Chief Justice Pearson stated, "The law gives the husband power to use such a degree of force necessary to make the wife behave and know her place."[35]

Deponents and litigants in Virginia divorce cases also drew attention to the ways in which the hierarchical system of slavery created and distributed power through the entire household. Though Elizabeth Jackson's petition focused on her husband's abuse of her, her attorneys questioned his abuse of his family and his enslaved people, a demonstration of how mastery created violence against multiple household dependents.[36] Eliza Rowen testified that she saw Jackson "beat his servants in the most shocking manner."[37] In an interesting twist, in order to demonstrate his wife's temper, Banks Menefee charged her with violence toward the couple's slaves. When she came home from her brother-in-law's (whom Banks had charged with convincing his wife to leave him), she would inevitably be in a fiery mood. Banks stated that she would then "call for a cow hide and a rope and would whip the servants most cruelly subjecting them to tortures . . . and exhausting herself would send them bleeding to him to be whipped again." If he objected, she cursed him and told him he could not compare with John Branaugh, her brother-in-law.[38] Households in Virginia were, therefore, not immune to the corrupting influences of ultimate power and mastery on both husbands and wives.

A violation of the strict racial code in place in the antebellum South could, in fact, be one of the only acceptable reasons to take such an extreme step as divorce. Harriet Wingo's case for divorce against her husband, John, hinged on his failure to uphold this code. In her petition, Harriet danced around the central issue, charging her husband with adultery and accusing him of having affairs with multiple women in the neighborhood during their seven-year marriage. However, the deponents in the case all focused on one particular affair, clearly finding this relationship to be the most odious. Lawrence Man reported that John frequently visited a "free col'd girl" in the neighborhood and that she had given birth to a mixed-race child that "favours him very much." Lawrence insisted that John had even acknowledged the child as his own. Another deponent, R. T. Wilson, also stated that John visited this free black woman, although he was less sure that her child was John's.[39]

During the colonial era, Virginia had been the first colony to pass a law that banned "miscegenation," or interracial relationships. Their 1691 law was the model for other colonies and future states, beginning a pattern of anti-miscegenation laws that would last until the Supreme Court ruled them unconstitutional in 1967.[40] However, the fact that a white man in the South was having an affair, potentially coercive, with a black woman, enslaved or free, is not a revelation and, as much as they tried to claim otherwise, probably was not for the participants in this case, either. The revelation of an interracial relationship was much more advantageous for a cuckolded man than an abandoned wife. Especially when adulterous white women gave birth to mixed-race children, courts readily agreed to give their husbands a divorce. If such a couple were to remain married, the husband could be responsible and legally liable for these children. As Thomas Jefferson noted, "While [they] continue man & wife, law of England will make her children his." Such questions threatened to expose the tenuous social construction of race in the slave South.[41]

White women could not expect the same intervention from courts if their husbands transgressed the color line. Joshua Rothman has argued that most white women in the South struggled in silence with their husband's indiscretions, especially because they "understood that white male infidelity with black women was common and usually went unpunished."[42] In Harriet's case, the child at the heart of this relationship may have been the reason the Amelia County Circuit Court ruled in her favor. In another case, for example, fifty years earlier, the circuit court in a neighboring county granted Mary Hawkins a separate maintenance from her husband, John, after she revealed his affair with one of her enslaved women, Suckey. Significantly, Mary wrote, "Deft instead of blushes appears to pride himself in" the relationship.[43] While white southern men could conduct affairs with enslaved women, society drew the line at flaunting the relationship or placing that woman on the same level as their white wives.[44] In this case, that transgression could have been so extreme as to necessitate the court's assumption of his masculine authority. John's potential decision to recognize a mixed-race child as his own was especially threatening. By giving his relationship a status that the law did not allow, John was potentially blurring the meaning of race and hierarchy in a society built on maintaining fictitious categories of difference. This, then, may explain Harriet's success, since her divorce was one of only two in her county before the Civil War.

For households built upon the idea of black dependence, any inversion of power relations could mean the ultimate humiliation for its white members. After nearly twenty years of marriage, sixty-year-old Maria Patterson, of Fauquier County, Virginia, sued her husband, John, for divorce in 1857. The couple had initially lived in "peace and quiet," but after the death of their only child and Maria's passage into non-childbearing years, John had become violent and cruel, beating her until she feared for her life. Yet, perhaps most disturbing to southern social mores, Maria stated that, with John's "full knowledge and approval," she was subjected to the "insubordination, insolence, and often violence of the negroes, all of whom are upheld and encouraged in their maltreatment of your oratrix, by the said Patterson."[45] For Maria, neither her whiteness nor her femininity protected her from a husband's abuse or earned his protection from the abuse of her slaves. In addition, by allowing such abuse to occur, John Patterson challenged the racial power structure of his home, giving his twenty-two enslaved people authority over his wife.[46] Though Maria told the court she had determined to bear John's abuse, as a wife and a white southern woman, she found the abuse of her slaves too much to endure. As Maria's and Harriet's divorces show, slavery played an important role in solidifying many of the traits of marriages in the eastern section of the state, differentiating it from Kentucky and western Virginia.

Western Virginians and Kentuckians abused their wives, too, and public opinion was not always disapproving. However, one court case from Wheeling, in western Virginia, suggests that the community tried to limit male authority. When Margaret Bole sued her husband for divorce in 1855, her neighbors testified about William's abuse and how they had tried to prevent it. Anne Elizabeth Moore was appalled to find Margaret Bole working behind the counter only a week after giving birth. When she told William Bole that his wife should be in bed, he replied that it was "his business." She responded that she would make it hers soon and warned him that she would check to make sure Margaret left the store. Western Virginians such as Anne Moore resisted husbands' excessive use of power toward their wives. Another neighbor, Martha Keating, testified that when she went to William's store to buy shoes, he was reading and refused to help her, calling his wife "to leave her domestic work" and help in the store instead. Keating told the court that his tone was "that of a master to his slave."[47] Clearly, William's actions crossed a line and did not reflect the proper way a husband should treat his wife. To Keating, wives had roles that were clearly distinguished from those of household laborers, such as enslaved people, and should be treated in such a fashion. Finally, another neighbor commented that William's "manner towards [Margaret] . . . was harsh and dictational."[48] Many deponents in Margaret's case made similar comments, showing some rejection of unchallenged male dominance in the border South.

Eastern Virginia men saw their wives' departure from their household, whatever the cause, as a rejection of their authority. Most expressed a willingness to allow their wives to return, on the condition that they show the proper deference they believed a husband was due from his wife. Others expressed disbelief that women could even act without the aid of a man, whether in court or in the decision to desert their abusive or intemperate husbands. Even when faced with charges of violence, husbands defended themselves, stating that their role as masters called for reprimand when wives acted disobediently. Male authority depended on the deference of their dependents. In a slave society, their status was also dependent on the permanence of social institutions, including slavery and marriage. Thus, eastern Virginians rejected contractualism and made it difficult for unhappy couples in their midst to achieve a divorce.

While some western states saw a legal evolution in divorce, older states along the eastern seaboard remained more rigid in their rejection of divorce. As the "defender of the organic model of the household," the South also resisted this movement toward a more contractual model of marriage and divorce law, which grew out of the notion of individualism.[49] Especially in a society built upon the intertwined concepts of mastery and slavery, the dissolution of the marital relationship represented a dangerous crack in the seemingly solid foundation of household hierarchy.[50] Even as southern and eastern legislatures and courts eventually grew to accept some measure of marital dissolution akin to the rest of the country, social acceptance of divorce remained low, reflected in the hesitance of many to petition for divorce and in the language of petitioners themselves. Petitioners faced an uphill battle to prove the necessity of separation and often utilized a gendered language of fault, necessity, desperation, and accusation to do so.

In eastern Virginia, divorce plaintiffs continued to fill their petitions with dramatic language designed to make them sympathetic to disapproving judges. As the Civil War approached, the legal and social atmosphere of Kentucky led plaintiffs there to feel less need to justify their decision and less need to use dramatic language. While western and Appalachian Virginians had to justify their divorces because of the harsh Virginia legal code, the high rate of nonresponse from accused spouses indicates that they felt less social pressure to object to these divorces than did their eastern Virginia counterparts.

In his recent work on divorce in North Carolina, David Silkenat uncovers a greater use of "emotional language" in antebellum divorce filings, in contrast to the more legalistic narrative found in postbellum cases. He argues that litigants who employed these "narrative strategies . . . sought to minimize divorce's social stigma by crafting a narrative that absolved them of all guilt in the marriage's demise." By contrasting their moral behavior even in the face of a partner's failings, plaintiffs might give the judge reason to believe they were worthy candidates for separation and that their decision was "necessary rather than voluntary."[51] This sort of narrative was still used by Fauquier and Amelia County residents in the antebellum years, whereas citizens in Franklin and Warren Counties began to use a more legal rationalization for their actions, which reflected adaptations in the law itself and in their attitudes. As mutuality and contractualism gained acceptance in these border regions, couples grew to believe that their divorce could be voluntary, not just necessary. In addition, the courts themselves may have become less demanding, allowing couples to adjust to this change.

In Fauquier and Amelia Counties, Virginia, moral and emotional language can be found in a number of antebellum petitions. In her 1851 petition, Martha Bayliss charged her husband with conspiracy to defraud her of her rightful property, intemperance, "rough" behavior toward her, and unwillingness to work or support her. Despite her ensuing poverty and emotional heartache, Martha told the court that she "determined to abide her lot." During their marriage, Martha Bayliss pleaded with her husband, telling him that she would live with him even in the "humblest cabin." Scorning the offer, Marshall left for Tennessee, leaving Martha without support for over seven years. Yet, when he returned, she repeated her willingness to make a home with him, if he would only supply a residence. Once again, Marshall refused and left the state, taking more of her money. Only after twenty-five years of marriage and multiple separations did Martha sue for divorce, claiming that Marshall's "habits pursuits disposition & tastes," plus his frequent abandonment, made it necessary.[52] Her claims seemed especially poignant when contrasted with the numerous occasions on which she had tried and failed to make her difficult situation work.

Maria Patterson of Fauquier County had been married to her husband, John, for almost twenty years when she sought a legal divorce from the courts in 1856. During that time, she wrote, John had given her "little if any of the affectionate kindness that should characterize the married life." Instead, she testified that she endured repeated abuse, physical and mental, before making her case public. However, she had "borne for years" such behavior. In fact, Maria told the court that it was only when she began to fear for her life that she sought legal remedy.[53] Similarly, Elizabeth Jackson had been married over thirty years when she sued her husband, John, for divorce. In her petition, she stated that she had "faithfully discharged all the duties that devolved upon her, as a wife and mother." In return, John Jackson had been increasingly cruel. Elizabeth chose to blame his actions on his growing addiction to alcohol, rather than an unkind nature, and "bore up under it long and patiently." She told the court she tried to win him over with kindness but failed. Yet, Elizabeth stayed with Jackson until he found her breaking point—adultery. Blaming his infidelity for his cruelty, she at first tried to "remove these evils," but, as she stated, "There is a point where forbearance even in a wife ceases to be a virtue."[54] She left him and filed her first suit for divorce.

Judges could, and did, deviate from the literal statute, depending on a number of factors. Often, when plaintiffs' charges did not adhere to the letter of the law, plaintiffs claimed more than one charge, attempting to strike the right chord with fickle judges. While a large number of petitioners from all six counties charged their failing spouses with more than one offense, Fauquier and Amelia County residents seemed to take advantage of this method most frequently. In only two prewar Fauquier County cases did litigants use one charge alone. In Amelia County, for instance, Frances Cole charged her husband of "many years" with cruelty, desertion, neglect, and adultery, all before he was finally sent to prison. As Maria Patterson's and Frances Cole's petitions reveal, Fauquier and Amelia County residents knew they faced a divorce code with few options for relief. Some probably believed that the more possible reasons for divorce a petitioner cited, the more pity they could earn from the judges.

In her divorce case, Maria Patterson stated that her husband had beaten her with his hands, her own hands, canes, and "other rude instruments"; in addition, he had whipped her, bruised her, pulled her hair, and dragged her by her clothes. To literally add insult to injury, John Patterson also threatened her, "wound[ed] her mental feelings," and "alienat[ed]" her affection. Yet, Maria Patterson was forced to admit that her husband, cruel though he was, had not actually abandoned her, a fact that made her case more difficult to sell to the court. Maria tried to convince judges that he had, for many months, "absented himself" from her bed and stayed elsewhere. This did not qualify as a legal abandonment, but she asked the judges to consider it, in combination with the listed acts of cruelty, a situation "which makes it unsafe for your oratrix to remain longer under his control." Maria never gave the courts a chance to test the limits of the desertion and cruelty requirements, though. Within eight months, she withdrew her case, citing a "compromise" between the parties.[55]

Details about this compromise are absent from the court records. Perhaps Maria chose to return to John, despite his cruelty. After all, she admitted in her petition that she had repeatedly been "induced to return by lies" and John's promises to stop his abuse, only to find her faith sadly misplaced when he began beating her again.[56] John may have convinced Maria once again that he had seen the error of his ways. On the other hand, Maria might have sensed that the courts of Fauquier County were not prepared to grant a woman a divorce on the grounds of cruelty alone and would not accept her interpretation of "abandonment." Therefore, her extralegal compromise may in fact have been a separation agreement, which allowed her to obtain some relief, if not full legal rights and freedom.

Fauquier County wives were not alone in these claims. Responding to the request of his wife, Susan, for divorce, Banks S. Menefee denied all her allegations of abandonment and cruelty. Banks turned the tables on Susan, painting her as a woman of ill temper, "feeble intellect," little cultivation, and violent passions. His home had been like one of the "damned," he wrote. Yet, he endured her flaws because "she was the mother of his children." For over twelve years, he "bore his lot with what philosophy and resignation he could," throwing himself into his work to escape from his troubles at home. Even after his wife told him that she thought she might take a friend's advice and poison him, Banks told the court he still sought to discourage her from a separation. At the very least, he asked her to remain in his house, in a separate room, and agreed never to enter there or to pursue "intercourse between them."[57] Yet, Susan refused this offer and demanded a separation. Even when he agreed to a separation agreement, she sought the aid of the courts. Utilizing similarly emotional language, Banks Menefee tried to show the court that he had attempted to salvage his marriage and had separated from his wife only when forced to do so.

Yet, many border South residents did not focus on the moral failings of their spouse. In fact, the more effective route seems to have been to stick to the legal requirements in the statutes for divorce. Located on the northern and western borders, states like Kentucky were on the front lines as ideas of contractualism and individualism trickled below the Mason–Dixon in the antebellum era.[58] Many prewar divorce cases from Virginia display the highly emotional and gendered language found by Silkenat; but, in Kentucky, petitioners' bills became shorter, less flowery, less dramatic, and more straightforward as the antebellum era wore on, especially in the second half of the 1850s.

While earlier, female plaintiffs had highlighted their wifely virtues, their sorrowful abandonment, their struggles to make ends meet, and their husbands' tawdry affairs, in the late 1850s and early 1860s, wives, such as America Palsgrove, stuck to the letter of the law. In her January 1861 petition, she noted the date of her marriage (March 1859), its location (Henry County, Kentucky), and the residence of the defendant (Franklin County). She concluded by echoing the state statute, stating that she had lived in Kentucky for more than five years, that her husband, Benjamin, had abandoned her more than one year before the suit, and that the cause of divorce had occurred within the state. America called two deponents, who stated that they knew the parties to the suit, that the couple had been living apart for more than a year, and that they would not reconcile. Within a month, the court ruled that she and Benjamin be divorced, both be given rights as unmarried people, and Benjamin pay the costs of her suit.[59]

Even when these litigants mentioned lurid details, they were far less likely to elaborate on these issues than earlier deponents. As with America Palsgrove, Nancy Hulett's July 1860 petition contained only a few lines, merely stating that she married the defendant, Joseph Hulett, in 1835, that she lived with him until September 1855, and that at that time, "without any just cause or provication," Joseph had deserted his wife. Following the law, Nancy assured the court that the separation had occurred more than one year previous to the initiation of the suit (in fact, four years prior to it). While Nancy did mention that she had "performed all the duties and obligations of a wife," she did not give details of this performance, nor did she attack the character of her husband (other than noting his abandonment). To support her case, she filed only one deposition. The sole deponent, James White, merely verified his acquaintance with the plaintiff and defendant, the date of Joseph's desertion, and the fact that he lived in the neighborhood where the abandonment had occurred. White closed his deposition with the intriguing statement that "the defendant took up with another woman and went off with her," but he apparently felt no further details were necessary.[60] Both America and Nancy received divorces within the year, perhaps due to their straightforward cases that followed the letter of the law.

Whereas Fauquier and Amelia County residents filled the pages of their petitions and depositions with assurances that they had not filed for divorce lightly, that they believed divorce was wrong, and that they had repeatedly tried to find another solution to their marital problems, Franklin and Warren County citizens began to trim down the content of their cases. Many of the late 1850s petitions from Kentucky are only one or two pages long and feature little of the dramatic, maudlin testimony of their Virginia neighbors. Social attitudes and the law both adapted to reflect a society in which divorce could be obtained more easily and with less justification.

Although Kentucky and Virginia had many cultural and geographic similarities in the years preceding the Civil War, their destinies would diverge as the country split apart. Kentuckians, torn between both sides, tried to claim neutrality. Their indecision reflected their true identity as a border and a middle ground. Virginia, on the other hand, ultimately became the capital of the Confederacy. That decision would eventually fracture the state, as western Virginians finally saw an opportunity to assert their own border identity and enact a divorce of their own—from their former leaders. The reasons for these varied paths are numerous and complex, but an examination of the differing social patterns in this region as the war approached gives insight into that ultimate conclusion. Patterns of marriage and divorce are only one facet of this borderland culture and its counterpart in eastern Virginia.

In eastern Virginia, white men and women maintained a household structure and pattern of gendered norms that differed from those of Kentuckians and western or Appalachian Virginians. In the plantation regions of the state, populated by high numbers of enslaved people, a strict patriarchy held sway, and vital to its maintenance was a sense of hierarchy. Without that, any number of social arrangements—from marriage to slavery itself—might be called into question. Eastern Virginians' behavior and attitudes toward divorce reflect their underlying assumptions about power, social structure, and regional identity. As the words of many litigants reveal, they took pride in maintaining marital permanence. Eastern Virginians were a bulwark in the face of dangerous reform movements percolating out of New England, whether abolitionism or women's rights. In their minds, liberalization of divorce laws was intertwined in the same radical sentiments that led reformers to call for freedom and equality for black men and women and for equal rights for women. As abolitionist and feminist reformers became increasingly associated with New England, resistance to their demands for social change and equality became part of defending southern identity against northern intrusion. In this sense, defending the institution of slavery against abolitionists was of a piece with defending the male-dominated household against early feminists.

In eastern Virginia, residents rejected many aspects of the mutuality and contractualism so sought after by their border neighbors in Kentucky and western Virginia. They did not see marriage as a relationship built on mutual interests and needs, but as an arrangement in which women exchanged obedience for protection and support. Their few divorce cases reflected relationships that had broken this dynamic by challenging the demand that wives remain submissive and that husbands act as loving authority figures. Of course, we cannot ignore the influence of slavery in this equation. Despite the fact that slavery was a part of life in every other county in this sample, Fauquier and Amelia County residents wove the peculiar institution more often into their narratives. Their decision to do so reflects how intimately connected gendered hierarchies and racial hierarchies were in these plantation homes. This connection made it unlikely that spouses, especially wives, would easily be able to break the ties that bound them. In fact, only under extreme and exhaustive circumstances would courts grant divorces in this environment. To allow couples to more easily divorce, or break their contract, would call into question other social ties. Yet, despite their best efforts, Virginians would witness a nationwide separation in a few short years, an attempt by the southern states to, in some ways, divorce themselves from what they viewed as a tyrannical household head—the United States government.

Part 2

Weathering the Storm

4

Irreconcilable Differences

During the fall of 1861, after he became governor of Kentucky under the provisional Confederate government, fifty-year-old George W. Johnson traveled throughout western Kentucky with the Confederate army, leaving his wife of almost thirty years at home in Georgetown. Kentucky was home to two governments during the Civil War years, but once the Confederates abandoned the Rebel capital, Bowling Green, Johnson's shadow government essentially became another arm of the military. Like other men of this era, Johnson's absence from home made him reflect on his priorities and personal life. In October, he wrote his wife, Ann:

> My dear Wife, I never knew till now how much you constituted as it were a part of my own life. How . . . dear are the pleasures of home, and the love of wife and children. When the passions of men or devils I hardly know which, disturb and convulse society, then come back to mind, pictures of the pleasures of Home, which delight the mind. How insignificant by the side of these, appear the ordinary pleasures of life—the pursuit of money or . . . of honour and fame.[1]

War opened Johnson's eyes to the power of the domestic sphere and the love he shared with his wife. He filled his letters over the next few months with professions of love, poems, and best wishes to his children. He spoke longingly of their lives together once the war ended and he could go home. Unfortunately, George never returned to his wife. In April 1862, he was shot and killed at the Battle of Shiloh. He left a simple note for Ann: "My wife knows how well I love her and she needs no message from me to tell her how I love her."[2]

War is always disruptive, and a civil war especially so. The citizens of Kentucky, West Virginia, and Virginia learned this lesson quickly and harshly between 1861 and 1865, as husbands, fathers, sons, and brothers left home and the region felt the hard hand of war. For many soldiers and officials, like George Johnson, separating from their wives and leaving them vulnerable to attack forced them to reevaluate their attitudes toward their homes and their relationships, laying the groundwork for a further embrace of marital mutuality and contractualism in the postwar years. These ideas had been firmly established in some communities before the war, and they were developed further as border couples relied on their partners to comfort and inspire them in conflict. Left behind during the conflict, white women of the border South dealt with a difficult emotional separation from their husbands, the threat of battle, and, for some, the escalated resistance of enslaved people. For many of these women, the Civil War confirmed the necessity for a more mutual relationship, as they were expected to take on more responsibility in the household than ever before. Many husbands, rather than try to direct household affairs themselves from the battlefield, urged their wives to assume greater control over the household economy and decisions. Eastern Virginians also experienced many of these wartime trends, but their defeat—and black emancipation—led them to challenge these ideals and value a strict social hierarchy. Any marital changes brought on by war collapsed in the face of Reconstruction. For Kentuckians, West Virginians, and Virginians the Civil War brought physical, financial, and demographic disorder, but it also disrupted courtship and marriage rituals, separated husbands and wives, and contributed to the overall evolution of marital roles in the border South.

As this chapter shows, the initial years of the conflict created anxiety for border South white men and women. Couples were separated emotionally and physically, and both those at home and those at war faced daily hardships and dangers. As a result, men and women turned to each other for support and love, something that they had learned to do even before the war. While southern couples throughout the border states and Confederacy found solace in loving relationships, in the upper South this trend was intensified. Their location between the Union and the Confederacy and their perceived importance to the cause brought an especially high level of internal and external conflict to the border South states of Kentucky and West Virginia, and to the Confederate state of Virginia as well. Fighting in and near their homes, as Aaron Sheehan-Dean has shown, impressed strongly upon men in this region the importance of their domestic world and their families.[3] The correspondence and personal records of Civil War Kentuckians, West Virginians, and Virginians share a similar emphasis on economic mutuality, men's emotional reliance on their wives, and growing female independence; however, the Confederates' loss—coupled with the blow of black emancipation—threatened white Virginians' desire to maintain these wartime adaptations. The challenges of physical and emotional distance, as well as the trials of wartime conflict, reshaped many established marriages during the war and left a lasting legacy pivotal to understanding marriage in the postwar years.[4]

This chapter opens with secession, a confusing time that forced those in the border states to choose between their loyalty to North or South. In both Kentucky and Virginia, the decision, far from clear-cut, contributed to the wartime atmosphere of conflict. It also became a defining moment for western Virginians, who, frustrated over decades of inequality and alleged political and economic neglect, broke from eastern Virginia to establish their own state. Created from a Confederate state and recognized by the Union, the newly established state of West Virginia exemplified the multifaceted identity and divided loyalties of the border South. This discord extended beyond politics, economics, and military conflict, and into discussions of gender roles, specifically with regard to married women.

After decades of division between the two regions, Virginia's vote for secession in April 1861 gave western Virginians the excuse they had long sought to sever their ties with the rest of the state. Their differing perceptions of gender roles within the household were certainly not the motivating factor in their decision, but they did reflect their increasingly distinct identity, separate from eastern Virginians. This identity stemmed from their frustration with the eastern elites, as well as their growing connection with their midwestern and mid-Atlantic neighbors. During the decades leading to the Civil War, western Virginians fought against underrepresentation in the state legislature, a tax code that benefited large slaveholders, and a government that made economic decisions based on the eastern elite's needs, rather than the burgeoning industrial needs of the western part of the state. As West Virginians, they aligned themselves with the border states, rather than Virginia, now home to the capital of the Confederacy. Like Kentuckians, they saw themselves as moderates, possible sources of a compromise, and a unique middle ground between two extremes. As the words of state lawmakers reveal, during the secession crisis, this identity helped shape the decisions of westerners and motivated them to resist secession. It also fueled many of their choices during the new state's constitutional convention in 1862 and 1863, in which they tried to distinguish their new state from their old one. The Civil War allowed West Virginians' attitudes about marriage, often disguised and hidden by antebellum Virginia's laws, to come into their own. In the border South, the Civil War challenged and clarified residents' acceptance of mutuality, individualism, and contractualism.

Events moved quickly in late 1860 and early 1861. In November 1860, Abraham Lincoln won a tightly contested election, and just over a month later, South Carolina seceded. By April, six other states had followed the Palmetto State's lead and formed the Confederate States of America. Yet, while sympathetic to their fellow southerners' demands, Virginians and Kentuckians hesitated, and debate over the necessity of disunion raged in the two states' streets, legislative halls, and homes.[5] On January 10, 1861, forty-one-year-old Ellen Kenton McGaughey Wallace of Hopkinsville, Kentucky, wrote in her diary: "The whole country is fearfully agitated and apparently on the eve of Civil War. Men's hearts failing them from fear of the terrible conflict and its consequences."[6]

Like other border South residents during this period before Fort Sumter fell, Wallace expressed a great desire for moderation, compromise, and peace. Similarly, other Kentuckians argued that Lincoln's election did not give the state reason to leave the Union. The *Lexington Kentucky Statesman,* a Democratic paper, stated: "The election of Lincoln *per se,* under all forms of law, ought not to be made the occasion of severing the present relations of the States."[7] Governor Beriah Magoffin agreed, although he also supported slavery and states' rights. Fearful about secessionist fever, Unionist legislators resisted calls to hold a special secession convention in Kentucky.[8] However, when Lincoln issued a call for troops following the attack on Fort Sumter, Governor Magoffin responded by telegram: "I say, *emphatically,* Kentucky will furnish no troops for the wicked purpose of subduing her sister Southern states."[9] In May, a special session of the legislature agreed, declaring that Kentucky would maintain a position of neutrality in the conflict between the Union and Confederacy.[10] Fearful of losing his birth state, Lincoln did not antagonize Bluegrass residents, and a tense peace held during the summer months.

Uncertainty about the state's position led to disagreement and confusion among Kentuckians. "It is my candid opinion," Henry Haviland told his fiancée, Susan Scrogin, "that Ky should occupy strictly neutral ground until she is better prepared." He believed that Kentucky should remain in the Union. Like many other border southerners, he believed that slavery would be more, not less, secure in the Union. In the border South, Union support did not necessarily go hand in hand with opposition to slavery. Even if Kentucky did secede, he figured, "We can be in Ky and be for union."[11] Susan did not agree. As a member of a slaveholding family, she worried that enslaved people might run away or be taken by invading Union armies. Henry assured her that slaves were more secure in Kentucky than elsewhere in the South, but she disagreed with him and called the Union army a "horde of Tyrants."[12] Especially in the correspondence and records of Kentuckians and western Virginians, the discussion about secession continued into late fall of 1861, while battles between the Union and Confederacy had already begun.

By September, though, Kentucky could no longer maintain a strictly neutral position. On September 18, 1861, Ellen Wallace wrote that Confederate troops had invaded Kentucky and her hometown. Within a week, both Union and Confederate troops were in the state, and the state's government abandoned its neutral stance.[13] Kentucky was now officially a Union state, though the state's Confederates formed a breakaway government, led by the homesick George Johnson. Ellen, a Unionist, faced an occupying force of Confederate soldiers. Kentucky's divided Civil War experience had begun.[14]

Virginians' loyalties also fluctuated in the months following the election of Lincoln and the secession of South Carolina. In the early months of 1861, both secessionists and Unionists held county meetings throughout the state, attempting to mobilize public opinion in their favor.[15] At one Fauquier County, Virginia, meeting, a secessionist declared the Union a "brute god," and the audience cheered when another man declared that Virginia should "Go out with her!" if the Deep South joined South Carolina in seceding.[16] Yet, Unionists still held the upper hand throughout much of the region before April 1861. Especially in northwestern Virginia and the Shenandoah Valley, unconditional and conditional Unionists formed a strong and vocal group, and they dominated the Virginia secession convention, held from February 13 through April 17.[17] According to William Link, of the 152 delegates elected to the convention, the "overwhelming majority were either conditional or unconditional Unionists," while only fifty were outright secessionists.[18] As these delegates debated the legitimacy and viability of secession, they also drew from their conflicted views of manhood, exposing another area of disagreement between Unionists and secessionists, westerners and easterners, and, ultimately, demonstrating the unique identity of border South residents.

Virginia secessionists labeled Unionists "submissionists," attacking their honor and manhood. Such rhetoric had been used throughout the

South for decades to imply a division between "'manly resistance' and womanly or slavish submission." It insinuated that Unionists were unmanned by fear, which prevented them from embracing secession.[19] Yet, while many grew angry at these slurs, others argued that their actions reflected a different—and more progressive—manhood. Many western Virginians prized moderation and deliberation and used the secession crisis to demonstrate their devotion to these traits.[20] Although they referred to moderation and deliberation in their political characteristics, it is not difficult to assume that these traits may have extended to their household roles and relations as well. Western Virginians prided themselves on their moderate manhood, which valued compassion and domesticity.[21] Westerners applauded their leaders for having the "true and unmistakable materials of manhood, in the most emphatic sense . . . to resist the overwhelming tide of hostility and bitterness for the Union."[22] One westerner wrote to his secession convention representative that westerners should not join in the "hot, inconsiderate, haste, the mad scheme of secession."[23] Hearing his constituents and speaking his own mind, Morgantown delegate Waitman T. Willey warned against "madly rush[ing] into the perils of disunion."[24]

Northern panhandle political leader, Chester D. Hubbard, a future US congressman, believed that these differences were sectional, implying that the restrained view was a northern one and that southerners were more likely to be rash. He wrote: "I know the Northern mind with its cool calculations can not understand this and will only consider a man, who lets his passions run away with his reason, as a fool or mad, but unfortunately we have too many such in the South."[25] Hubbard valued rationality and calm reflection over the emotional volatility he saw in his fellow southerners. Still, Hubbard bristled at being called a "Submissionist" by "those traitors at Richmond."[26]

Others defended their decision to "submit." The *Wellsburg Herald,* a northwestern Virginia paper, argued that there was "nothing dishonorable in being coerced" or in "rendering obedience to the laws under which we consent to live."[27] At a local meeting near the future West Virginia–Virginia border, one man argued, "If to contend for the honor of that flag for which Washington fought, and for which many of our soldiers gave up their lives in the revolutionary war, and again in the war of 1812 . . . if that constitutes a Submissionist, I am one."[28] These bold statements asserted that obedience could be manly, something that would have seemed contradictory to many white southern men. To be a white man in the antebellum South was to be a master, and a master submitted to no one.

Western Virginians' attitudes toward secession were shaped by years of perceived political and economic inequality between western and eastern Virginia. Even while elevating a different perspective of manhood, men like Hubbard believed that the use of "submissionist" language undermined their honor and masculinity. They also believed that to submit to the easterners again, after years of second-class treatment, would be following "like the cattle on the hills or the slaves on their plantations."[29] Western Virginians rejected eastern Virginians' aggressive stance on secession, criticizing their form of manhood as violent, illogical, and emotional. Nonetheless, the sting of the "submissionist" label revealed that they had still absorbed some aspects of white southern masculinity. They did not fully embrace "restrained manhood," but instead "moderate manhood," which combined the calm, rational behavior of the North with some aspects of the masculine honor of the South.

Still, these men attacked Virginia elites by using language that revealed a unique perspective, distinct from that of their eastern neighbors and more aligned with their western neighbors in Ohio, Indiana, and Illinois. The eastern Virginians were a "negroocracy," according to Fairmont's Francis Pierpont, future governor of the Restored State of Virginia.[30] The "slavery oligarchy are impudent boastfull and tyranical," wrote another westerner—asserting that they were made so by the peculiar institution itself.[31] No longer could westerners tolerate eastern Virginians' feelings of superiority. The state's division was an inevitable consequence of the continued trampling of westerners' rights and beliefs by easterners.[32] Westerners' language suggested that slavery made easterners less democratic. Implicitly, westerners rejected some of the hierarchy that typified eastern slave society, and this extended into western homes as well.

Secessionists slandered western Unionists and called them weak for resisting the pull of the Confederacy, but other Unionists also grew angry with them for "submitting to the indignities that are being heaped upon them, in Richmond."[33] Still, while many submitted to the secessionist attacks, western Virginians remained steadfast.[34] Their ability to do so, as well as their attempts to reshape the discourse in their favor, indicates that they had a different understanding of manhood than their eastern neighbors. Armed with a new understanding of moderate manhood, haste and anger had little appeal to them. Many defended obedience to the law, turning what some southerners might see as a womanly trait into a sign of manhood. Some border men did occasionally employ a modified version of southern masculinity through their use of "submissionist" language, but this too reflected their border identities. Border South men drew on competing gender ideals when making their Unionist stand.

In 1861, it initially seemed as though moderates might carry the day at the Virginia secession convention, but the events at Fort Sumter and Lincoln's call for troops led to adoption of the secession ordinance, eighty-five to fifty-five, on April 17, 1861.[35] The western delegates, seeing their interests ignored for one last time, walked out on the convention. Though secessionists may have painted the Unionists as cowardly submissionists, the western papers and public highlighted the courage and danger of their stand, which, it was rumored, had forced them to "flee for their lives" from Richmond.[36]

Throughout the western part of the state, public meetings of "Union men" sprang up to support the decision of western Virginians not to secede. Many of the leading voices in the new state movement organized and attended these meetings.[37] In May 1861, a convention of westerners met in Wheeling to discuss the repercussions of Virginia's secession and agreed to reconvene after a public vote on the secession ordinance. In June, a second Wheeling convention "disavowed the act of secession" and unanimously elected Francis H. Pierpont governor of the Restored State of Virginia.[38] Moderates argued that because Virginia had seceded, they forfeited the legitimacy of the Richmond government, giving the new Wheeling government the power to recognize a new state. The Second Wheeling Convention drafted a dismemberment ordinance, which the public ratified in October.[39] With this, a new state began its path down the road to formation, and the men in charge had the opportunity to revise their former state's legal legacy toward married women. Their rhetoric at the subsequent constitutional convention reflected their border beliefs about the proper position of husbands and wives.

The same public vote that overwhelmingly approved the proposition to split Virginia and create a new state also elected a committee of delegates to draft a new constitution. The meeting consisted of sixty-one members from forty-seven counties, all in present-day West Virginia. A mix of lawyers, ministers, farmers, and teachers, only 5 percent owned slaves at the time of secession.[40] While many delegates hoped the constitution would reflect Virginia law, decades of disagreement over constitutional issues and the unique demographics of the convention ensured that there would be significant changes.[41] Often, Virginia law provided little precedent, and westerners had to look outside the state's boundaries for inspiration. In some ways, this constitutional fusion reflected the region's attitudes in the antebellum era, which had been influenced by western Virginia's midwestern and northern neighbors. The debate over a proposed married women's property law revealed the social attitudes of delegates in this borderland, as well as their slowly growing belief in mutuality in marriage.

On January 8, 1862, the constitutional convention debated and passed the forty-second section of the proposed West Virginia constitution, which stated that "the legislature shall pass laws to protect the property of the wife against the acts and debts of the husband."[42] At the time of secession, Virginia had no formal married women's property law, and as they drew up a new one, the delegates were inevitably forced to evaluate other states' laws.[43] The discussion surrounding the possible passage of such a law shows the extent to which western Virginians challenged Virginia's social and legal rules, much as Wheeling residents had through their manipulation of divorce law. After splitting from a state that had no formal married women's property law at all, merely having this discussion showed a desire for change and adaptation. Yet, while many men drew from the ideal of mutuality, others still supported a patriarchal view of the household.

Many delegates argued that the property law was necessary because women, as the "weaker" sex, needed protection from the men in their lives. Abraham Soper, of western Tyler County, maintained that many women were vulnerable to bankruptcy and ruin because of intemperate, financially irresponsible, or misfortunate husbands.[44] During the antebellum period, legislators throughout the country had used a similar defense to enact married women's property laws. In Mississippi, the site of the first married women's property law, wealthy planters saw the measure as a way to protect their daughters' property from fortune-hunting husbands. These lawmakers still saw women as dependents in a patriarchal system. Through these laws, women did not gain control over their property; families merely protected their property interests from interloping men.[45]

Strenuously opposed to the measure, James Brown, of southern Kanawha County, made his point clearly. A married women's property law, he believed, would un-sex women, who gained their femininity from their submissive role in the marital relationship. If such a measure were passed, he asked, why not give women the vote? Why not allow them to join the military? And finally, he stated, "Why not make a man of a woman at once?" He argued that the new provision would lead to a situation where the woman "wears the 'breeches.'"[46] Brown's attitude reflected the perception (and reality) that in many places, calls for married women's property laws came from women's rights groups and others advocating gender equality. By 1860, outside the South, married women's property laws focused more on women's ability to control and convey property, not just own it. Brown could not support the implied mutuality that this change allowed.

Others criticized Brown's notion, using the language of mutuality and even equality. One legislator wondered aloud who would consider a "man degraded because his wife happened to be on an equality with him?" Some argued that the new motion would actually strengthen the marital relationship, by making each member more content financially and obligating the husband to be more "humble [and] amiable" toward his wife.[47] Legislators even disputed the legitimacy of the *feme covert* doctrine. Daniel Lamb of Ohio County argued that property was "made common by transferring everything to the husband and leaving no right to the wife" and that "a wife ought to have some rights." He rejected the very core of the *feme covert* ideal, stating: "When the law assumes that a wife is nobody I take the liberty of saying it is not a fact."[48]

This discourse reveals an ongoing debate in this divided state between two different marital ideals, one attached to their old identity as "Virginians," the other reflecting their long-term resistance to Virginia and their growing economic and cultural ties with northern and western states. Prewar western Virginians in Ohio County manipulated the Virginia legal system to grant them divorces, based on a new contractual philosophy toward marriage. Likewise, delegates to the mid-war constitutional convention demonstrated views toward marriage at variance with the Virginia legal system. Delegates openly acknowledged this divergence.

One delegate argued that many other states "in this Union" had passed such married women's property laws and that West Virginia should follow suit. When one man argued that the provision should be optional, another shot back that he supposed "the legislature would have the right at any time to pass laws for the protection of the married woman" but that "it has never been done, I think in this State."[49] Many believed that West Virginia needed to go further than Virginia in advocating mutuality in the marital relationship.

Despite these persuasive arguments, the amendment was overturned a month later and removed from the draft before ratification. The historical record shows no debate or reason why the tide shifted against it. Oddly enough, Chapman Stuart of Doddridge County made the move to strike this section of the constitution. He had not only voted for the proposition a month earlier but had fought for its existence as a measure for the "protection of the female portion of our country."[50] Stuart's arguments had not been as progressive as those of others, and his moderation may have caught up with him. Perhaps he realized that giving married women power over their property would liberate them in some ways. White men in West Virginia remained divided: some saw these laws as a way of protecting patriarchy and property and some supported them as an extension of a progressive notion of mutuality in marriage.

West Virginia finally passed a married women's property law in 1868, as part of the new West Virginia Code. Modeled after New York's law, the new law stated that "all real and personal property, heretofore conveyed directly to a married woman . . . by any person other than her husband, as her sole and separate property, and the rents, uses, and profits thereof shall be and remain her sole and separate property, as if she were a single woman; and the same shall in no way be subject to the control of her husband, or liable for his debts."[51] While there were some limitations (for example, the new law allowed a married woman to sell her property without her husband's permission only if she lived separately from him), in framing new laws West Virginia leaders chose to look northward to a state where the push for married women's property laws came through a combination of male legislators and the budding women's rights movement.[52] Women also received control of their earnings, something that southern states had hesitated to allow before the war and that only about a quarter of them would permit by 1870.[53]

In the midst of a national debate over contract and its role in a free society, West Virginia's formation and new legislation on women's rights led to discussions of *feme covert,* property rights, and women's abilities to contract as equals, once again demonstrating the influence of mutuality on the new state. Married women's property acts allowed women outside the home to keep their wages, thus verifying their contractual rights, while in some ways stifling the husband's contractual rights to his wife's property.[54] In addition, the language and perspective of some legislators reflected a growing respect for mutuality, especially economic, in marriage. While this ideal had existed before secession, the war itself created a crisis in many relationships that forced men and women to either recommit to or reject this notion.

From 1861 to 1865, two armies vied for control of Kentucky and Virginia. During the first two years of the war, the Confederate army invaded and occupied many parts of Kentucky, including its state capital (the only loyal capital to be occupied during the war). By late 1862, however, the Union army had pushed the main Confederate force out of the state. Nonetheless, the Confederate military conducted periodic raids into Kentucky throughout the war, forcing many Kentuckians to remain on their guard for the next three years.[55] The Union military established a firm hold on West Virginia early in the war, but, as in Kentucky, although the largest battles ended quickly, raiding and guerrilla attacks continued until 1865. Meanwhile, Virginia served as one of the main theaters of the war, beginning with the first major land battle of the war (the Battle of Bull Run) and ending with the Army of Northern Virginia's surrender at Appomattox Court House in April 1865.

While soldiers faced the harrowing dangers of battle and camp life, their wives endured their own set of trials. In Kentucky, West Virginia, and Virginia, many women found themselves directly on the battle lines, caught between two sides, and without male support for much of the war.[56] In Virginia, almost 90 percent of military-aged men eventually served in the military.[57] The number was much lower in Kentucky and West Virginia, but this did not mean that women could always depend on the presence of their husbands or male relatives.[58] Although often exhausted, frightened, and frustrated by their ordeal, many border South women grew more confident in their own abilities, as they defended their homes against enemy soldiers, scavengers, thieves, and guerrillas.[59] At the same time, as enslaved men and women embraced their freedom and fled the plantations, white slaveholding women in the border South shouldered additional household duties and responsibility for running the region's farms and plantations, while trying to maintain control over a potentially mutinous enemy within.[60] By empowering the region's married women, the Civil War further solidified the acceptance and expansion of mutuality in marriage.[61]

Not only did white women take on additional work and responsibility within the household during the war, many quickly came into contact with occupying male forces, forcing them to take an assertive position antithetical to passive feminine ideals. While many women were victimized on the ravaged home front, especially in areas of high guerrilla conflict, others took action, confronting the enemy and fighting back.[62] For those who lived in the border South, these sorts of experiences were made even more fraught by military occupation and the conflicting loyalties of the states' citizens. In Kentucky, with neutrality null and void, the Confederate and

Union armies fought for the loyalty of the border state's residents and for control over its land and resources, leaving women vulnerable.

In October 1862, Fanny Bell reported to her aunt, Mildred Bullitt, that Danville, Kentucky, was home to over three thousand Union soldiers and a hundred sick Confederates. Every public and private building was bursting at the seams, and the soldiers' diseases were quickly spreading to the civilian population. Yet, as bad as it was in Danville, she was grateful to be living in a town. Outside of Danville, bands of lawless men "are roaming the country over, frightening the people and taking every thing left by this army and that was little enough."[63] Kentucky women lived in constant fear of both Union and Confederate attack.

Ellen Wallace worried about putting on her nightgown "for fear of a sudden alarm at night of some sort or other." One night in December 1862, ten robbers descended on her home and ordered her to open her stores for them. "We live as it were by chance without any security from the law, but only the mercy of God," she reflected.[64] Mary Johnstone was similarly unnerved by her close encounter with war. "The firing seemed to come nearer every minute," she wrote her aunt, Mildred Bullitt, in November 1862. As her house was near the road, she could see everything that was going on. People streaming by told her that the Yankees were coming quickly. When Mary and her mother at last decided to leave, a man came and tried to take their wagon. Mary's mother confronted him, bribing him with some grapes to leave them alone. He then told her not to leave the house. Mary told her aunt, "It is very well we didn't as every house where families had left was broken open and things taken out."[65]

Hula Winston, a Unionist in Paducah, experienced a local raid. She was "frightened to death" by the gunfire and shells and ran for "two miles with out stopping." At one point, a shell hit a house just behind her and her children, showering them with pieces of wood. She pushed her children to run one more mile before she reached a safe house and waited "untill the rebels left." Women like Hula lived in constant anticipation of attacks or guerrilla raids. For them, the war demanded new vigilance and new responsibility. "My children never think of undressing at night but sleep in their clothes," she wrote. "I keep a change of clothes up in a pillow case I can sling across my shoulder and run."[66]

Though invading soldiers sometimes saw women as helpless, submissive creatures, women in the border South reacted to war in ways that proved them anything but. As Jacqueline Glass Campbell argues, the "emotional ties that bound Southern women to their homeland often led them, not to passivity, but rather to a fierce defense of hearth and home."[67] Women like Fanny Bell, Mary Johnstone, and Ellen Wallace knew that their gender provided little protection and that they must face the horrors of war, often alone. Yet, in the border South, this burden may have been eased by a greater prewar acceptance of household mutuality. Because of this, white border South women drew upon their antebellum ideals, giving them greater confidence in their ability to care for their homes, protect their families, and defy the enemy. At home, women all over the upper South faced soldiers who demanded part of their dwindling food and provisions. Susanna Gordon Waddell, a West Virginian, appreciated the Union army "robb[ing] us in the politest manner imaginable," but she still grew frustrated at their repeated visits. She confronted the intruders, begging them to leave her family alone and challenging them to find any food to take (she hid it over and over).[68]

In West Virginia, an early Union occupation ensured the new government's viability and suppressed its Confederate population. As one woman put it: "We are all divorced from our rebel husbands but I can inform Uncle Abe that I would rather be called the wife of the poorest meanest soldier in our army than be the wife of a brigadier general in his army or his wife either!" Like other Confederate West Virginians, she scoffed at the new state, calling its founders "traitors."[69] She represented the many Confederate sympathizers in the border South, whose frustration lay with the Union military. These women, who demonized northerners, or "Yankees," complicate our understanding of border South women's behavior. Confederate border South women challenged women's traditional roles as passive onlookers to the war, but this is not to say that they were antislavery or even pro-Union. In the border South, acceptance of mutuality and individualism in the household did not necessarily translate into anti-Confederate views. These women's beliefs and presence in these divided communities highlight the inherent messiness of the border, where mutuality could stand uneasily alongside a belief in racial hierarchy.

In addition to confronting troops and running their farms, women in these divided regions took on the additional responsibility of hiding their husbands, whether from enemy troops, guerrillas, or home guards.[70] In some areas, a change in the occupying force could lead to the departure of a town's male inhabitants. In late 1864, Hopkinsville, Kentucky, for example, fell into the hands of the Confederate army, and all of its male inhabitants reportedly left town, "fearing that they would be conscripted."[71] Women hid husbands who were unable to flee their homes from enemy troops. In 1864, Sarah Duval, whose husband was an invalid "scarcely able to sit up," had to care for their children, exert authority over their slaves, and help move the family, despite a violent snowstorm, when the Union army invaded and burned their home. She was not alone. With few men around, the other women of her community also packed up their children and fled. Sarah had to be constantly vigilant; at the slightest hint of a Union soldier approaching, she would whisk her husband upstairs, to hide until the danger passed.[72] Women served as protectors, upending the traditional marital bargain in which men provided protection in exchange for obedience. Drew Gilpin Faust has argued that this reversal threatened to destabilize household relations after the war. If men could not protect them, why did white women owe them obedience? Yet, this argument assumes that this understanding of marital roles was intact at the outset of the war. In the border South, that deal had already begun to falter in the antebellum years.

Stories of the vitriolic response of southern women to the invading Union armies are legendary. White southern women aggressively refused to accept Union occupation or control.[73] In New Orleans, women left streetcars or crossed the street to avoid Union soldiers; in one case, a woman "spat in the faces of two officers." In response, General Benjamin Butler issued General Order No. 28, warning that any white woman who continued to behave in such a way would be treated as a "woman of the town plying her avocation."[74] In the border South, however, such reactions were not confined to Confederate women. Unionist women resisted Confederate occupation and raids with a similar level of fiery anger, and guerrilla conflict drew white women from both sides and a variety of classes into the conflict.

Jacqueline Glass Campbell argues that displays of female anger unsettled Union soldiers because of their northern values, particularly the ideal of women as pious and pure moral beings at the center of a domestic haven.[75] In the border South, however, women may have drawn from this very ideal of domesticity to establish themselves as assertive domestic defenders, rather than "she-devils." Also, the Unionist loyalty of many border South women gave northerners a reason to glorify their actions, rather than disparage them as they did those of southern women.

Defying the male authority of occupying armies and invading raiders gave white border South women a way to assert their rights to protection as women and, at the same time, to challenge their submissive positions. In addition, while many white southern women continued to expect deference and special treatment throughout the war, women in divided regions—heavy in guerrilla warfare and bushwhacking—learned quickly that their gender provided little protection against the ravages of war.[76] Women in the border South may have come to accept their altered position more quickly because of the high levels of conflict within the state.

Because the border states harbored their fair share of both Unionists and Confederates, residents closely watched and policed one another. Loyalty, and what it meant to be loyal, was often in question. In this tense atmosphere, women's words took on added weight, no longer protected by the shield of gender. Especially in a region with high levels of extramilitary combat, women's actions took on greater political meaning. However, to acknowledge women as political actors was to acknowledge them as individuals, capable of independent thought and action. This would have implications for their relationships within the household both during and after the war.

Not all border South women, for example, shared their husbands' or lovers' national loyalties, and they confronted them about this. John Davis, a young Unionist Democrat from West Virginia, faced criticism and teasing from his Maryland "secesh" fiancée, Anna Kennedy. Though the two gently quarreled about the war, they married in 1862, despite his involvement in the West Virginia statehood movement.[77] Meanwhile, when Susan Scrogin contemplated moving farther south, away from Yankee invaders, her fiancé argued that Kentucky should stay in the Union.[78] To win the debate, Susan, like many other women, leveraged her affections to persuade her fiancé to support her side in the conflict.[79] In December 1861, she wrote Henry, alternating between assurances of her deep love for him and a discussion of the Union's intentions toward slavery. "Dont for one moment think that I would hesitate to trust my happiness to your care," she told him. A few lines later, she added: "Remember my dear that you told me if you thought that this war was waged for the emancipation of Slavery that you was right with the South."[80]

Such disagreements could threaten fundamental conceptions of marriage and women's role within the institution. Women who disagreed with their husbands' or fiancés' perspectives on national political affairs resisted male authority and asserted their own identity as citizens and political actors.[81] In a region rife with political disagreement, this not uncommon situation further solidified women's individualism in the marital relationship. Additionally, in the border South, some men actually used the notion of marital mutuality to accommodate and forgive their future wives' disloyalty, even if it initially disturbed them. Women's independent political thought forced border South men to apply their new ideals, and the test often exposed their conflicted attitudes toward such a relationship.

In this divided region, the treatment of women's political activities, especially through their correspondence, demonstrates an even more noticeable change in their overall social position. As the war went on, women's correspondence came under increasing scrutiny, especially letters to enemy soldiers. No longer could domesticity and femininity protect women, and men wrote to warn their female relatives or sweethearts of this possibility.[82] Charles Simrall wrote to his former fiancée, Belle Price, that he had heard that the Federal authorities were arresting women as well as men, and asked for the "priviledge my friend, to remind you that caution in speaking, and acting, your feelings cannot be too much exercised."[83] Belle teased him, "How timid you have grown about me great big man that you are." She reassured him that she would not get into "political trouble" as she had "grown to be a perfect pattern of prudence."[84] Belle chose to address these activities in a joking tone, but her letter suggests she fully realized that her gender no longer protected her against even "political" charges. The war profoundly reshaped the private and public identities of white southern women, as wives and as citizens. With their loyalty in question and sometimes distinct from that of their husbands, married women gained a new independent identity, which further challenged the concept of *feme covert*.[85]

With men gone or incapacitated, border South women also took on greater economic responsibility in the household during the war. Husbands and wives in antebellum Kentucky and West Virginia had begun to seek a sort of economic partnership in their relationships, so they were often better equipped to handle this transition. Antebellum court documents praised the industriousness of both sexes and disparaged those who failed to contribute toward the family's support. Some Virginia couples also expressed a growing sense of economic mutuality during the war years, but this was more a response to specific wartime needs than the sort of economic partnership that was developing in antebellum Kentucky and West Virginia. After the war, while some sense of economic mutuality remained in Virginia, it did not reflect a broader change in household hierarchy. On the other hand, the wartime experiences of Kentuckians and West Virginians had a more lasting impact, since they built upon, rather than challenged, their prewar traditions.[86]

In early 1865, Kentuckian Mary Ford was busy dealing with her family's health problems, hiring slaves, purchasing food, arranging her daughter's education, haggling over old bills, raising her chickens, mending clothes, and attending church. Like many other women during the Civil War, she shouldered increasing responsibility in the household, including economic support and management.[87] Women ran farms and plantations as "deputy husbands," something they had long done without substantial challenges to gender norms.[88] Yet, coming as it did during a pivotal point in the evolution of marital roles and women's rights, the Civil War threatened to effect permanent changes to women's status in the home.[89] With men's departure for the battlefield, the rise in female heads of household spurred a rethinking of postwar marital roles. The absence of thousands of men left women to carry the household mantle and to reevaluate their potential position in marriage. Additionally, because many of these men did not return home after the war, wartime independence did not end for some women with the cessation of hostilities.[90]

In Fauquier County, Virginia, Ida Powell Dulany had been alone since her husband, Henry ("Hal") Grafton Dulany, left in July 1861 for training in the Confederate cavalry. She became "the decision maker" at Oakley, the family's 850-acre plantation, and "had to provide food, clothing, and medical care for everyone on the place." She stepped outside her role with the help and support of her husband. For example, after she sold some cattle in October 1861, she received a letter from Hal, commenting, "I think you did excellently well with your cattle."[91] Concerned with battles and other pressing matters, many men urged their wives to take on these additional responsibilities and relieve them of the burden. While many may have seen it as an extension of women's antebellum role as plantation mistress, this abdication of household responsibility to wives inevitably emphasized the mutual responsibility of men and women in the household. Therefore, when George Johnson, the Confederate Kentucky governor, cautioned his wife, Ann, that he would no longer give her instructions and that she should now manage his affairs "in any way you think best," he signaled his shift toward a broader understanding of mutual economic responsibility.[92] For other couples, the "deputy husband" role built on a border tradition of mutual household economy. Many border South men found it prudent, even before the war, to include their wives in their financial and economic dealings and no longer saw them as incapable of managing the larger affairs of the household. For these couples, the war further solidified an existing evolution.

For many West Virginians and Kentuckians, these attitudes remained after the war. In 1870, West Virginian Semantha Morgan chafed under her limitations as a wife and longed to help support her husband. While he left to earn extra money, she lived with his father. "I am so helpless from my position in your fathers house, and am only an additional weight about your neck," she wrote her husband, John. "That renders me so miserably unhappy."[93] The Morgans struggled economically, and both John and Semantha longed for an "independent" life together. Their prolonged separation prevented them from forming the sort of domestic relationship they, and many other border residents, sought. John took joy, at least, from the fact that they worked together to make their financial decisions, even if they struggled. He told Semantha: "Nothing gives me more pleasure than to know that we have made up our mind to use the means we have, and those we have not, to do without."[94] His emphasis on "our" decision shows his belief in mutuality in their relationship.

As Kentuckians Susan Scrogin and Henry Haviland prepared for their wedding in the years following the war, she asked him not to worry about how he would provide for her in the future. "It is realy something strange to hear anyone even hint that they have a thought of assisting me in taking care of myself, or providing for my future wants," she told Henry. Having supported herself alone for six years, she was proud of her "self reliance." This behavior, she wrote, had helped her endure her troubles and rise above want. She would continue to do so, even after their marriage, as long as her health allowed. If he insisted on supporting her, however, she promised to "assume my portion of responsibilities that will naturally accrue to the Married Life."[95]

Certainly, not all men came to see their wives as mutual partners after the war. Robert Page, a doctor in Petersburg, though loving, also maintained a particular view of the relationship between himself and his future wife, Pattie. When planning their wedding ceremony, Robert wrote to Pattie, "I'm sure I dont care much who I go in with, so I come out with you, as a piece of my property." Robert struggled to find a proper home for them after their wedding, but when Pattie suggested that her father help pay for their board, Robert immediately took offense. "It is not your place to support me, and far less your Father's—it is mine to support you, and I have an abiding faith that I can & will do it," he told her.[96]

The war could also strain a relationship that had not always been based on mutuality. Virginian Carter Harrison clearly placed himself at the head of the household during the early years of his marriage in the 1850s. Alice Harrison respected his views and his authority and looked to him to make decisions, run the household, and manage their affairs. When Carter left to join the military, however, Alice took on a new role in the family, and the pair seemed to struggle with this altered balance of power. When Alice asked him mundane questions about household management and buying food, Carter snapped back at her, "I can't possibly answer your questions about the eggs &c—Can't even take time to think about such matters."[97]

While his dismissal could have been an opportunity for Alice to claim more responsibility in their relationship, she clearly struggled with this possibility. "Oh me if I was only well & hearty (& a man to boot) I know I could go . . . dispose of your horses raise money & get you a good house servant," she sighed. "I am going to try my best anyhow." By July 1861, though, Carter realized that the war might last longer than a few months and that he needed to prepare his wife for this possibility. He told her to economize and prepare for a winter away from him. He tried to encourage her, "You must show yourself a brave hearted woman (as I know you are)." He told her to occupy herself by looking after their farm and raising the best possible crop of corn to store for the winter.[98] Although Carter had not willingly embraced her changing role, the realities of the war forced him to adjust his expectations and encourage his wife to do the same. We can only hope she took his advice, as Carter Harrison was killed on the eve of First Manassas, forcing Alice into the new independence she so struggled to accept.[99]

In the border South, however, many women accepted their new roles more quickly than Alice Harrison, reshaping their attitudes toward both themselves and their marriages in the postwar years. One West Virginia woman confessed, "I get much out of heart sometimes when I think how we have been broken up & seperated so far apart." While she understood that every man needed to serve his country before enjoying "the quiet of home," she worried that her husband was over two hundred miles away from her. Yet, she knew that their distance also gave her an opportunity to explore her own abilities. For example, she traveled by herself for the first time and cared for their children. "We do not know what we can endure until we have the trial," she realized.[100] Another West Virginia woman was also surprised at her own independence. "I used to think that if my husband would ever have to go to war I could never survive it," she admitted to her friend, Helen Robinson, "but he has been in the army seven months & I am still living though I have felt very uneasy about him."[101] By the time Lee surrendered at Appomattox Court House, many border South women shared these sentiments. Surprised and pleased at their own abilities and strength, many would use these attitudes in the postwar years to further embrace and solidify a sense of mutuality in their marriages.

In some ways, the war actually strengthened relationships. Certainly, it created new ones. As Drew Gilpin Faust puts it, "Separation paradoxically seemed to encourage a new frankness, a new emotional accessibility, and a new intensity of feeling between husbands and wives."[102] Kentuckian Charles Simrall, for example, confessed to his fiancée, Belle, that he cried openly when he left her to travel overseas. She assured him that "to me tears are but testimonies of sensitive nobles," and "I like you all the better for them."[103] For other men and soldiers sent to war, such emotional intimacy and sensitivity became increasingly common. In the border South, war, as it often does, led to a spike in marriages, but it also deepened the emotional connections between men and women and gave men a higher estimation of the domestic sphere. More men began to use strong romantic language in their letters to lovers or wives and emphasized their desire to be with them. In other words, women's wartime empowerment *and* men's glorification of domesticity cemented the establishment of mutuality in marriage in the postwar years.

Under these circumstances, marriage took on an added importance—and immediacy—for many men. In their correspondence, upper South residents commented frequently upon the growing number of wartime marriages.[104] In Petersburg, Robert Page commented, "There seems to be a matrimonial force in town now."[105] Charles Sydnor called it an "Epidemick of Matrimony . . . spreading over our land with a rapidity unequaled by any contagion since the breaking out of the measles."[106] The violence of war increased the value of marriage in men's minds.

"Oh I tremble when I think how very fearful I am Death may be very near to me," one young soldier wrote to Helen Robinson, a resident of north-central West Virginia, in late October 1863. Ominously, he predicted, "I may be cut off in one short hour."[107] During four long years of battle and camp life, death remained a constant presence in many soldiers' minds.[108] Yet the possibility of death, though final, was only one of the forms of separation they dealt with during that time. For many, living apart from their wives, mothers, and children for months or years could be devastating enough to make them reflect on their priorities and values. Many, like

George Johnson, came to realize that the domestic world held a primary place of importance in their hearts. As the war raged on, many turned to the supposedly safe haven of their homes and families to keep them mentally and physically afloat. As they did so, they strengthened the importance of mutuality in marriage by glorifying male domesticity.[109] In addition, they recognized the power of their wives' support and attempted to encourage the women back home who were left vulnerable to conflict and attack. Especially in a divided region, the war pushed husbands and wives to lean on each other and to see the marital bond as one of mutual support, encouragement, and love.

Fifty-year-old George Johnson knew clearly what mattered most to him in the world, despite the importance of war and politics at that moment. Ranking his affections, he placed his wife first, then his family and children, and finally his country: "Oh, how inexpressibly dearer to the human, is the wife of a man's early manhood, and the mother of his children, than all other affections of the human soul." If there was any doubt about his meaning, he went further, "I think I love my country, but far beyond is the interest I feel in you."[110] George found consolation, at least, in the thought that he fought to protect his wife and family and to ensure their happiness once peace came. Although he had been married for decades, the war heightened his feelings and put things in new perspective.

Men throughout the upper South felt the same as George Johnson. Protecting the domestic sphere justified their absence and inspired them, while incidentally increasing the emotional power of their homes and wives. After he was wounded in late 1862, Oscar Styron told Mollie Burroughs how much she meant to him. "The thought of having you nearer me was alleviating & oh how your presence would have cheered up my spirits," he told her. He confessed that he lay awake at night, dreaming of her and his home. "I love my home better than I ever did," he realized. If he could get home again, he told Mollie, he would be "content to remain there."[111] The war, Oscar told her, had calmed him down and changed his habits and outlook for the better. Especially for young Virginians like Oscar, the war could provide an opportunity to reorient their philosophy on manhood and domesticity.

To these men at war, the domestic sphere gained prominence as a source of pleasure and contentment. Charles Sydnor, stationed at a hospital in Virginia, wrote to his fiancée, Mollie, that as he dealt with "fatigues and hardships . . . my thoughts ever turn to thee as the emboddyment of all my future happiness."[112] Men fighting an exhausting and bloody war glorified the purity of their homes and the power of their wives to support them emotionally. As Charles told Mollie, "It is in times of distress as well as in times of prosperity that I look to you for comfort."[113] In addition, as Aaron Sheehan-Dean has shown in his study of Virginia soldiers, "The pressures of military service encouraged men to identify their families' immediate and future well-being as the most important reason to participate in the war."[114] Men wrote repeatedly of the dangers suffered by their wives, daughters, mothers, and sisters, a fact that only pushed them to fight harder, while also emphasizing the importance of women and the domestic sphere. Oscar Styron wrote to Mollie, "I often think of you, my home and my native county and the thought that they are in the possession of the enemy animates and nerves me to fight harder and if necessary die for their delivery."[115]

Kentuckian George Johnson admitted that thoughts of how long he might be separated from his family sometimes overwhelmed him, but said that he never wavered in his commitment to the Confederate cause. "I console myself," he told his wife, Ann, "with the reflection, that when I return to you it will then be the day of my compensation."[116] Being home and holding his family would be his just reward. Such thoughts increased the value of home by linking it with victory or defeat in the war. It also gave men something to inspire them and keep them fighting when victory seemed unattainable. Susan Scrogin even used married men's attachment to home to justify their being drafted after the second year of the war. "I am truly glad that the married men have to go," as she defiantly told Henry Haviland, her fiancé, "they have no more right to stay at home than single men has. they should fight for their Wives."[117]

Border South residents continued to value male domesticity after the war ended. To them, the home was a shared space, reigned over by two complementary partners. In this way, the war's ravages had only solidified their commitment to mutuality and domesticity. Living in postwar Poca, West Virginia, Semantha Morgan urged her husband to remember her and their "sweet children" when he worked. He would not be able to enjoy the fruits of such labor and might be taken from them if the stress or exertion became too much. "You must take care of your health, it is the most precious of all Gods good gifts," she wrote.[118] In her view, his time at home and with his family took precedence over their much-needed economic support.

Kentuckian Sallie Bullitt rejoiced over her son's character and told her daughter Julia that his wife, Jinnie, was fortunate to have such a husband.

"His tender thoughtfulness and watchful care must to a good extent alleviate and soften her grief," Sallie stated. In exchange, Jinnie made "every effort to make him happy."[119] Sallie commended her son's caring behavior, as well as the mutual exertions of the couple to help one another. Wives also dedicated themselves to their husbands, especially their husbands' emotional and spiritual needs. Many newly married men in the postwar period focused on their resulting happiness, possibly relieved to find something good in the midst of loss. Writing to his mother, one Kentuckian wrote, "It is useless for me, Mother to tell you how happy I am now and how blessed I think I have been in getting such a woman for a partner in life."[120]

By glorifying the domestic sphere, encouraging their wives to shoulder greater economic responsibility, and accepting, in some measure, their wives' independent opinions, men further strengthened the power of the ideal of mutuality in the postwar years. As A. P. Farnsley wrote to his fiancée, Bettie, "I would not like for two weeks to elapse without hearing from you, even in ordinary times . . . much less in times like the present, when we hardly know whom to claim as friends and whom to claim as enemies; when we feel like clinging closer and closer to those whom we love and whom we know to be true to us."[121] The messy and complicated world of the border South during the Civil War drove men and women into one another's arms and forced them to reevaluate their importance to one another. Certainly, this also happened in places like Virginia, but there, the changes brought about by the war years did not have the same impact in the postwar years.

"Love is a singular Commodity," Kentuckian James Carter told his wife, Melville, and in the postwar border South, both newly courting couples and long-married partners worked to cultivate this commodity, with a marriage of mutuality as the ultimate goal.[122] For many, this goal had become even more vital because of the war itself. During the Civil War, Kentucky, West Virginia, and Virginia experienced near constant conflict as the Confederate and Union armies crisscrossed their borders. At the same time, Kentucky and West Virginia also faced internal conflict, as their borderland collection of economic, cultural, racial, and political differences threatened to tear them apart. Such a vast upheaval reverberated in the states' households, challenging women left at home and men sent to war to reassess and redefine their marital roles. In this environment, marriage could provide a sense of stability or of volatility. The adoption of mutuality in marriage before the war enabled many Kentucky and West Virginia couples to adapt more easily to the challenges of civil war. Many white women in the border South already viewed marriage as based on economic mutuality, which would lessen the shock of their husbands' absence for years at a time. Similarly, many border South men applauded and supported the efforts of their wives to maintain their households in their absence. Facing similar combat scenarios, Virginia couples also saw a shift in responsibility away from the husband and father to the wife and mother. However, without a stable ideological foundation for this change, the shift was a temporary one, seen as an extreme response to extraordinary circumstances.

The period of secession and civil war was the moment when the borderland identities of Kentucky and West Virginia stood out most clearly, a moment in which residents defined themselves as distinct from either their Union or Confederate neighbors. Kentucky's attempts to maintain a fraught neutrality reveal their attitudes as unique or separate from these two battling sides. Similarly, West Virginians embraced Virginia's secession as the moment to declare their independence and establish themselves as a state. The process of statehood allowed residents to declare and establish their regional and state identity. During a war in which some declared that they fought exclusively for their state, the creation of a new state and defining oneself as a citizen of that state had tremendous meaning. The battles over secession and the debates at the subsequent constitutional convention provide a clear window into one facet of that identity—their understandings of manhood and marriage. In these areas, West Virginians saw themselves as moderates and as distinct from their eastern Virginia neighbors. The war would further crystallize this identity, at least for the first few years after the Confederacy's surrender.

During these years, courtship and marriage remained an integral part of border citizens' lives. Certainly, the outbreak of war would change the courtship process in many ways, and of course, the loss of thousands of young men limited many women's options.[123] However, many couples overcame the obstacles of distance, inconsistent mail service, and military conflict to form lasting bonds. Many married, some more quickly than they might have in peacetime; others struggled to adapt the ideal of mutuality, which required emotional intimacy and mental connection, to the difficult circumstances of the war. Marriages constructed in the harsh environment of war could strengthen the bonds between couples or tear them apart through their own desire for closeness. Throughout Kentucky, West Virginia, and Virginia, married couples often expressed their undying affection and devotion for one another. In the face of incredible hardship and sweeping change, many border southerners chose to turn inward and rebuild their relationships, often on the foundation of mutuality and respect, rather than patriarchy and dominance.

The close of the Civil War left men and women across the border South uncertain about their public and private roles, including their position within the household and their marriages. Four years of war had challenged and solidified the power of mutuality in the border South, as men came to value the domestic sphere, women grew confident in their own independence, and both leaned on each other to survive the trials of war. Yet, the Civil War also created vast changes in the southern landscape, including, most notably, black emancipation.[124] The postwar period would test whether border South marriages were truly partnerships, with obstacles best faced together, or not. As Charles Sydnor expressed to his fiancée, Mollie, in mid-1864:

> It is true we will have to begin the world as others placed under similar circumstances and as I fear all others what ever may have been their condition before the war, commence life anew relying on our own efforts and exertions for prosperity & success. Yet I fear not but am willing yea even anxious to begin the contest . . . with you for a connector and partner the difficulties and obstruction that constantly present themselves to a pleasant and happy journal through life, would be bravely encountered & overcome.[125]

For Charles and Mollie, as for other couples, their ability to face this "contest" together would be given its ultimate test in the coming years.

5

Torn Apart

On a late September day in 1861, Lewis Long, a resident of the northwestern panhandle of what was then Virginia, joined the Union army as a private. Under the terms of service specified in his enlistment, he was to serve "three years or during the war." Like many soldiers, his decision to leave home affected more than himself. Lewis left behind Rosanna, his wife of barely two years. Absences such as these strained many marriages, and Lewis and Rosanna's relationship proved no exception. In August 1863, Lewis discovered Rosanna committing "lewd and improper practices" with another man and refused to live with her again. By the time the war ended, Rosanna was living with James B. Hays, even buying supplies with his credit. Within a year, Lewis filed for divorce, citing adultery as the cause.[1]

Lewis and Rosanna Long's tumultuous relationship was just one of many failed border South marriages in the early postwar years. The Civil War may have ended in April 1865, but its impact on the region's relationships continued to reverberate for years to come. How could a war that had devastated the southern environment, economy, and household (through emancipation) fail to also wreak havoc on the romantic relationships of those involved? Four years of war had a profound impact on people's psyches and emotions, and for those caught up in the turmoil of the conflict in the border South, this was exacerbated. In the postwar years and even beginning during the war itself, outside pressure on marriages created irreparable cracks that would soon give way.

Marriages collapsed for a number of reasons. Many men and women left their partners or saw their partners leave them for the same reasons that had always ended marriages. However, other cases reveal the very particular impact of the Civil War on border South relationships. One of the biggest causes of marital dissolution in the postwar years was the lengthy absence of so many men during the conflict. Like Lewis, men left expecting to earn a good living, defend their country, and attain glory and honor in battle. They probably expected to come home as conquering heroes, but many returned to empty houses. Left behind, women like Rosanna sought comfort and support in the arms of men who remained in their community.

The experience of battle also shattered many men. In an era before medical science had given it a name, many soldiers suffered from undiagnosed posttraumatic stress disorder. Their untreated trauma hurt their ability to maintain healthy marriages and may have created more tension in border South relationships. The chaotic postwar environment also gave many unhappy partners the opportunity, in addition to the motive, to leave their marriages. The postwar South was characterized by the movement of people—freedpeople searching for family and work, former soldiers traveling home, and white southerners returning to farms and plantations they fled during the conflict. In this atmosphere, abandonments increased, as many spouses grabbed their chance. This, of course, does not take into account the impact of emancipation, which drastically altered relationships within the postbellum household.

Finally, two traits of life specific to the prewar and wartime border South contributed to the rise in divorces immediately following the war. First, the antebellum acceptance of marital contractualism and mutuality made much of this possible. Marriages were contracts, and many signatories had failed to maintain their agreement during the war. Therefore, divorce was the only solution. For some, long absence during the war revealed a more mundane fact—the couple no longer loved one another. In West Virginia and, especially, Kentucky, this could be reason enough to file for and even obtain a divorce. Second, the fervor with which soldiers pictured the domestic sphere during the war led to many quickie marriages, marriages with little thought or love behind them. These marriages could quickly fall apart under the realities of peace.

The end of the Civil War shaped marriages in the border South differently than in the rest of the South. The border states, after all, had never seceded, and therefore, many soldiers returned home victorious. However, this earned glory could be deeply disturbed by the return of neighbors who had fought on the opposite side and whose return was far less triumphant. Additionally, this region had felt the hard hand of war and had experienced loss—economic and otherwise. Border southerners, although they did not experience the same military loss and military Reconstruction as the Confederate South, did experience the social change created by black emancipation, which differentiated their postbellum world from that of the northern states. As before the war, the border South continued to forge its own unique path through this pivotal era. This chapter places the end of many border South marriages in a specific historical context—the years following the conflict, in a region whose laws and social practices were especially conducive to this spike in divorce. Nonetheless, many of these stories have a timeless quality to them, reflecting that war, any war, can devastate long after its end.

During the Civil War, thousands of Kentucky, West Virginia, and Virginia men served in the Confederate and Union armies.[2] They left behind women and children, who had to deal with deprivation, societal changes, and internal conflict on the border South home front. As the Civil War raged on, men and women struggled to maintain their marriages, now strained by time, distance, and economic and physical hardship. Although mutuality and love often sustained beleaguered soldiers and their families, others saw their bonds break and crumble in the face of such trials.

In the border South states of Kentucky and West Virginia, the postwar years saw a continued rise in the number of divorces, for a variety of reasons.[3] While many can be traced to a change in the legal requirements for divorce and to the impact of the evolving economic and social system on marriage, many divorces stemmed from the pressures war put on the marital relationship. Women blamed men for failing to support them when home front deprivation became overwhelming, and men blamed wives for a lack of emotional support and devotion when they faced death and danger on a day-to-day basis. In Kentucky and West Virginia, frustrated spouses filled pages of their postwar petitions and depositions with stories of admirable soldiers with unfaithful wives, financial neglect or abuse by both husbands and wives, and rash wartime marriages that failed to meet the new companionate standard. These stories demonstrate the tumultuous environment of the postwar years, as well as the willingness of spouses in the border South to bring these common travails to the attention of both the courts and the community.

Many relationships, such as that of Lewis and Rosanna Long, were relatively new when the war began and could not withstand the stress of separation. Off fighting with the Union army, Lewis lived apart from his wife longer than they had lived together before the war, and in this case, absence did not make the heart grow fonder. Within two years of his departure, Rosanna moved in with another man. Although she may have been motivated by many factors, some of Lewis's charges in his divorce petition suggest a potential explanation. In his bill of complaint, Lewis charged that

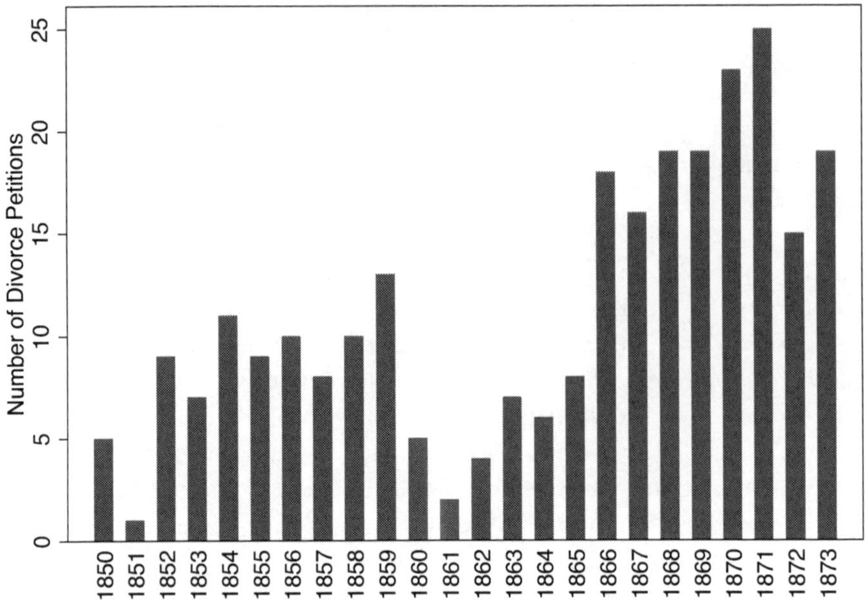

Divorce petitions filed, 1850–1873. Graph by William Hicks.

James Hays bought Rosanna's groceries and paid her rent.[4] While Lewis saw these as proof of an improper and illicit relationship, they also suggest another motive: money. Civil War soldiers were notoriously poorly paid, and the working-class background of many divorce petitioners in the border South meant that Civil War deprivation would fall even more harshly upon them. Rosanna may have gotten fed up with receiving little or no money or support from her husband and turned toward a more financially secure, and certainly more physically present, man in the community.

Still, even a long-term marriage could be vulnerable under the strain of war. William and Rebecca Ferrell had been married for twenty years when he left to join the Confederate army in July 1861. He returned home to Tazewell County, Virginia, only once during the conflict, in March 1862. Yet, in March 1864, Rebecca gave birth to twin boys, who she obviously had to admit were not her husband's. William Ferrell filed for a divorce before he even returned home.[5] Giving birth to a child during a husband's long wartime absence was the clearest way to reveal a wife's unfaithful behavior—and for a cuckolded husband to obtain a divorce. Sabra Ann Wimmer had a child in 1864 while her husband served in the military. He had been absent from home for more than twelve months before the birth. Similarly, Martha Runyon and her husband had been married for eight years when he joined the Union army in 1862. By the time he returned home in 1865, she had been living with another man for a year, with whom she had a child.[6]

Many Union and Confederate recruits pleaded for furloughs so they could go back to check on their wives and homes. Some worried about their families' safety; others believed their families could not survive without male support and aid.[7] When military leaders denied these requests, women at home had to fend for themselves, which often led to actions their husbands deemed worthy of divorce.[8] While her husband, Jacob, served as a soldier in the Union army "engaged in fighting rebels," Ellen Stroble of Wheeling, West Virginia, maintained an ongoing relationship with John Hunter. Residents spotted Ellen and her paramour, John, about twice a week at market days in Wheeling, where they met in the back room to discuss their sales over hot whisky punches. When they finished, John would say, "Let us go home now" and pick up both market baskets, and the pair would leave together. A saloonkeeper on Market Street testified that he "took them to be man and wife," as they brought their marketing together and "took it home together."[9]

With her husband at war, Ellen maintained a long-term extramarital relationship, resembling that of a husband and wife, with John. Jacob Maser saw the pair buggy riding on multiple occasions and testified that John Hunter had been staying at Ellen's house "all summer and fall." Joseph Kramer, who owned a hotel on Main Street in Wheeling, stated that Ellen frequently came to his hotel with John Hunter for dinner. Taking on the husband's role as breadwinner, John always paid, and he bought goods for her and left packages at the hotel for her to pick up. Another neighbor, Arthur Higgins, saw the couple check into the same hotel room in Columbus, Ohio, and register as "John Hunter & Lady or wife."[10] Ultimately, the community condemned Ellen Stroble's actions and how she flaunted her illicit relationship. Maser stated that Ellen had a poor reputation among "the people in our town West Wheeling." Both Maser and Higgins agreed that she was "known by reputation as a prostitute."[11] Yet her actions may not have been simply those of the average unfaithful wife but may have been inspired by financial need or turmoil.

A husband's absence could significantly change a woman's financial situation and living arrangements. When her husband, Archibald, left to fight,

Susan White was forced to live with a neighbor, Elizabeth Sargent. While there, she began an affair with a man named William Smith, and eventually left Tazewell County, Virginia, to cross into Kentucky and live with him there.[12] This was not an uncommon reaction to male absence during the war. In their divorce petitions, border South men went out of their way to prove that infidelity was not a reflection of a husband's poor support, suggesting that some might draw such a conclusion. In his 1870 divorce petition, John R. Hutchinson, a Wheeling cigar maker, told the court that while serving in the First Virginia Infantry, he sent his wife "a large proportion of the pay which he was receiving from the Government for his service, to wit: the sum of ten dollars per month." Despite this, his wife, Mary, had been chronically unfaithful, almost from the moment of her husband's departure for war in September 1861. In fact, Mary had been so notoriously unfaithful that "she was arrested for public lewdness in the City of Wheeling, by different Aldermen, and fined for that offence, and imprisoned in the County Jail of Ohio County for such offence." When John was honorably discharged in November 1864, he learned of his wife's actions during his absence.[13] Similarly, when asked whether neighbor William Prophater had provided properly for his unfaithful wife, Julia Chesnell stated that "she always looked to have plenty" and that "their house was very nicely fixed." Nonetheless, while William was in the military, Isabella took up with another man and eventually left Wheeling with him to bear his child. William's witnesses universally painted Isabella as unchaste and unrepentant about her infidelity.[14]

In his Tazewell County petition, William Cecil assured the court that he had left his wife, Emma, in a good financial position when he joined the Confederate army in 1862. He stated that he had left provisions for both his wife and his son and had arranged for them to stay with a local widow who lived in "good circumstances." Because of this, he felt that her alleged behavior after his absence was especially unwarranted. He charged Emma with "strolling about the country" with various soldiers and even committing adultery, before leaving for "some one of the Northern states." Yet, a closer look at the depositions and his subsequent amended petition reveals a different story. No witness had explicitly seen any evidence of adultery, and most merely stated that Emma had left her husband in late 1862 to return to her mother's home in New York City. Because of this, William changed his cause of divorce to abandonment, which the court accepted.[15] We will never know if Emma was actually unfaithful to her husband, or if she had another reason for leaving. Perhaps she did not find his financial support as extensive as he suggested. Perhaps she saw an opportunity to leave a husband she no longer loved. Perhaps she, like many others on this border, could no longer sympathize with her southern husband's attitudes, beliefs, and behaviors. As a New Yorker, she may not have wanted to remain in the Confederacy, married to a Confederate soldier.

A wife's use of her husband's wartime pay could also cause rifts in a marriage. Like John Hutchinson, Louis Lindemuth told the Ohio County Circuit Court that while he was a soldier in the Union army he had sent his wife "all his earnings and wages as such which were received and appropriated by said defendant to her own uses and purposes."[16] When Louis returned in 1865 to his Wheeling home, his wife, Augusta, refused to tell him how or where she had spent this money. Though it appears their separation did not occur until 1867, Louis's choice to mention their financial rift in a short 1871 divorce petition reflects the importance he placed on his role as a provider. At the same time, he expected Augusta to use his earnings prudently and frugally, for the betterment of their home and future. His petition suggests his anger and suspicion at her refusal to disclose what she did with his money.

The Civil War also gave some husbands an excuse to escape their financial obligations to their wives, following a pattern that had begun before the conflict. Elizabeth Goudy's husband, James, had refused to live with her since their 1860 marriage because of her class and German background, and once in the Union army, he gave her money only when forced to do so by the governor.[17] Another Ohio County couple, Catherine and John Heston, had had a tumultuous relationship since their 1850 marriage, living together off and on while he worked at various jobs: in a cotton factory, on the river, for a boot and shoe dealer, and eventually as a counterfeiter. During the war, she returned to her father's home while John served in the army. Her father, Samuel Litten, stated, "What assistance [John] gave her, I cant say" but pointed out that it had come to his attention that she was living in Parkersburg "in a suffering condition."[18]

As with the Hestons, the war further disrupted Eliza and Robert Hawkins's already rocky relationship. Married on Valentine's Day 1855 in Louisville, Kentucky, Robert and Eliza lived with her father, first in that city and then, after 1859, in Franklin County for the bulk of their marriage. After his 1862 enlistment in the Confederate army, Robert saw Eliza only three times, the last time in early 1865, before he completely abandoned her and their seven-year-old child, leaving her "entirely dependant upon the kindness of her father."[19] In such cases, the Civil War exacerbated problems caused by financially negligent spouses, but because of a sympathetic court system, every one of these wronged spouses found quick relief with a successful divorce petition.

Some men, such as Wheeling resident Xavier Keefer, made it clear that military service provided a method of escape from their marriages. After leaving his wife during the war, Xavier ran into an old acquaintance in Ohio, and told him that he had joined company K of the Twenty-Eighth Ohio Regiment under a fictitious name. When asked about his future plans, Xavier replied that as soon as he had raised a few hundred dollars in service he would "run off from the company and go to Switzerland." When Henry asked what would happen to his family, Xavier replied, "I dont care a damn they can do as they please."[20]

Many of these wartime marital crises differed little from their prewar predecessors. After all, men leave their spouses for reasons other than wartime service, and wives are not unfaithful only during national conflicts.[21] And of course, any accusation of adultery could also be a manipulation of the legal system by a couple, or spouse, trying to obtain a favorable verdict. It can be difficult to determine whether wartime marriages ended in adultery charges because marital problems led to real infidelity or because marital problems necessitated using adultery as an excuse to end a relationship.[22] However, wartime marriages existed within altered environments that could provide additional opportunities or explanations for infidelity and divorce. The tendency of wives to leave their husbands, supportive and unsupportive alike, can be partially attributed to the rash of hasty marriages many border South residents entered into during wartime. Courtships grew considerably shorter, and couples found even less time than in the prewar years to get to know one another before heading to the altar.[23]

Sometimes, shaken by the dangers and terrors of war, men pushed the women in their lives to commit to a more serious relationship than they desired. In some cases, men's eagerness to enter into the stability of marriage may have led hesitant women to make rash decisions. As men increasingly turned to marriage and the domestic sphere for comfort, women gained greater power in relationships and acted boldly in response. Others, though, maintained the same level of hesitation and high standard for companionate partners as their antebellum counterparts.[24] Belle Price, of Covington, Kentucky, accepted Charles Simrall's proposal before she truly knew her own wishes. After he was released from Ohio's Camp Chase, nineteen-year-old Charles, a Confederate prisoner of war from Kentucky, planned a lengthy overseas trip to avoid being drafted into the Union army. On the eve of his departure, he asked Belle to be his fiancée, and she agreed. His impatience to cement their relationship may have pushed her to agree too hastily. When he arrived in Europe, Charles wrote to Belle that he loved her more than his own life and that "the belief that you will one day belong wholly to me nerves me for the conflict of life." Only four months after his departure, though, she changed her mind. She admitted that she had acted with "rash impetuosity" in accepting his proposal but wrote that, after much reflection and after the "excitement is over," she realized she loved him "as your Sister only could love a favourite Brother." Charles wrote back, "Oh how this one has wrung my heart. . . . To find that you, who I loved better than my life, You in whom my future was so wrapped up who formed the highest dreams of my existence, to find that you have deceived me . . . that you loved me not."[25] Heartbroken, he insisted that she had deceived him, accepting his love while they were together and waiting until he was gone, "alone in a strange land," to level the blow. "Our engagement is cancelled," he wrote angrily. "Remove my ring."[26] Though Charles had insisted that absence "instead of conquering only strengthens love," Belle's actions, like those of other young women left behind, hint that absence may also have led some hearts to wander. During Charles's absence, Belle wrote to another man, who urged her to marry him and "to look upon me with your sweet smile—to love me."[27]

One ill-fated wartime couple, Pierson and Lucy Clifford, married shortly before he left home to serve in the Union army in April 1863. Pierson filed for divorce in the Franklin County Circuit Court within a year of the war's close. In his petition, he told the court that he and his wife had lived together only a short time, which had given him little opportunity to become acquainted with her. In fact, he assured the court that he had been unaware of her pregnancy (allegedly by another man) at the time of their marriage and was therefore unprepared for her "lewd conduct and illicit intercourse with other men" afterward. Deponents stated that Lucy Clifford had had two children since her marriage, neither of which were her husband's, and had been seen "frequently passing along the public highway with other men in the absence of her husband with verry unbecoming intimacy."[28]

While some found the adage "marry in haste, repent at leisure" all too applicable to their situations, other wartime changes in the border South exacerbated marital conflict. For example, not only did soldiers' long absences from home lead some wives to seek other male companions to fill the void, but particularly in the border South, there were increased numbers of available partners for such forays. Lying along the Union–Confederate border, Kentucky and West Virginia were frequent sites of battle and hosted numerous soldiers, from both sides, during the four years of the war.[29] Lonely, homesick men from either camp might find willing company in some of these border women.

In August 1866, Thomas Young, a Franklin County resident, charged his wife, Sarah, with adultery and fraud, stating that she had been pregnant at the time of their marriage and had committed adultery before, during, and since that time. Numerous deponents testified to her "impruden[ce]" with other men. Many charges were related to her premarital lovers, including two whose timeline coincided with the conception of her child, but others were in regard to her marital affairs. John Riddle, who lived within four hundred yards of Sarah's family, cited a number of specific incidents, including the time he had seen her riding by his house with Captain Hick of the Second "Meraland ridgment infrantry," who was, incidentally, a married man.[30] Mary Carpenter's affairs were as apparent to her Tazewell County community as Sarah Young's had been to her Franklin County community. However, she did try to conceal the illicit nature of her behavior from some of her paramours. When she began her flirtation with Lieutenant Slack of the Union army, she misled him about her marital status, "produc[ing] a letter stating that P.M. Carpenter [her husband] was dead." She then asked him to "right" to her.[31]

Not all women had questionable intentions with the men they met through military occupation, though; many met their future spouses this way, which increased the region's borderland fusion of marital ideals. Young men who joined either army generally served far from their home communities, often meeting women—both friend and foe—that they would never have encountered in peacetime. Women, in both the Confederacy and Union, came into contact with occupying forces. Wartime refugees entered new communities, and those who ventured into nursing or voluntary activities met men from outside their normal social circle. Moreover, as Drew Gilpin Faust argues, "The powerful feelings inspired by wartime danger combined with the desperation of many women for mates to yield unconventional alliances."[32] In the border South, all of these wartime forces were particularly evident. New wartime relationships built on antebellum traditions of travel and interstate courtship, and they challenged couples to renegotiate their marital roles in light of new perspectives.

During the war, both armies alternately occupied Hopkinsville, Kentucky, allowing young Annie Starling to meet numerous new suitors. Despite her staunch Unionism, Annie met various Confederate soldiers and flirted with some of them. In December 1861, she went with two friends to her sister's to meet a group of Confederate officers. "I was particularly interested in Lieut. Cowan," she admitted. "He is very handsome, dark hair, and beautiful clear dark hazel eyes, and a pretty mouth."[33] A few weeks later, two other Confederate officers paid her a visit and stayed until midnight. "I must say I liked Lieut Hughes very much," she wrote. "He talks so much like a gentleman." He flattered her, too, by wishing that some Kentucky women could be transplanted to "our Sunny South."[34]

Like many women, Annie seemed captivated by the allure of the military, and for young girls in small villages or towns, the exposure to dashing new suitors and the expansion of social activity could overcome worries about political differences. Like many border South women, Annie may have fallen in love with the uniform more than the man. She daydreamed of another officer, Colonel Murray, taken by his "noble figure" and "brown waving hair," and most especially his "beautiful eyes which could burn with patriotism and the thought of hard fought yet victorious battle field or flash with scorn but often welling with love."[35]

After his 1862 visit to Hopkinsville, James B. Bullitt, a Confederate soldier from the Louisville area, wrote to his sister that he had met three young women there he much admired. "Without being in love at all, I have determined that if ever the war is over and I come through safe, I shall return here to make a visit," he told her.[36] Unfortunately, James was killed in Lebanon, Kentucky, riding with John Hunt Morgan, and would never return to the ladies of Hopkinsville. Many others managed to make those visits, though, and took up a courtship with women they met during the war. Benjamin Field, a sergeant in the Tenth Kentucky Cavalry, waited for years after the war to marry a girl he had met while traveling with the army in Virginia.[37]

Unfortunately, not all of these relationships ended in bliss. For example, Fannie Hall met James F. Anderson, a carpenter from Owen County, Kentucky, while he was serving in the Thirtieth Kentucky Regiment of the Union army. Soon after the war ended, the couple married in Garrard County, Kentucky, and before long, had two children together. Yet, in

December 1868, he abandoned Fannie and their children, making "no provision" for the trio. Ten months later, James, still a married man, tied the knot with Eliza Vallandingham in Gallatin County, Kentucky, and the pair left for Indiana. In fact, Fannie's own marriage was on shaky legal ground, as one witness contended that James was already married to a woman named Mary Owen before Fannie. Ultimately, the court determined that their marriage, valid or not, was at an end.[38]

At the end of the war, Nancy Ballard found herself in a similar situation to Fannie Hall. She had met her husband, Jacob, when he traveled with his unit from Kentucky to Tazewell County, Virginia, during the war. She fell in love with him and agreed to marry him in 1865. Not long after their marriage, however, she learned that he had a wife and children still in Kentucky. Her husband then fled Virginia. Interestingly, a local man named A. J. May had been Jacob's commanding officer during the war. He stated that he knew about Jacob's Kentucky family because Jacob had frequently requested leave to visit them. This may have been how Nancy learned of her husband's bigamy, but the information had clearly not reached her before Jacob convinced her to marry him. Whatever Jacob may have told his commanding officer, though, he conveyed a different story to others. While he admitted to having a wife, he told William Steel that he had no plans to return to her because "she had done badly."[39] Perhaps Minnie, his first wife, had been unfaithful to him during the war, and he did not want to pay the costs of a divorce suit (which seems likely to have been successful in Kentucky on those grounds). Perhaps he was merely making excuses for his own choice to be unfaithful during the war. Either way, during wartime, it seems, both men and women found ample opportunity for extramarital liaisons.

War and the dangers of spinsterhood also encouraged women to be bolder in their courtships, sometimes exceeding the dictates of antebellum etiquette in ways that could be confusing for their potential partners. Annie, for example, seemed shocked at her own "daring" when she sent her love to Colonel Murray in May 1863. She wrote that the chances of his returning her love were slim but worth the risk.[40] However, when "Dear 'Cousin Tom'" left Hopkinsville for battle a few months later, she impulsively told him she loved him, "when really my heart was all anothers." When she began receiving letters from him filled with the "deepest, purest love," she wrote of her anguish and guilt.[41]

Men also acted in unorthodox ways. E. G. Davison wrote to Helen Robinson, of Taylor County, West Virginia, without ever having met her.

He excused his presumptuous action by stating that her cousin, who served in his company, had allowed Davison to read Helen's letters. "I would like to corespond with you," he told Helen. "A soldier has a great deal of lasier time and I wold as soon spend a portion of the time in writting to an inteligent lady as not."[42] Helen received letters throughout the war from men she had never met. Her first in August 1861 was from James Boyd, a young soldier looking to "ad[d] one personal friend to the list of my . . . Secession friends."[43] Though Helen's paramours often initiated contact with her, her choice to continue the correspondence indicates that she did not mind communicating with men she had never met, a bold decision in itself. The war caused some women to adapt their behaviors to challenging new circumstances and take a more assertive role in the courtship process. Such changes suggest the overall evolution of women's position in romantic relationships, both married and unmarried. However, her brother, W. J. Robinson, wrote to their mother that Helen should be more careful about her correspondents. "One of the Yanks we captured last month was sporting a letter he had recd from her that I would consider bad work," he wrote animatedly. "If I had knew he had it I would of taken it from him or broke his neck."[44]

The Civil War strained marriages in the border South. Left to struggle on their own, some women turned to alternative providers and ended up in extramarital affairs. Some wives had no such excuse, as their husbands insisted that they had properly provided for them. Other husbands grasped the opportunity of wartime absence to escape from the burden of marriage and its incumbent financial responsibilities. Wartime marriages themselves were inherently risky. Some couples had little time to learn about one another before a husband went off to war; others had a shallow emotional attachment, increasing the chances of infidelity on either side. Especially with soldiers frequently occupying border South communities, chances for meeting an illicit lover increased. Whatever the circumstances, it is clear that the Civil War played a strong role in a number of marital breakdowns in Kentucky and West Virginia. Its impact would continue in the postwar years as well. While many deserted their husbands or wives during the war, others did so after the fighting stopped, perhaps influenced by the upheaval, displacement, and uncertainty of the Reconstruction era.

While cases of abandonment were always common in the border South, they soared in Kentucky, West Virginia, and Virginia during the eight years following the end of the Civil War. For example, in the 1850s, 43 percent of Franklin County's divorce cases involved abandonment charges, and in

Ohio County the number was only slightly higher.[45] In the postwar years in Franklin and Ohio Counties, petitioners now utilized the charge of desertion in 70 and 69 percent of all cases, respectively.[46] While few cases (other than those mentioned above) directly cite the war as a cause of the abandonment or separation, it is likely that the turmoil of the postwar period influenced this trend.

For one thing, movement became a common theme in the post–Civil War South. Former enslaved people traveled dozens, hundreds, and even thousands of miles to reunite with lost family members.[47] Other freedmen and freedwomen took the opportunity to leave plantations, change employers, flee to the city, or move elsewhere. While black southerners sought to build new lives in freedom, white southerners' lives were disrupted in other ways. In war-torn areas such as the border South, white southerners found their homes destroyed and their communities in disarray. With their main source of wealth walking out the door, most saw their financial prospects decline.[48] In some places, wartime farmers had flocked to towns, unable to staff their farms or protect them from guerrilla attacks.[49] Movement reshaped the postwar border and contributed to its fluid state. Searching for new opportunities, many white southerners left their failing farms and plantations and headed for the city, while others merely went farther west. Within this fluid environment, it is unsurprising that marital ties lost some of their hold on restless spouses.

To use one example, the divorce records of the Franklin County Circuit Court suggest the mobility of many of its citizens after the war. Most of those who abandoned their spouses left the state upon doing so, usually staying in the surrounding states. This reflects the interconnectedness of their region, especially as many returned to their home states. Martha Montgomery, Thomas Boyd, and David Waits all fled to Missouri.[50] Jacob Beamer skipped across the river to Ohio.[51] Leonard Zimmerman and William Marshall turned south to Tennessee.[52] John M. Smithson departed for the Lone Star State.[53] Finally, the highest proportion of abandoners went north—to Indiana. There, away from the reach of their spouses, Catharine Sayre, Belle Morten, James Anderson, George Ritchie, Cynthia Warren, and Nancy Lynn all started new lives.[54]

Tazewell County residents seemed to have a propensity for abandoning their spouses and moving to West Virginia. The number of residents who fled to the newly created state reveals the fluidity of this new border. The counties in West Virginia had been part of a different state for only two years when the war ended, and McDowell County, West Virginia, across the state line had been carved out of Tazewell only in 1858. This decision by state lawmakers had, in a ten-year period, divided residents into two counties and then divided them into two countries and into two states. It is not surprising, therefore, to see West Virginia as a common destination for fleeing spouses.[55]

Kentucky judges, understanding that sometimes partners left, wanted to ensure that outdated ideas of womanhood did not prohibit women from obtaining legal relief from abandoning husbands. In 1870, the Kentucky Supreme Court upheld a wife's right to sue for divorce if her husband had fled the state, a ruling necessary because of judicial precedents that considered a wife's formal residence to be wherever her husband lived.[56] Yet, in the 1870 case, Chief Justice George Robertson warned that it would "be a reproach to our legislation if a faithless husband in Kentucky could by leaving the state deprive his abandoned wife of the power of obtaining a divorce at home."[57] The justice's ruling weakened the legal fiction that husband and wife were one and further contributed to the atmosphere of contractualism and individualism in postwar Kentucky.

Some spouses took advantage of the atmosphere of movement to escape prior marriages and form new ones without disclosing their preexisting legal ties. Temperance Allen moved to Warren County, Kentucky, from nearby Logan County after the war ended. She had until recently been enslaved in that county and had had one child there before being widowed. She came to Bowling Green to start a new life and to support herself and that child. In 1867, she met William Roberson, a carpenter, and fell in love with him. Within months, they married. A week after they married, William accepted a job with a local man to drive stock to the southern markets. While he was gone, Temperance received a visit from a woman from Nashville, who showed her a marriage certificate proving that William Roberson was still married to her. When William heard about this visit, he fled, most likely to Texas.[58] Apparently, William realized that moving only one state away was not far enough to escape his past.

The financial strain experienced by many southerners in the postwar period created or exacerbated tensions in many relationships.[59] Moreover, the psychological blow to both the male ego and the southern ego brought on by the simultaneous loss of a war and a way of life aggravated an already volatile situation.[60] Emancipation shook the very core of white male identity and made southern men feel "marginalized."[61] It is not unreasonable to assume

Table 5.1. Number of Charges in Divorces by County, 1865–1873

	Franklin County (KY)	Warren County (KY)	Ohio County (WV)	Tazewell County (VA)	Fauquier County (VA)	Amelia County (VA)
Charge other than abandonment	29.2% (19)	46.2% (12)	30.6% (15)	54.3% (19)	41.7% (5)	42.9% (3)
Abandonment as single charge	47.7% (31)	26.9% (7)	40.8% (20)	2.9% (1)	8.3% (1)	14.3% (1)
Abandonment and one other charge	18.5% (12)	19.2% (5)	16.3% (8)	40.0% (14)	33.3% (4)	28.6% (2)
Abandonment and two other charges	4.2% (3)	7.7% (2)	6.1% (3)	2.9% (1)	16.7% (2)	14.3% (1)
Abandonment and three other charges	0.0% (0)	0.0% (0)	6.1% (3)	0.0% (0)	0.0% (0)	0.0% (0)

Note: These data are derived from all cases encompassing these years found at the Library of Virginia, accessed through the online Chancery Court Records Index; in circuit court cases on microfilm at the West Virginia and Regional History Center, Morgantown, West Virginia; and original copies of the circuit court records at the Kentucky Department for Libraries and Archives, Frankfort, Kentucky. All statistics reflect the number of cases found, since numerous natural and man-made disasters may account for cases missing or destroyed.

that some men took out this frustration on the dependents who remained—their wives.[62] While abandonment charges increased throughout Kentucky, West Virginia, and Virginia, one difference among these states is apparent. Virginia residents were, by far, the least likely to charge their spouses with abandonment alone; instead, most combined abandonment with another charge, usually adultery or cruelty. While 40 percent of Ohio County's cases, almost half of Franklin County's cases, and more than a quarter of Warren County's cases involved the single charge of desertion, only 14 percent of divorce cases in Amelia County used this single charge—even fewer, 8 and 3 percent, respectively, in Fauquier and Tazewell Counties.

Of course, Virginia judges may have applied a harsher legal standard to postwar cases, leading litigants to pile on more charges to get the same results. So, Fauquier, Amelia, and Tazewell County litigants seeking divorce in the volatile postwar world may have manipulated their cases, playing up their woes, to obtain these more favorable verdicts.[63] However, another explanation is also plausible. With the social upheaval caused by southern surrender, emancipation, and women's changing roles, Virginia marriages may simply have become more acrimonious in the postwar years.[64] The lack of satisfaction on the part of both partners may have led to more quarrelsome and even violent relationships. If this is the case, the higher number of charges in the three Virginia counties suggests that couples there had a more difficult adjustment to the postwar world than many couples in Kentucky and West Virginia.

A sample petition shows the volatility of some marriages in the postwar years. Though they had been married since the 1850s, John and Virginia Walden's marriage grew increasingly acrimonious after the war. Shortly before their 1867 separation, John Walden's behavior had become unbearably cruel, Virginia told the Fauquier County Circuit Court. John cursed his wife, insulted her, and "wished she was dead." Once, he repeatedly punched her in the head, and another time, he "tried to throw her over the barristers of the stairway saying he would break her d-d neck." Finally, in 1867, he drove her from their home, lashing her with a carriage whip. She fled to Warrenton, unsupported and alone. John Walden told the court that his wife had been "insubordinate" and defended some, if not all, of his actions.[65]

Although she did not explicitly state that the end of the war caused the change in her marriage, Margaret Tunstall of Amelia County, Virginia, told the court that her husband's abuse worsened in 1865 before he finally abandoned her entirely. Her husband was neglectful, lazy, "thriftless," abusive, and frequently intoxicated. All this occurred before his eventual abandonment, an event that "compelled" her to apply for a divorce. Margaret, like many of her fellow Virginia petitioners, leveled a number of charges against George, her husband, and pleaded with the court that she had only taken such a drastic step because her life had truly been in danger. Her deponents reiterated her story of abuse, especially the abuse occurring in 1865. Her mother stated that George frequently hit her daughter and often expressed a desire to kill her. Another neighbor heard George whipping his wife. Margaret called out to the neighbor, pleading for him to stop George from "beating her to death." George, though, turned his anger on the neighbor and threatened him with a similar treatment if he moved from his seat to intervene.[66] Before 1865, the couple had been slaveowners, and it is possible that George's anger grew out of his loss of status as a slaveowner; his use of whipping, specifically, could have been a not-so-subconscious throwback to the type of violent coercion he had used on his former slaves. Although marriages throughout the South became more volatile in the years immediately following the Confederacy's surrender, cases like that of the Tunstalls reveal the subtle distinctions between marriages in a postwar Border state and a postwar Confederate state.

Postwar border South couples continued to receive manuals on their wedding days that contained advice similar to that given to many of their antebellum brethren. On his July 4, 1865, wedding day, Will Hays of Louisville, Kentucky, received a copy of *The Marriage Gift,* authored by Pastor James Petrie of New Jersey. One can only hope that he had already followed its instructions to find a "partner for life," who would do more than "please the eye." After the wedding day, though, Petrie advised his audience to cultivate respect and affection in their union, something that would only come if the couple had been "influenced by sincere love for each other" in choosing a mate.[67] Petrie's advice, like that of antebellum authors, stressed the mutual roles and responsibilities of men and women in the relationship, without gendering their duties. In marriage, he wrote, the pair should "bear one another's burdens . . . sympathize with each other in joy and sorrow—bear with and overlook each other's infirmities—watch over and administer to each other the cup of consolation in sickness . . . provide for each other the good things of this life."[68] He also encouraged married partners to use industry in their lives and economic cooperation to make their home a success.[69] The gift of such a manual to Will Hays upon his marriage to Belle McCullough in the first months after the war suggests that friends and family of the couple still wished a marriage of mutuality and love for the pair, even if the social structure around them was uncertain.

The years following the Civil War featured both change and continuity in the border South. Certainly, the tremendous loss of life and the economic and social disruption of battle could not fail to change the lives and loves of those in these states. As the cases in this chapter demonstrate, marriages crumbled in this environment. Whether because of wartime adultery, postwar abuse and stress, or the unprecedented wave of people moving throughout the region, many relationships did not survive the ten-year period following the war. Additionally, as slave states before the war, neither Kentucky nor West Virginia embraced emancipation or the dictates of Radical Republican rule during this era. Many, like Will Hays, turned to the past to learn how to rebuild their lives. In Kentucky and West Virginia, this provided a blueprint for relationships built on mutuality and contractualism—loving relationships that could be renegotiable. In Virginia, this meant rebuilding a sense of patriarchal control in households destroyed by war.

Among these states, any shared experiences of battle and chaos dissolved in the fact of antebellum differences, especially in their strikingly different reactions to black emancipation.

Emancipation and the turmoil of the Reconstruction years contributed to divorce cases in a number of ways. Rising levels of mobility and restlessness created an environment ripe for abandonment, as reflected in the surge in desertion-related cases. In addition, challenges to the southern way of life—produced by defeat and emancipation—created tension and hostility between husbands and wives in the home, especially in Virginia. Finally, many women seemed inspired to assert their independence in the household after freedom came to the other set of southern dependents: enslaved people. Of course, not all white households rocked by emancipation ended in divorce in the postwar years. Still, the process of divorce would be strangely analogous to emancipation in the postwar years. Divorcing couples exposed another pivotal household relationship, marriage, as impermanent and negotiable. This chapter has shown the immediate and visceral reactions many had to the turmoil, loss, and disruption of households in the wartime and postwar period. However, the success of these divorce cases depended on a legal establishment and social environment receptive to divorce as a solution to couple's problems. As the next chapter reveals, especially because of the dangerous connection between black emancipation and divorce, Kentucky, West Virginia, and Virginia would have widely divergent responses to these postbellum cases.

6

Stability in the Face of Great Distress

From the moment the first enslaved people took flight during the Civil War, the process of black emancipation profoundly shook the core of traditional white southern society. Throughout the antebellum slave South, law and custom reinforced a strictly hierarchical social structure that upheld elite white male authority over both social inferiors and household dependents. Many southerners understood slavery and gender roles within the household as irrevocably linked and viewed an attack on one as an attack on the other. By the 1860s, secession debates and Confederate rhetoric urged southerners to defend their households, both black and white, as well as their way of life against northern attackers.[1] Yet, by taking up arms to defend their homes, white southerners unintentionally brought about the end of the slave system and threatened the household itself. With the end of the war, both emancipation and divorce exposed the inherent dissolvability of social relationships, which ultimately threatened to reveal white male authority as tenuous and unstable. If ties such as marriage were not obligatory but voluntary, how fixed could other social contracts be?[2]

As enslaved people left plantations from Texas to Virginia, both slaveholding and nonslaveholding white southerners reevaluated their gender roles within the home. With emancipation, the southern household became a newly contested landscape, as white men and women struggled either to redefine their positions or to maintain the social order that typified southern life before the war.[3] Black emancipation was a messy and uneven process, and its impact on the South's white population and their attempts to reorder or reclaim the household were equally uneven. A comparison of divorces in eastern Virginia with those of West Virginia, Appalachian Virginia, and Kentucky reveals how emancipation's effect on border gender roles was muted by the region's hybrid culture and antebellum experiences. More specifically, in postbellum Kentucky, residents used rhetoric and motivations for separation that were consistent with that used in antebellum cases, reflecting their continued desire for mutuality and individualism in their relationships. The number of divorce petitions in Ohio County, West Virginia, freed from Virginia law, rose almost 300 percent, while residents' use of adultery charges declined dramatically. Across the border, Appalachian Virginians also filed for greater numbers of divorces but were still forced to manipulate the strict Virginian law. On the other hand, eastern Virginians decried the breakdown of racial mastery, connected it with potential disruptions to their hierarchical households, and demanded obedience and loyalty from both formerly enslaved people and spouses. The only exception in the former plantation counties of Fauquier and Amelia was the dramatic rise in filings by black couples, many—if not all—formerly enslaved.

Black freedom represented disruption and tumult to white southerners, and many fought back as best they could. Inevitably, many white southerners clung to the past, refusing to adapt to the changes wrought by emancipation. With the passage of the Black Codes and the initial rejection of the Fourteenth Amendment throughout much of the South, former Confederates made it clear that changes in the racial order would not come easily. Additionally, because of the close connection between a gendered hierarchy and racial mastery, these same white southerners were in no hurry to reform marriage or marital roles. Alongside a racial backlash, many white southerners reinforced their support for a patriarchal household structure based on female dependence and male authority.[4]

Since slaveholding border states such as Kentucky and West Virginia never technically seceded, the process of emancipation in these places differed from that in Confederate states such as Virginia. In addition, a lack of large-scale warfare and its accompanying displacement and destruction allowed Kentuckians and West Virginians a smoother transition, in some ways, into the postwar years.[5] Nonetheless, many border residents shared the animosity of their former Confederate neighbors toward racial progress. As Aaron Astor and Anne Marshall have demonstrated, in the years following emancipation Kentuckians passed some of the harshest racial laws in the South and began to reimagine and reassess their wartime allegiance.[6] However, in contrast with many other southern states, the impact of emancipation on white border southerners' marital relationships was surprisingly minimal, reflecting the region's history as a flexible borderland long before the war that placed it on the line between two nations.

The connection between black emancipation and white marital roles, so well documented in other regions, proves tenuous at best in the border South.[7] In a pattern established before the war, the attitudes of antebellum border southerners toward household gender roles proved adaptable and allowed for greater numbers of divorces under more flexible statutes than in eastern Virginia. However, while firmly part of a national trend toward greater mutuality and contractualism in marital relationships, border southerners did not extend this same enlightened attitude toward their relationships with enslaved people or free blacks, nor did their use of this philosophy in their marriages lessen their attachment to a racial hierarchy. Two explanations prove useful. First, compared with other parts of the South, the border South had a greater percentage of small farms and hired slaves. In Kentucky and western Virginia, slavery existed alongside an already flourishing free labor market and an industrial sector.[8] Second, and most crucially, their border mentality of compromise and fusion allowed them to accept multiple philosophies and ideologies without necessarily viewing one as threatening the other.[9] Free labor did not necessarily threaten slavery. Likewise, changes to slavery did not necessarily threaten white families. Because of a culture built on the middle ground among many different geographical, economic, and political views, border southerners disassociated rival philosophies in a way that differed from other white slaveholding southerners. Thus, black emancipation was a threat to race relations, but not necessarily to gender roles within white households. Additionally, although most white southerners saw the reestablishment of racial and gender hierarchy as essential to restoring a prewar social system, the same was not true of Kentuckians and West Virginians.

Border southerners experienced a resurgence in white supremacist attitudes in reaction to the loss of their enslaved people and the slave system as a whole, but there was no noticeable shift away from the antebellum pattern of mutuality and contractualism.[10] In the demands they made against partners in divorce cases, Kentuckians continued to express the same antebellum ideals for marriage that typified their complicated prewar border households. West Virginians moved away from their antebellum pattern to more closely mimic this border South model. Appalachian Virginians, still legally bound to their eastern neighbors, continued their antebellum pattern as well, as they used adultery charges to manipulate the courts. Although divorce itself is a disruptive process, the marital separations in Kentucky, West Virginia, and Appalachian Virginia reflect continuity with the prewar era and an attempt to uphold the ideals of that era.[11] The fact that Kentuckians and Appalachian Virginians could continue to divorce at the same antebellum rate and West Virginians at a much higher rate, despite the fact that divorce threatened social unity, demonstrates that they did not draw the same connections between gender and emancipation as did other white southerners in the postwar period.

Of course, notwithstanding many white southerners' best efforts to maintain the organic structure of household hierarchy, emancipation and the end of the Civil War brought slow change to the political and social landscape, moving the South toward what some historians have termed a more "mainstream . . . American development."[12] For example, while southerners still trailed northerners and westerners in rates of divorce, liberalization in the law occurred. Often through the efforts of Reconstruction governments, constitutions and state codes evolved to allow more divorces.[13] In contrast to other southerners, Kentuckians and West Virginians experienced this postbellum adaptation through the unique lens of their border experience. First, in their case, the change began before the war, not as a result of it. Kentucky's divorce code remained unaltered in the wake of the war, and their postwar petitions built upon the sense of contractualism cemented in the 1850s. West Virginians' manipulation of the law in the antebellum era revealed their deeper attachment to contractualism as well, giving context and meaning to their postwar changes. Changes in West Virginia divorce law occurred during the process of statehood, rather than being imposed by a Reconstruction government. Second, while the number of divorce cases and minor aspects of the law changed in states like Virginia, the core content of divorce petitions and the fundamental nature of the law stayed much the same, reflecting a greater resistance to a contractual and individualistic form of marriage.[14] Kentucky, West Virginia, and Appalachian Virginia do not fit into the current narrative regarding emancipation's influence on white families. Some historians argue that the threat of emancipation caused white southerners to reinforce antebellum gender roles, while others contend that emancipation led to a flood of changes in the household.[15] However, in the border South, the end of the war and emancipation may not have had the disruptive effect on marriage it had elsewhere.

In the antebellum era, especially in the Bluegrass region of central Kentucky and the farms and mines of southern and eastern West Virginia, slavery formed a critical part of the economy. In the decades leading up to the Civil War, enslaved people made up almost a quarter of Kentucky's population, and while most Kentuckians did not own enslaved people, the system had a pervasive influence on the state. Nevertheless, by the Civil War, Kentucky slaveholders had begun to sell many of their slaves "down South," and neither Kentucky nor West Virginia's attachment to the institution was strong enough to make the state secede.[16]

West Virginia became the first southern state to "abolish slavery at least partially of its own volition" when it became a part of the Union in 1863. Attached to the statehood bill, the Willey Amendment freed all slaves born after July 4, 1863, and by the end of the war, the state had freed all slaves.[17] Still, West Virginians were no abolitionists. Lawmakers had been told that statehood would not pass without some form of manumission or emancipation. Although enslaved people never formed as large a percentage of the population as in eastern Virginia, their economic contributions and position in the social hierarchy were still pivotal in the region. Especially in the southern parts of the state and the eastern panhandle, slavery collapsed with considerable resistance from the local population.

Kentuckians neither sought nor desired emancipation at the beginning of the war, and most reacted angrily to that eventual outcome. During the first years of the war, Lincoln worked to maintain the vital border state's shaky loyalty by shielding it from the blow of emancipation. Early attempts by Union leaders to encourage emancipation and freedom among the slaves of the border states met with angry resistance from Kentucky's citizens and with Lincoln's ultimate disapproval. "I hope to have God on my side, but I must have Kentucky," Lincoln reportedly said of his birthplace. However, by mid-1862, Lincoln decided the military benefits of emancipation outweighed its drawbacks and announced the preliminary Emancipation Proclamation. The document freed only those enslaved people who lived in areas under rebellion and did not apply to Kentucky. Kentucky's enslaved people refused to wait, however. As early as 1861, many fled to the Union army, and although Lincoln's initial call for black troops also did not apply to Kentucky, thousands of the state's slaves enlisted elsewhere. By 1864, the Union army agreed to accept those still remaining in the state. Because of Kentucky's resistance to emancipation, most of the state's male slaves actually obtained their freedom through their military service.[18] Nonetheless, at the end of the war, about a third of the state's slaves remained in bondage.

After the war, Kentucky refused to ratify the Thirteenth Amendment and even tried to reject a March 1865 congressional act that freed all slaves who had served in the Union army. Many slaves in Kentucky only became free with national ratification of the Thirteenth Amendment on December 18, 1865. (Kentucky itself refused to ratify the amendment and would not do so until the late twentieth century.)[19] Emancipation, however, did not end the debate regarding the status of blacks in the state. In Kentucky, a fierce resistance sprang up, and a wave of racial violence swept the former Union state. Additionally, because many of the state's most virulent opponents of racial equality had actually fought for the Union, few were disenfranchised in the postwar years, which allowed a more conservative government to control the fortunes of freedpeople. Blacks, never a majority in the state, could not form the same protective political coalitions as in the Deep South. Eventually the Freedmen's Bureau intervened, despite Kentucky's wartime status, to stop the state from stripping blacks of their rights to a fair trial and other crucial civil liberties.[20]

Emancipation's implications for household relations had long struck a chord of fear in the hearts of white southern leaders. Antebellum northerners, many linked to the abolition movement, urged reforms for married women's property rights and began the liberalization of divorce, both of which threatened what Peter Bardaglio calls a southern "network of households grounded in dependence and inequality."[21] Southerners resisted such reforms in the years leading up to the war, and many feared that Reconstruction governments might impose these changes upon southerners' households without their approval. In fact, they were not wholly wrong. In the wake of Congressional Reconstruction, new legislatures convened and revised state constitutions, many of which included changes to divorce statutes. Although southern Redeemers repealed many of these provisions when they gained power in the early 1870s, ideas of contractualism in marriage infiltrated the South. Exacerbated by the collapse of the slave system and the growing reintegration of the nation, slow changes occurred within southern households, especially in the rate of divorce. More southerners filed for divorce, and divorce laws themselves became less rigid, allowing for separation in a greater number of cases.[22]

Yet, the unique pace and quality of postwar marital evolution in West Virginia and Kentucky and its relationship to emancipation are reflected in the states' rate of divorce, charges filed, and language and rhetoric. While the number of divorces increased (to varying extents) throughout the South, their continued growth in West Virginia and Kentucky built on antebellum changes, not outside disruptions specific to the postbellum period. In addition, the rhetoric used in divorce petitions in West Virginia and Kentucky, including a higher number of references to no-fault divorce and "mutual" needs, as well as less justification for the decision to separate, indicates that the character of those divorces also differed from those in other southern locales. For example, in comparison with Virginians, Kentuckians and West Virginians divorced after shorter marriages, waited less time after a marital crisis to petition the chancery courts, and filed using fewer charges. In Kentucky and West Virginia, divorce laws and attitudes toward marriage continued to evolve based on ideals such as mutuality and individualism. Rather than turn to a patriarchal model of household gender roles, West Virginians and Kentuckians used prewar changes to weather the storm of emancipation. Because they still labored under a strict Virginia law, Appalachian Virginians fell somewhere in the middle of these two groups, staying married for longer and using adultery, rather than contractualism, to obtain divorces, but filing at the rate of a border South county.

In the postbellum years, Virginia residents in Fauquier and Amelia Counties exhibited only a slightly greater desire for divorce, despite the enormous disruption of soldiers' absences, women's wartime independence, and emancipation itself. During that period, wives and husbands in Fauquier County filed for divorce a dozen times, and only seven times in Amelia County. Meanwhile, sixty-five Franklin County residents and fifty Ohio County residents sought a divorce from their spouses, many citing adultery, abandonment, or just a loss of love. Tazewell County petitioners, using adultery as the primary charge, filed thirty-five cases in the nine years following the war. With almost thirty cases, Warren County was on the low end of the border South spectrum. Statewide, stark differences are also apparent between Kentucky and Virginia's postbellum records. Although both states had roughly the same population (1,321,011 and 1,225,163, respectively), Kentuckians petitioned for over thirty-five hundred divorces, while Virginians requested one-fifth that amount—about seven hundred—from 1867 to 1875.[23]

The number of divorces filed in Ohio County, West Virginia; Franklin County, Kentucky; Warren County, Kentucky; Tazewell County, Virginia; Amelia County, Virginia; and Fauquier County, Virginia, rose during this period, with a dip during the war years (Table 6.1).[24] Breaking down these numbers, though, reveals variations among the rates of growth in these six counties. Although Fauquier and Amelia County petitioners filed more divorces, they still did so in far smaller numbers than Franklin, Warren, Ohio, and Tazewell County residents. During the decade before Fort

Table 6.1. Number of Divorce Petitions

	1850–1861	1865–1873
Franklin County	48	65
Warren County	23	26
Ohio County	13	50
Tazewell County	21	35
Fauquier County	8	12
Amelia County	2	7

Note: These data are derived from all cases encompassing these years found at the Library of Virginia, accessed through the online Chancery Court Records Index; in circuit court cases on microfilm at the West Virginia and Regional History Center, Morgantown, West Virginia; and original copies of the circuit court records at the Kentucky Department for Libraries and Archives, Frankfort, Kentucky. All statistics reflect the number of cases found, since numerous natural and man-made disasters may account for cases missing or destroyed.

Sumter, Fauquier County citizens sought divorce eight times, and in the nine years following the war, county residents sought twelve divorces.[25] Although Amelia County residents appeared to make a dramatic shift in their rate of petitioning (from two filings in an eleven-year period to seven in a nine-year period), a closer look reveals that at least five of the seven petitioners were black, a group that would not have been able to file in the antebellum era.

Especially in Franklin County, Ohio County, and Tazewell County, the upward trend in the numbers is more noticeable. For Franklin County residents, the numbers reflect the liberalization of the antebellum legal system, which had contributed to their high number of prewar divorce filings. On the other hand, in antebellum Ohio County, although local courts granted an especially high percentage of divorces filed, the actual number filed was much smaller than in Franklin County, Kentucky. In the postwar years, freed from the restrictive Virginia divorce laws, Ohio County residents submitted a much higher number of cases.[26] Tazewell County residents found themselves on a new border after the Civil War, between Virginia and the new state of West Virginia. Although they did not benefit from the new legal code of West Virginia, they did see an uptick in the number of cases filed. In their case, they continued to use their effective antebellum strategy, manipulating the Virginia legal code with a dramatic number of adultery charges, while residents of Ohio County, West Virginia, diversified their charges. Even as Ohio County residents' use of adultery as a charge dropped from almost two-thirds to only one-third of their cases, Tazewell County residents filed for divorce on the grounds of adultery over 90 percent of the time both before and after the war. This supports the conclusion that many of those who charged adultery were manipulating the law.

Postwar divorce had different implications for Kentuckians, West Virginians, and Virginians. Kentuckians and West Virginians, living in a border culture, had drawn their ideals from both slaveholding and nonslaveholding regions and adapted more easily and with less resistance to post-emancipation household upheaval. Many Virginians, meanwhile, believed that society itself was under attack. Antebellum Kentuckians and West Virginians had embraced mutuality and contractualism in marriage and divorce while they still maintained the slave system. Therefore, postwar border southerners could simultaneously urge a return to strict racial hierarchy and continue an ongoing evolution in gender relations and household structure. Virginians struggled more noticeably with the transition because they did not share this pattern of compromise and fusion with border residents. To them, reconstruction of the antebellum social order included clinging to a patriarchal system in the household and reinforcing the permanence of all relationships. Often, judges stood on the front lines of this battle, stabilizing an unsteady social order.

In 1867, Georgiana Bailey sued her husband, James, for divorce *a mensa et thoro* in the Wythe County Circuit Court, citing abandonment, adultery, and cruelty. James Bailey, a widower, father of nine, and professional gambler, traveled frequently during their short marriage. After he left indefinitely without wishing her good-bye, she wrote to him and received a curt answer. Although James agreed to support Georgiana, he wrote, "As for ever living together as husband and wife, that is played out. . . . I have no love for you, nor never will again, for the simple reason that you are not what I believed you to be."[27] The Wythe County Circuit Court, located in southwestern Virginia, granted her a legal separation.

When the case reached the state's court of last resort, the Supreme Court of Virginia, the judges were not entirely unsympathetic. Judge Joseph Christian concluded that James Bailey had sought a young, impressionable woman to take the place of his first wife and to care for his children. Ultimately, he argued, "She is entitled to a divorce from the bed and board of a man who has so utterly disregarded the marital rights of the wife and marital obligations of the husband as to reject and desert her to whom he had solemnly pledged his vows to love, cherish, and protect." However, this case was the exception, not the rule, he wrote. He rejoiced, "Happily for the interests of society, and the sanctity of marital rights and relations, suits of this character are not of frequent occurrence in this State." According to Christian, Virginians rarely filed for divorce because of the "purity of social life and the inviolable sanctity of the marriage bond" in Virginia.[28] Though he and his fellow justices upheld Georgiana Bailey's divorce from her husband, James, they expressed "hope that such cases may be in the future as infrequent as they have been in the past." Gesturing to the recent loss of the war and the slave system, they tellingly prayed that

> amid the whelming tide of social and political revolutions which threaten to sweep away all the forms of our cherished southern civilization, one pillar at least of the social fabric may still stand firm, and that the time may never come when the sacred bond of matrimony can be lightly broken, or the holy duties and high obligations it imposes, can be disregarded with impunity; but that marriage may be in the future, as it has been in the past, be ever recognized in Virginia as an institution to be cherished by law and sanctified by religion, as one upon which alone the happiness and purity of social and domestic life must ever depend.[29]

With the end of slavery, marriage became the next threatened institution of patriarchal control. White Virginians such as Judge Christian felt that society was changing rapidly enough without dangerous "experimentation" with marital law. Throughout the South, many former slaveholders turned inward, relying on their domestic relationships to bolster their shaken masculinity. As a result, they sought to maintain some form of dependency within the home, even without their slaves.[30] Yet, in Kentucky and West Virginia, this "pillar" had begun to collapse even before emancipation began. As a result, it did not become the last vestige of white southern civilization, as it was for some like Judge Christian.

Other Virginians shared this attitude. For example, John Craig, a Fauquier County resident, echoed Judge Christian's sentiments about marriage and divorce in postwar Virginia. In response to his wife's 1870 divorce bill, John Craig wrote that he was "advised that the marriage tie is one of love solemnity & obligation & not dissolvable at the caprice of parties—and that although rapidly advancing in radicalism the state of Virginia is not yet up to Indiana in the cause of free love & general licentiousness."[31] Like Christian, Craig argued that Virginia was radicalizing too fast and fought to maintain the antebellum structure of marriage and divorce in the state. Both focused on the ease of divorce and, more specifically, individuals' *choice* to end their relationships. Divorce, like emancipation, revealed the impermanence of household relationships and hierarchical roles. After all, if a slave did not owe his master obedience and allegiance, did a wife owe her husband the same? Additionally, although neither Craig nor Christian mentioned the role of gender, the fact that both objected when a wife filed for divorce suggests that giving women the ability to end these relationships, especially without cause, was especially dangerous to white southern social hierarchy.[32]

Despite Virginians' resistance to divorce and its impact on social relationships, West Virginians demonstrated a greater willingness to consider such actions in the postwar period. Legislators modified Virginia's divorce law, loosening many of the strict limitations that had hampered divorce filings in the 1850s and demonstrating a greater commitment to a contractual understanding of marriage. Whereas Virginia's laws allowed for full divorce only for adultery, impotency, and imprisonment for seven or more years, the newly adapted law allowed for full divorce in West Virginia if the "husband without the knowledge of the wife, had been a notoriously licentious person." Legislators also decreased the number of years after which a person could sue for divorce after desertion from five to three, and the new West Virginia code allowed for a full divorce in such a case, rather than just a divorce from bed and board. Finally, the bill voided the fourteenth section of the Virginia code, which forbade the guilty party in an adultery case from remarrying.[33] In making these changes, West Virginians leaned further away from their Virginia roots and toward a more contractual understanding of marriage.

In the years following the war, West Virginians, as represented by Ohio County, went from a heavy reliance on adultery charges in divorce cases to using a greater variety of charges. Some of this may have been due to the sheer growth in volume of cases, but that very growth demonstrates that West Virginians had felt limited under the previous Virginia legal system. The passage of new, more flexible state laws allowed them to file for a greater variety of reasons, and more people felt free to file than before or to change the charges under which they filed. Either choice reflects their embrace of contractualism. The first indicates that removing Virginia law allowed West Virginians to more easily end their marriages, something they had been waiting to do but could not before the war. The second indicates that they no longer felt the need to manipulate the legal system through their use of adultery charges alone. When adultery was one of the only charges under which a person could obtain a full divorce, it was the most popular charge. When other charges, like abandonment, allowed petitioners to achieve the same goal, they used that instead.

In their divorce records, Kentuckians display less panic than their Virginian counterparts. While Kentuckians disparaged the racial changes occurring upon emancipation, their divorce petitions reflect less resistance to postwar adaptation in the home. Whereas Virginians such as Craig and Christian fought to defend marriage as a sacred "obligation" for both parties, Kentucky law allowed residents to end their marriages for a wide range of reasons, including a loss of affection. Kentucky couples might even agree to end their marriages, a rare concept at the time. Although no state yet embraced modern no-fault divorce, Kentuckians' use of mutual separation indicates a greater acceptance of contractualism and individualism in the state. In other words, Kentuckians more readily accepted the impermanence of marriage as a contract and the individual's role in forming and ending that relationship. Both beliefs, taken to their extreme, had profound implications for gender roles and hierarchy in the home.[34]

Kentucky judges upheld this view, allowing colluding couples to get divorces and accepting the contractual nature of marriage itself. By contrast, others, like Judge Christian of Virginia, sought to defend and keep permanent the hierarchical antebellum notion of family roles.[35] Christian argued that courts needed to "prevent parties who were weary of the bond of matrimony, and impatient of its restraints and obligations, from obtaining the aid of the court through their own collusion and default."[36] In Kentucky, though, an antebellum acceptance of contractualism continued even after the social turmoil of emancipation. Kentucky judges certainly did not welcome divorce and marital dissolution, but they reflected more on the personal tragedy of it than the social ramifications. After listening to one divorce case, Judge Belvard J. Peters ruled that when "neither party is shown to be without fault and the allowance for maintenance is reasonable, a decree of divorce will not be disturbed upon appeal."[37] His unruffled attitude suggests that this concept had gained some acceptance in the state.

In their desire for more equitable roles for husbands and wives in their relationships, as well as in their desire for divorce when this did not happen, Kentuckians reflected a greater acceptance of contractualism and individualism in the post-emancipation years than Virginians. For example, E. Hensley, a middle-aged man from Franklin County, Kentucky, cited "irreconcilable differences" with his wife when he filed for divorce in September 1867. Divorce for Hensley was not a dramatic reaction to an unforgivable sin such as adultery, but a remedy for his failed companionate relationship. The Franklin County Circuit Court upheld this as a viable argument and granted both spouses a divorce.[38] Provided that couples met the basic requirements of the law (no cohabitation for five years and no intent to reunite), judges continued to view these charges as valid, despite their implications for the permanence of the marital relationship.

Kentuckian A. P. Carr also sought a marriage based upon mutual interests and affection. She called her marriage "an unfortunate one" in her June 1869 divorce petition. Unfortunately, the couple's "dispositions, education, and temperaments were so different, they did not and could not agree," she complained. Her husband, W. H. Carr, responded to her petition, "unit[ing] in her prayer that they both be divorced."[39] The court quickly divorced the two. Others were less clear about the exact cause of their separation but fully admitted that both partners desired it. John J. Crittenden, a man "of color," married Agnes Jane Wilson in July 1866, but the couple lived together for less than a year before separating in May 1867. In his 1872 petition to the Franklin County Circuit Court, John stated only that the pair separated by "mutual consent." The court called two witnesses to confirm the marriage and separation (a deviation showing the court's suspicion of the legality of some black marriages), before granting John's request.[40]

Similarly, some residents of Ohio County, West Virginia, saw little problem with two people agreeing to end their marriage when it made them unhappy. For some, this belief may have led to misunderstandings of the law, which suggests that social attitudes progressed more quickly than statutes. Ephraim and Amanda Trimble's rocky relationship was well known to their Wheeling neighbors in the late 1860s. The pair took turns abandoning one another, fleeing to neighbors for sympathy. Yet, for one of Ephraim's friends, the solution was simple. When Ephraim complained to R. W. Strobel that he "couldn't live with that 'hellcat,'" Strobel simply said that "if they could'nt live together, that if they would both go to the Court House and both of them would swear that . . . that I thought they could be separated."[41] However, West Virginia law did not yet allow mutual agreement as a cause for divorce.

Kentucky courts granted divorces for mutual separation even before the war, but the implications of this decision became even more radical in the postwar era. Allowing couples to decide collectively to end their relationship recognized the authority of both partners in marriage and in the household. It undercut the hierarchy at the foundation of many southern homes. Just as emancipation threw one form of household dependence into question, mutual separation and collusion undermined another. Additionally, divorce itself suggested that certain social and familial ties were dissolvable, a dangerous suggestion in the era of emancipation. In spite of this, though, many Kentuckians chose to end their marriages through divorce, which demonstrates that emancipation's impact differed depending upon the place and culture in which it occurred. Black freedom affected white Kentuckians and white Virginians differently; both feared racial turmoil, but emancipation did not threaten white gender roles in Kentucky to the same extent as in Virginia.

As Bluegrass courts granted more divorces on the grounds of mutual separation, some Kentucky couples chose to admit their mistakes and partners joined in requesting a divorce. Therefore, even petitions that charged adultery, abandonment, or neglect reflected the same attitudes as those that cited mutual separation—a growing acceptance of divorce as a legitimate solution to marital grievances. Over half of Franklin County's accused spouses who responded to a divorce petition either filed a cross-bill or acquiesced to the divorce. For example, when B. B. Sayre charged his wife, Catharine, with abandoning their marital home a mere three months after their wedding, she admitted freely that she "left his house with the intention of abandoning him as her husband." She would never live with him again, she vehemently assured the court. Therefore, she was "satisfied that it will be best for both him and herself" that they obtain a divorce.[42] The Franklin County Circuit Court agreed.

Did those accused spouses who did not respond to their partners object to the divorce? Why did they not also file and agree with their spouses that divorce was necessary? It can be difficult to tell, and less than a fifth of Franklin and Warren County spouses responded to their accusers. Many had left the state; others may have thought a silent assent through non-reply was more effective in obtaining the desired divorce than any answer at all.[43] However, another possibility remains. Kentucky residents may have felt little need to defend their reputations and to object to a divorce. In Fauquier County, Virginia, on the other hand, almost 60 percent of spouses responded to their partners' claims. Some, like John Craig, fought against the divorce, citing the indecency of such an action. Many sought to clear their good names from the shame of divorce and accusations of adultery or abandonment.

Certainly, not all Kentuckians so willingly embraced the end of their marriages. When his wife, Viola, filed for divorce in 1869, John Lackey promptly filed an answer denying her right to a separation of any kind. Viola accused her husband of having been a "confirmed drunkard," of having failed to provide for her or their child, and of having abused her. John denied every charge and told the court that Viola's petition did not reflect her true wishes, but rather the "persuasion and malevolent influences of another." He hoped, instead of a divorce, that Viola would change her mind and return to him. The case never reached the decree stage, so it is quite possible he received his wish. John may have been motivated by love for Viola, or worse, by a twisted emotion such as possessiveness, but he may also have been threatened by her desire to claim alimony, as well as a divorce. In her petition, Viola requested, and was granted, an injunction preventing John from having any control over their estate. Similarly, John Metzger denied his wife's charges of abuse or her right to a divorce. He pleaded with the court that he was a sick man and would much prefer to live with his family, but, he quickly noted, "if a divorce be granted," he wanted to keep his house.[44] John's last-minute admission suggested that he was more upset over losing his house than his wife.

In Fauquier County, even a spouse who agreed to a partner's divorce strenuously denied all charges filed by the petitioning spouse. Joseph Brent, for one, objected strongly to his wife's accusations of abuse and abandonment. Ultimately, he did not want to "throw any obstacle" in the way of a divorce, but to set the record straight. According to Joseph, his wife, Sarah, had been another man's mistress before the couple's marriage, rather than the "virtuous maiden" he believed her to be.[45] Virginian Arthur Sullivan also agreed with his wife's request for the couple's divorce, but he denied her accusations of neglect and abandonment. He had tried "in every way to promote their [his wife and her children's] welfare by rendering such aid advice and assistence in all matters that concerned them as he could." He did not choose to leave but was forced to do so by Mary Sullivan's "violent and unreasonable temper."[46]

Virginians Joseph Brent and Arthur Sullivan agreed to a divorce, a small step toward the mutuality of Kentucky divorces, but neither was willing to take any blame and, in fact, felt obligated to shift blame fully to their spouses. This reflects the harsher social judgment against divorce in their Virginia county than in Franklin or Warren County, Kentucky. Both men felt it necessary to protect their own images and tarnish those of their wives. The legal system in Fauquier County required finding one party at fault, in contrast to the law in Kentucky. Divorce cases, after all, were crafted narratives, designed to obtain the goal of separation. While Kentuckians began to forgo emotionally fraught language in their antebellum divorce petitions, choosing instead to rely on the letter of the law, Virginians in postwar Fauquier County still felt the need to spin a tale of woe for the courts.[47]

Similarly, Tazewell County residents only tiptoed toward signs of collusion or agreement in their petitions. In his 1866 divorce petition, Rees Turley accused his wife, Susan, of adultery. Her hastily filed response did not even acknowledge the charge, a striking omission. Instead, she tried to convince the court to see her side of the story. After fifteen months of marriage, she wrote, Rees left her. In a short time, he returned and "with tears in his eyes effected a reconciliation." He would go on to repeat this pattern five times in the coming years. Exasperated, Susan admitted she was "almost inclined to be rid of a husband who has acted as strangely & unnaturally."[48] Unlike many respondents, she did not deny that the court should grant her husband a divorce but just asked that they protect her financial interests if they did so. However, the court never granted a divorce. Perhaps Rees was successful at persuading Susan to take him back a sixth time, or perhaps the court did not like the appearance of collusion in the case.

Virginia spouses emphasized the moral failings of their partners and, ultimately, their own innocence, knowing that the court would only allow a divorce under such stringent circumstances. Perhaps many petitioners knew that Judge Christian's view was common—that "amid the whelming tide of social and political revolutions which threaten . . . our cherished southern civilization, one pillar at least of the social fabric may still stand firm."[49] White perceptions of emancipation had profound effects on gender roles in the years following the Civil War. Because many Virginia judges, unlike some in Kentucky, saw emancipation as a threat to white household roles, they resisted other forms of social change such as divorce. As a result, litigants in the Old Dominion had to work harder to prove the necessity of their separation.

Married to William T. Suddoth in the summer of 1841, Susannah lived with him only occasionally during the twenty-five years before her divorce petition to the Fauquier County Circuit Court. Their first separation occurred in April 1842, when she fled to her father's home after enduring months of drunken violence. After William returned from the Mexican War in January 1849, she agreed to live with him again, believing the war had changed his intemperate and dissolute ways. It had not. She left him again in 1852, due to William's "returning habits of drunkenness maltreatment and neglect," according to her brother.[50] Thus the pair may have continued, if not for William's wandering eye.

In her petition, Susannah told the court that she truly preferred "long to suffer in silence and carry with her uncomplainingly through life the burden of her blasted hopes," than to "brin[g] her grief upon the public gaze." She could have dealt with separation; if William had requested her to come back, she might even have endured more neglect and "harshness," but she could not stand "the greater offence of conjugal infidelity." According to Susannah and her deponents, William had recently taken up with another woman, installing her in his home and introducing her to friends and neighbors as his wife.[51] Susannah's statements make it clear that she did not see all offenses as divorceable crimes, and the court probably agreed with her. She had to prove that she chose formal marital dissolution as a last resort, not a frivolous impulse or "caprice," and her length of marriage and moral credentials make that clear.[52]

Susannah, like her fellow Virginians, stayed in her marriage longer than the average divorce petitioner from Kentucky or West Virginia. Half of those Fauquier County residents who filed after the war had been married longer than ten years; a quarter had actually been married more than twenty years. On the other hand, three-quarters of Franklin County petitioners and 70 percent of Warren County residents had been married less than five years. In Ohio County, West Virginia, only 15 percent of litigants had been married over ten years before filing.[53] Border southerners had more faith in their ability to obtain a divorce quickly and with fewer charges than their Virginia counterparts. Not only did Virginia couples endure longer marriages before divorce, they also waited much longer than border residents to ask for said divorce. Whereas only 10 percent of Franklin County petitioners, 9 percent of Ohio County petitioners, and 5 percent of Warren County petitioners waited more than five years after a known marital crisis to file for divorce, more than 40 percent of Fauquier County petitioners did.[54]

Mary Sullivan, for instance, waited well over a decade to petition the Fauquier County Court for her divorce. A widow with children, she married Arthur Sullivan in September 1853. They lived together only five months before he abandoned her home, never to return. Their marriage was a tumultuous one. Arthur had been frequently intoxicated and treated her in an "unkind" manner. He failed to support the couple, despite having access to her property. Mary waited until after the war to file and insisted that "although maltreated, [she] would not ask for the interposition of a court of equity if she alone were involved in the misfortune." She only did so for her son, she assured the court. Her child from her first marriage, he lived with her, and she considered it unfair that he should support her when her property was tied to her drunk and lazy husband. The court sympathized with her and granted her the divorce.[55]

Arthur Sullivan also employed the language of forbearance in his answer to Mary's petition. Denying her charges, he accused her of possessing a violent temper and of making his home "intolerable" with her "unkindness." Despite this, he "bore with patience and for a long time by a course of conduct that he thought would soften her endeavored to bring about happier relations." Instead, "his submission seemed rather to exasperate than mollify and finally in despair of any change for the better he was compelled to leave a house . . . which had become too intolerably uncomfortable for him to remain longer."[56]

West Virginian Hattie Arthur began her petition with a suggestion of being the same sort of long-suffering wife. She had "since the solemnization of the rites of matrimony as aforesaid, been to . . . Jesse Arthur, a constant and faithful wife." Yet, her marriage had barely existed. Married on February 13, 1867, Jesse Arthur abandoned his wife the very next day, refusing to recognize their marriage. Anne Hamilton would have sympathized. She and Smith Hamilton married in Wheeling on January 17, 1867, and spent one night together as husband and wife before he deserted her.[57] Both women waited the requisite three years before filing and quickly received a divorce. West Virginians felt less need to craft a narrative about desperation and endurance when the courts allowed for simple divorces.

In addition to the length of their marriages and their use of fault-based language, Virginians resisted post-emancipation legal change in other ways as well. A third of Fauquier County petitioners asked only for a divorce *a mensa et thoro*. Divorce *a mensa et thoro*, or divorce from bed and board, amounted to little more than a legal separation, granting a couple the right to live apart but denying either party the right to remarry.[58] Those requesting divorce *a mensa et thoro* may have objected to a full divorce upon moral grounds, a reflection of Virginia's postwar social attitude, or they may have believed the court would not grant them a full divorce for their charges, a reflection of Virginia's strict legal code. Kentucky state statutes, conversely, granted full divorces for numerous reasons, including abandonment, cruelty, and adultery, while Virginia law continued to maintain adultery as the sole cause for absolute divorce. West Virginia modified Virginia's divorce statutes specifically to expand the number of reasons for which one could get an absolute divorce.[59] The comparison between Fauquier County and Franklin and Warren Counties is especially stark. In the two Kentucky counties, not a single petitioner chose to file for a divorce *a mensa et thoro,* and they still achieved a higher rate of success with their petitions than residents of Fauquier County.[60]

Kentuckians such as Catherine Bailey and Mary Mack exhibited a greater tendency toward legal simplicity in the postwar years, knowing that both society and the courts were more receptive to divorce in their state. Born Catherine and Mary Ridley, the two sisters from Franklin County married within a week of each other in early February 1866. The pair shared more than the timing of their nuptials, however. In August 1866, George Bailey abandoned Catherine, and by September, Horace Mack abandoned Mary as well. As the sisters experienced so much together, it is perhaps fitting that they filed for divorce in the Franklin County Circuit Court on the same day—June 11, 1868. Displaying a rare bureaucratic desire for efficiency, the court allowed their mother's testimony to be used in both cases, the only witness for either sister. Within weeks of her deposition, the court gave both sisters divorces and full rights as unmarried women.[61] Their simple and effective cases reflect the spirit of contractualism and legal continuity found in post-emancipation Kentucky cases.

Furthermore, in Fauquier and Amelia Counties in Virginia, married women continued to sue with their next friend, suggesting that the law still considered them incompetent to stand alone and independent in their own divorce cases. A next friend (usually a male friend or on rare occasions a single woman) made it possible for married women, previously incapable of suing in court, to file for divorce. Courts obligated minors, those labeled mentally incapacitated, or others unable to act for themselves to sue with a next friend. Even Tazewell County residents used the device from time to time, although less frequently than their eastern Virginia counterparts. Formerly Virginians, residents of Ohio County, West Virginia, retained the device for the first few years after the war, but its use disappeared after 1871. Kentucky judges, even at the more conservative appellate level, viewed the concept of a "next friend" as outdated.[62] According to Judge George Robertson, a wife had the "right to sue in her own name for alimony and divorce."[63] Franklin and Warren County residents clearly agreed, because not one woman filing for divorce there mentioned a next friend. However, in Fauquier County every woman who filed for divorce, and in Amelia County all but one, did so with a next friend. Virginia's retention of the "next friend" standard reflects an unwillingness to believe that women could be legal actors on their own, or further, rational, decision-making partners in marriage. As previously stated, women's growing independence could be especially threatening to white men in the postwar years, when emancipation already threatened patriarchal control.

After the war and, more importantly, after the division of Virginia and West Virginia, Tazewell County residents experienced their own transformation. As many historians have shown, the war crystallized the regional identity of many Americans. The war forced many on either side of the Union–Confederate divide to declare and defend their loyalty and to define what made someone a northerner, southerner, or westerner. This certainly was true of those living in the border South states of Kentucky and West Virginia, although in many ways, their identities shifted during the postwar years. Immediately following the war, they maintained their blended identities, reflecting their status as victorious Union states who still had to undergo a federally imposed emancipation process. For this reason, states like Kentucky and West Virginia only became "southern" in their identity after Reconstruction and the imposition of Jim Crow laws and other racially restrictive measures in the late nineteenth century. In this environment, how did Tazewell County residents grapple with their regional identity?

While the rest of the country struggled to grasp the appearance and then disappearance of a border between the Confederacy and Union, those living along the edges of the new state of West Virginia dealt with the creation of a different border. Tazewell County residents certainly had close ties with West Virginia. Residents of the new state had, after all, been Virginians like themselves only a few short years before. Now, they had rather arbitrarily been separated into two states. In some ways, it seems strange that an invisible line should create difference between those living in McDowell County, West Virginia, for example, and those living on the other side in Tazewell, but it appears to have done so. After all, those invisible lines had real ramifications for residents. As previously stated, Tazewell County residents still operated under the Virginia legal code, including, in this case, a more restrictive divorce statute.

Additionally, Virginians, as this chapter has shown, felt the loss of the war and black emancipation strongly. They sought to prevent further social change by defending marital permanence as a glorious sign of southern strength and morality. Maintaining a gendered hierarchy in the household became linked to their regional and state identities, a way to achieve stability in the midst of chaotic change and return to at least some prewar ideals. An analysis of Tazewell's divorce cases reveals how some of this rhetoric and behavior may have shaped even this rural Appalachian enclave. Tazewell County residents may have continued to file using the charge of adultery because they still labored under a restrictive Virginia legal code, and the evidence of their antebellum charges and the sheer number of filings suggests that this is, at least in part, true. To some extent, Tazewell County residents differed from their fellow Virginians in Fauquier and Amelia Counties in their understanding of divorce and contractualism. However, they did not mirror completely their West Virginia counterparts. In contrast to Ohio County, for example, men filed the vast majority of cases in Tazewell County.

Margaret and William Dillion had been married for fifteen years and had had eight children when he left her for another woman. William and Matilda Hash, without much attempt to hide their behavior, left for McDowell County, West Virginia, in 1870. William Dowland had lived with his wife, Susan, for only a year when she eloped with Frank Willis to Charleston, West Virginia. Archibald White's wife, Mary, stayed for an even shorter period—three months—before running off with James Carver. That couple chose to stay in Tazewell, however. In some cases, such as Henry Walker's 1866 divorce petition against his wife, Frances, the person with whom the spouse conducted an affair testified on behavior of the aggrieved spouse.[64] Nonetheless, the number of cases filed, as well as the success found by petitioners in Tazewell County, suggests that their beliefs were not completely in step with those of their eastern Virginia neighbors. In those counties, especially Amelia County, a different set of factors shaped some of their postwar experience.

Before the war, Amelia County's social and legal environment was not conducive to divorce. With an economy heavily based upon slavery and plantation farming, Amelia County represented many of the trends of other southern places: patriarchy was dominant, infused with a healthy dose of racism and violence. During the decade before the war began, there were two petitions for divorce filed in this county, compared with dozens of cases in the Kentucky counties of Franklin and Warren. In the years following the war, this number rose at a striking rate. Granted, the number of cases went from two to only seven, but this more than tripled the divorces heard before the local court. A quick glance at this shift suggests that Amelia County residents shifted their attitudes about divorce in the wake of surrender, a surprising change indeed.

However, a closer look at the cases and, more importantly, the participants, reveals a more complicated story. In fact, as many as five out of seven couples involved in these divorces were black. Before the war, over 70 percent of Amelia County's population was enslaved, a status that made it impossible for them to legally marry. In the antebellum American South, enslaved people formed monogamous long-term relationships that they and their owners dubbed marriages but that had no formal protection under the law. After all, to recognize the ability of enslaved people to marry would be to recognize their personhood in general. Although many owners encouraged such relationships and many enslaved people sought them, marriages formed during slavery were always precarious, subject to sale, separation, and violence from outside forces.[65] In the wake of black emancipation, many freedpeople knew that claiming legal protection for their marital relationships was a pivotal assertion of civil rights and their own humanity.[66] For these reasons, as well as from a personal desire to sanctify their marriages, many freedpeople scrambled to marry in the months following Confederate surrender. Additionally, working with the Freedmen's Bureau, many Reconstruction governments passed laws that legally recognized black relationships as marriages. Not all of the lawmakers' motivations were pure, however. Some, in the belief that black southerners were inherently immoral or licentious, wanted to ensure a sort of puritanical emphasis on marriage in these communities, assuming that such a mentality could only be imposed from without by white elites. Similarly, some worried about the financial burden of illegitimacy if long-term relationships did not have legal status.

In Virginia, the General Assembly passed the Cohabitation Act of 1866 in February of that year. The act, which legalized formerly enslaved people's marriages and gave their children legitimacy, was instigated by Governor Francis Pierpont, a West Virginian who headed the wartime government for the Restored State of Virginia. This government had complete jurisdiction over the state of Virginia once the war ended and could therefore pass such a law. In 1864, Pierpont had stated, "A perplexing question to the minds of many arises out of the marital relationships which now exist among the freed people. The code of slavery disregarded the marital rights of slaves, yet they formed their matrimonial relations." The governor then suggested that the assembly recognize the marriages formed, informally or otherwise, during slavery, that couples who had been separated during slavery be regarded as divorced, and that children of both types of relationships be given legitimacy. Although he did not succeed in convincing lawmakers at that point, he would shepherd these ideas through the Virginia assembly in 1866.

As passed, the law mandated that ministers and others who performed marriages make a record of the ceremony, for either a white or black person. Marriage licenses, which had to note the race of those marrying, would be collected by the county clerk. More specific to former slaves, the law stated that "where colored persons, before the passage of this act, shall have undertaken and agreed to occupy the relation to each other of husband and wife, and shall be cohabiting together as such as the time of its passage, whether the rites of marriage shall have been celebrated between them or not, they shall be deemed husband and wife . . . as if they had been duly married by law." The law accomplished many of Pierpont's goals, and many freedpeople welcomed the change. However, as Amelia County's records show, it also complicated other relationships.

In February 1871, Richard Craddock filed his divorce petition in the Amelia County Circuit Court. On the one hand, Richard's ability to file such a case and have it heard before a white judge reveals the tremendous shifts in the status of black Virginians' lives in the postwar years. On the other hand, his case speaks of the frustration many divorce litigants, white or black, felt upon taking such a step, and it also reflects the specific circumstances of black life in the post-emancipation period. Richard Craddock's relationship with his wife, Malvina, had been legalized under the 1866 Cohabitation Act, and he had lived with her from that point until 1870. In 1870, Malvina came before the Amelia County Court to be prosecuted for the charge of bigamy. She was quickly found guilty by a jury and sentenced to four years in prison. Neither Richard's divorce petition nor Malvina's indictment mentions the circumstances of her bigamous relationship, but it is possible that it related to the complications of relationships that began in slavery. Many freedpeople who cohabited as husband and wife in 1866 had previously had marital bonds with other men and women before they were separated under slavery. Could Malvina's second relationship have been such a marriage? Unfortunately, the case is brief, so we may never know. Within a few short months, the Amelia County Circuit Court granted Richard his divorce.[67]

Richard's success illustrates another interesting trait of postwar Amelia County divorce petitions—the frequency with which they were granted.[68] Samuel Minge filed his petition in March 1870 and received a positive decree within a month, a shockingly short time for divorce cases in this era. He and his wife, Laura, had been living together as husband and wife since well before the war, "as was the custom among slaves prior to their emancipation." As with Richard and Malvina's marriage, Samuel and Laura's marriage had been legalized by the Cohabitation Act in 1866. However, by 1868, Samuel worried that Laura was becoming distant. When he finally discovered the reason, he was shocked to learn that she had fallen for another man and was pregnant with his child. She quickly left the couple's home. His petition hinged on this alleged adultery. He called five deponents to support his case, including one man who had actually spoken with Laura after her departure. According to John Hill, when asked if she would return to Samuel, Laura emphatically stated that "she would never be Sam's wife again, . . . that Sam could never do enough for her when he had her and that Sam knew it."[69]

Obviously, the biggest explanation for the sharp uptick in postwar divorce cases in Amelia County was not a liberalization in sentiment born out of the wartime experience but rather the large segment of the population that was suddenly given access to legal rights previously denied them. For white petitioners, Amelia County's court system proved just as restrictive as it had been in the antebellum era, if not more so. Of the two cases likely filed by white residents, only one resulted in a divorce. Isolating these divorces demonstrates how Amelia County residents and judges, like their counterparts in Fauquier County and elsewhere in Virginia, chose to reinforce the permanence of marriage and the importance of household hierarchy in the wake of black emancipation. Especially in a county with such a large proportion of formerly enslaved residents, this would be vital. The Minges, the Craddocks, the Greens, the Jameses, and the Bookers could not have filed their cases before the war since their relationships were not legally valid. Still, the postwar white legal system showed a striking disparity in its treatment of white and black divorces. Whereas white divorces could imperil white male power in the post-emancipation household and society, it appears that black divorces proved no such threat. In the white mind, black relationships did not center on the same gendered relationships as white marriages. Black women had never been granted the benefits of femininity or black men the rights of masculine power in the American South, and they struggled to claim them in the postbellum world. To see black divorce as threatening, white Virginians would have to implicitly recognize black men as dominant and their dominance as something to be protected. They would also have to recognize black relationships as equally worthy of moral protection with white relationships, another thing most white Virginians proved unwilling to do. In Amelia County after the Civil War, black emancipation gave more people access to the legal divorce system. Although they found success in the courts, that success did not necessarily reflect racial progress and in fact suggests that white Virginians sought to place black marriages on a lower plane than their own. In this county, the impact of black emancipation could be felt in the differing treatment of white and black divorce.

In March 1864, Benjamin Mourning, a sixty-year-old widower from Franklin County, Kentucky, married Laura Alley, a widow and the mother of several young children. Although Lincoln's 1863 Emancipation Proclamation did not apply to Bluegrass slaveholders such as Benjamin, he, like other Kentuckians, nonetheless felt the effects. Worried that he would lose his remaining slaves, Benjamin feared the impact on his household. Before his marriage, he told friends that Laura seemed to be an "intelligent business woman and good housekeeper" and that he sought her hand in marriage to "keep his house" if emancipation occurred. Ironically, this marriage, created out of fear of emancipation, crumbled at the same moment that such a future seemed certain. By the end of May 1865, Benjamin threw Laura out of his house, which led to her successful 1866 divorce petition.[70]

Benjamin and Laura's tumultuous relationship symbolizes the domestic ripples that emancipation caused for white southerners during the immediate postwar years. Emancipation was a contested process with a variety of meanings for black and white southerners. The process differed based not only on one's color and class but also on one's region. As it did throughout the South, emancipation in Kentucky and West Virginia threatened public and private racial hierarchies, leading to a backlash within the states toward their newly freed population. In the years following the war, border southerners implemented harsh economic and political measures against blacks and participated in the wave of racial violence that swept the South.

However, as their divorce records indicate, black emancipation did not have the same disruptive impact on white gender roles within the household as it did in other regions.

Ultimately, the process of emancipation in the border South must be filtered through its unique antebellum experience. Because of their prewar hybrid border culture, Kentuckians and West Virginians exhibited a high level of adaptability within their households. In the 1850s, many residents embraced mutuality and contractualism, as seen in their liberalized divorce laws, while still maintaining a strong slave system in their state and in their homes. By the time emancipation did occur, ties between gender and racial hierarchy had grown weak, allowing citizens to experience seemingly contradictory views toward changes in the household. It is worth remembering how the process of emancipation could be fractured by the complex, divided culture of a southern borderland.

7

Never Happier in Her Life

On a bitterly cold and snowy night in late February 1870, Hettie and Romaine Trimble crept slowly across a two-foot gap between the roof of Hettie's Wheeling home and that of her neighbor, Amanda Trimble. The pair then crawled across the flat roof and crouched outside Amanda's bedroom window. Through a torn window blind, they watched for over an hour as Amanda sat by the fire talking with her nineteen-year-old nephew, William Sterling. Finally, their patience was rewarded. William got up, undressed completely, and climbed into bed beside his aunt, despite the presence of an available lounge on the other side of the room. Hettie, whose brother Ephraim was currently entangled in a nasty divorce case with Amanda, confirmed her suspicions about Amanda's infidelity and lifestyle. She told the Ohio County Circuit Court that she "would have waited three hours to see" evidence of the affair, despite the cold.[1]

Hettie's nighttime spying and the divorce case that prompted her actions illustrate the active and public role many working-class women played in regulating and negotiating marriage in the mid-nineteenth-century border South. Hettie and Romaine not only felt little embarrassment spying on their neighbor, they bragged about it to the county court. In the divorce case *Trimble, Amanda M. v. Trimble, Ephraim* (1868), male voices are muted, and women, especially Amanda and her sister- and mother-in-law, speak loudly and strongly in a public forum. The specific border environment of West Virginia and Kentucky led to their attitudes and gave them room to act in ways in which they could not elsewhere in the South. Ultimately, these two women, who braved wind and snow to spy on their neighbor, confronted her with the information and went before a court of law. They felt comfortable doing so because of the competing cultural, ethnic, economic, and regional borders in which they lived. West Virginia and Kentucky's borderlike environment created fertile ground for ideas of mutuality and egalitarianism. While this led many to pursue friendship, love, and partnership in their relationships, elite and middle-class husbands and wives of the border South still often adhered to a social ethic which dictated certain gendered behaviors to men and women. In working-class society, however, these philosophies gave women a greater sense of independence and authority that allowed them to push the boundaries of the household and assert themselves in new ways. In the border South, this created a unique opening for visible, self-confident women—women who actively monitored their neighbors' marital behavior, women who engaged in extramarital relationships, women who called upon the community to challenge their husbands' authority, women who freely abandoned their spouses, and women who supported themselves with or without their husbands' presence.[2] Victoria Bynum has shown how black and white women in antebellum North Carolina defied society's expectations for them, despite resistance from external forces. However, in communities like Wheeling, Frankfort, and Bowling Green, women were not so much defiant as adaptable. They did not resist a hegemonic social authority so much as they vacillated between different definitions of proper behavior.[3]

Viewing the postwar period through the eyes of working-class women also reveals how antebellum border communities began to differ in the years following the war. As the last chapter revealed, Tazewell County, lying along the newly created border of West Virginia and Virginia became, in a word, more "Virginian" in the postbellum period. As their community's identity as southerners and as Virginians crystallized, women in this county found fewer openings in society's formal gendered assumptions through which to assert their independence or to publicly display and defend any atypical behavior. Certainly, Tazewell County women defied social conventions—the sheer number of adultery charges successfully lobbied against wives reveals that. However, they were less able to mount defenses to these charges, and the voices of women in these cases, whether as defendants or deponents, are considerably muted compared to those in Ohio, Franklin, or Warren Counties. In Tazewell County, evidence suggests that white men tried to more closely monitor and control white women's behavior in the postbellum period, perhaps to maintain some semblance of social hierarchy in the wake of black emancipation and the loss of the Confederacy. Most of the women involved in the Tazewell cases shared a similar class background with the women in the Kentucky and West Virginia counties. Besides their identities as Virginians, the only other substantial difference between these places was the rural quality of life in Appalachian Tazewell County. Yet, this had not proven to be a substantial factor before the war. It was only after the battles ended, when state and regional identities hardened, that the urban areas of the border South began to substantially distinguish themselves from the rural communities. Nonetheless, this is not to say that Tazewell County residents became carbon copies of their eastern Virginia neighbors in Fauquier and Amelia Counties. Instead, their communities became places in between, borders between the border and the South. Women pushed against the growing hardening of social rules by displaying unconventional behavior, and men worked to maintain those conventions in the face of these actions. Neither were entirely successful.

Hettie Trimble's first run-in with Amanda Trimble was not on her roof in February 1870. She had been at odds with Amanda for years, even before Ephraim Trimble's 1864 abandonment of his wife. Despite her brother-in-law's departure, Hettie and her mother continued to live next door to his wife, a position that enabled them to closely monitor Amanda's actions.[4] When they swore they observed infidelity, Amanda accused Barbara and Hettie of encouraging her husband to seek a divorce, pestering her after he did so, and manipulating their neighbors into testifying against her in the subsequent case. Barbara Trimble allegedly asked the local grocer to refuse Amanda a line of credit after her husband left, and Hettie supposedly told a neighbor that "no one ought to help [Amanda] or give her anything because she was lazy and would not work."[5]

According to testimony, Barbara frequently stood in her door when Amanda left home, "hollow[ing] to her and ask[ing] if she was going out begging." Amanda told a former employer that Hettie and Barbara "suspicioned her," but that "none but decent people visited her." Nonetheless, "No one could come about the house without their watching them . . . sticking their heads out of the window" and yelling at them.[6] Hettie and Barbara both took action against their female neighbor, participating within the local community and the legal system to punish her for what they believed were improper actions in her marriage. In addition, they did not hide the ways in which they had obtained this information but freely admitted to the court that they had climbed onto a neighbor's property and interfered with her business. Amanda responded publicly to every one of their assertions, defending her social and sexual reputation for years.

Throughout the nineteenth-century United States, women expected some community regulation of their sexual and social behavior, but those who addressed these complaints defiantly often merely confirmed accusations of their "inappropriate" behavior.[7] Neither Amanda, nor Hettie, nor Barbara shied away from those labels, though. Assertive women throughout time, but especially during this era, have been labeled as volatile, angry, and bad-tempered. Most women flatly denied such charges when asked. In her case, however, Barbara merely replied: "My temper is like that of a great many others that when I am annoyed I am generally hasty."[8] Hettie, Barbara, and Amanda believed their roles were appropriate and acceptable, and many in their community may have supported them.[9]

In some ways, the urban and working-class environments of Wheeling, Bowling Green, and Frankfort encouraged women like Hettie and Barbara to monitor their neighbors' relationships, as close proximity bred intimacy and observation. In heavily working-class locales, evidence from boarders, neighbors, and houseguests reveals that some women engaged in socially questionable behavior. Additionally, boardinghouses and crowded neighborhoods increased the potential for adulterous activity.[10] While her husband traveled back and forth to Cincinnati for work, Elizabeth Firestone started a relationship with George Axel, a fellow boarder at the Franklin County, Kentucky, home of Rachel Dill.[11] In Wheeling, Malinda Watson, Caroline Brareton's former housemate, witnessed her frequent adultery. She told the court that a man named Charles Denis visited Caroline two or three times a week, often staying the night. As the house was small, only three rooms, Malinda saw them in bed together, even on Sundays. Besides committing adultery, Caroline's behavior further defied social expectations because Charles was black.[12] Border South cities, places of mixed cultures, ethnicities, and classes, seem to have fostered some interracial illicit relationships.[13]

Women in Tazewell County, Virginia, also provided some evidence of extramarital liaisons, but in this Virginia community, men seem to have generally been the witnesses in divorce cases. When women testified, it was in their capacity as housemates with other women. In a rural community with a high concentration of working-class couples, many husbands who were forced to leave their wives for months or years at a time for work or in the pursuit of military service took advantage of single women's generosity. For example, when he left to serve in the Confederate army, William Cecil moved his wife, Emma, into the home of Ellen Witten, a local widow. When he filed for divorce from his wife five years later, Ellen proved to be one of his most adamant witnesses. She stated that Emma had stayed with her only a few months before Ellen confronted her about her allegedly licentious behavior. Ellen felt that Emma was too intimate with soldiers in the neighborhood, especially one for whom she cared for while he was sick. She swore that Emma left the county with a company of soldiers and traveled to Charleston, West Virginia. Yet, the male witnesses did not corroborate her testimony, merely stipulating that Emma was now living in New York City, where her mother resided. Ellen failed to convince the court as well, who ultimately allowed William Cecil to change his charge to abandonment, rather than adultery, and granted his divorce.[14]

While Ellen chose to testify and voice her opinion, her opinion seems to have been given less weight than that of her male counterparts in the community. In most cases, if women testified, their narratives had to be corroborated by men. White men also acted as arbiters of female behavior by testifying repeatedly about the sexual or moral reputation of women in the community. When Mary Hall sued her husband, Alexander, for divorce in 1872, a number of male neighbors came to her defense. Joseph Harrison swore that he had known her for fifteen years and that "she is a woman of good character, that he never heard the slightest imputation against her in any way." Her doctor, R. W. Witten, reiterated these sentiments. James W. M. Witten merely corroborated her statement that her husband remained in Tazewell County after he abandoned her.[15] Not only did these male witnesses, when combined with one other, outweigh the sole female deponent, they also served in many ways merely to assure the court that Mary Hall was a trustworthy person. Mary herself had less standing than her witnesses. No husbands had to prove their moral reputation when they filed for divorce against adulterous wives. Many stated it in their petitions but seem to have assumed the court would take those statements as fact.

In 1871, Margaret Dillion alleged that her husband, William, had run off to McDowell County, West Virginia, with another woman, Matilda Hash. Every single person called to defend her charge was male, including Matilda's own father. James P. Hash readily admitted that his daughter had left the county at the same time as William Dillion, and the pair appeared to be living as husband and wife. Instead of defending his daughter, he strongly applauded the moral reputation of Margaret Dillion, a "woman who stays at home closely & attends to her own business."[16] Matilda, it seems, had so violated feminine convention that her own father would not defend her. Meanwhile, Margaret had earned his respect, in part for closely adhering to these norms and by playing the role of the domestic woman.

One member of the community defended William and Matilda's behavior—William's father, William Dillion Sr. He admitted their relationship, stating that they lived together in a one-room house purchased by his son. However, he seemed to feel that Margaret still had no grounds for divorce, since William Jr. had made accommodations for her when he left. William Jr. left his wife and children at his father's home, along with "plenty" of support. William Sr. then assured Margaret that she would be cared for permanently in that home. He said that she had begun to express frustration only when her brother visited from Indiana. Like many white southern men, he assumed that Margaret's feelings toward her husband could not have developed without outside (male) influence. William Sr. reiterated that if Margaret had only stayed with him, she would have had plenty of goods and support.[17] It was her choice to abandon that situation. William Dillion Sr. seems to have believed that Margaret should have remained a silent spouse and should have accepted her husband's behavior and absence, in exchange for the basic necessities of life and little else. In his view, a woman's job was to endure and not to complain in the face of her husband's behavior. In choosing to condemn Margaret's decision to make a public statement against her husband, however, he also failed to criticize the unconventional behavior of his son's new lover, Matilda.

Matilda falls into another category of border South women—those in adulterous relationships who acted quite publicly and proudly. As seen in chapter 5, some women took few pains to conceal their extramarital affairs. While her husband served in the Union army, Ellen Stroble traveled throughout Wheeling on the arm of her lover, John Hunter. The pair attended market days, visited a local hotel, and went buggy riding together.[18] Wheeling neighbors called Isabella Prophater unchaste and unrepentant after she became pregnant with her lover's child while her husband was at war.[19] In Franklin County, Kentucky, Lucy Clifford took advantage of her husband's absence, by frequently striding along a public highway in "verry unbecoming intimacy" with other men.[20] When Elizabeth Sargent confronted Lydia Martin about her affair, Lydia brazenly admitted that she was pregnant with another man's child and planned to leave her husband as soon as that child was born.[21]

In Tazewell County, over 90 percent of the cases filed in the eight years following the Civil War involved the charge of adultery. Additionally, most of these involved very specific charges, rather than a general charge of adultery. Most spouses alleged that their husband or wife had left them for one person, a charge that was simpler to prove and also supports the veracity of a number of these cases. Additionally, unlike in other border South counties, almost two-thirds of those adultery charges came from men. This could reveal a community in which men's voices held more weight and in which men were more likely to receive relief from their broken marriages in court. However, it could also reveal the unconventional and defiant adulterous behavior of women in Tazewell County.

Susan Turley was one of the women whose husbands charged them with adultery during this period. Interestingly, her husband, Rees, did not name a specific person in his adultery charge. Susan also proved an exception in responding to his charge. She neither denied nor accepted his accusations of adultery. Instead, she laid out the problems in their marriage, subtly implying that Rees had failed as a husband and that their marriage was effectively over regardless of her actions. During their marriage, Rees had abandoned her and begged forgiveness on multiple occasions. Because of this, she said, she was "almost inclined to be rid of a husband who has acted as strangely and unnaturally."[22] Susan's response is fascinating for not specifically engaging with the accusation of adultery, the only charge in Rees's very short petition. She cannot have missed the charge, and by sidestepping it, she brushes aside the seriousness of the charge and suggests that his behavior is more problematic and potentially renders her choices defensible.

Beverly Schwartzberg argues that for many nineteenth-century Americans practices such as bigamy reflected a "pragmatic flexibility that demonstrated both respect for marriage and a willingness to adapt households to meet need and fortune."[23] While neither Ellen Stroble nor Isabella Prophater formally married their paramours, their decision to abandon relationships that no longer served their emotional and financial needs reflects similar attitudes toward marital flexibility. Schwartzberg attributes some of these beliefs to "mobile societ[ies]," migratory occupations, and a legacy of frontier societies, such as in the West and Appalachia. Wheeling, an Appalachian city whose river location offered great mobility and migratory occupations, and Kentucky, which had once been the western edge of the United States, drew from all of these. Tazewell's identity, both Appalachian and southern, could explain the contradictions of numerous adulterous women and the patriarchal system men worked to strengthen.

In other cases, emancipation contributed to a new language of freedom, challenging the South's hierarchical social structure. Especially in the rhetoric of departing women in the border South, one can see evidence of rumbles within the traditional southern household. When Iva Boyd sued her husband, Thomas, for a divorce in 1868, she told the Franklin County Circuit Court that they had married in the months following the close of the war but he had abandoned her within one month. Though she made every "proper womanly advancement" to obtain his return, Thomas refused to ever live with her again and left for St. Louis. Iva steadfastly told the court that she did not "desire to be interfered with, or controlled by a man who loves her not."[24] Though Iva's statement seems to imply that she might allow a man who loved her to have authority over her, it also hints at the ways in which some border South women took back some power from wayward husbands and refused to submit unquestioningly to a subordinate position. While Iva Boyd employed the rhetoric of power and control to obtain relief as an abandoned spouse, Lenarca McDonald did so when acting as the abandoner herself. Ambrose McDonald married Lenarca Snelling in April 1863, and the couple lived together for three years before Lenarca left their home in late spring 1866. According to James Christopher, a boarder at the McDonald home, Lenarca told Ambrose that she was "a free woman" and "would go where she pleased."[25]

Similarly, Cynthia Warren, a Kentucky resident, employed the language of freedom to defend her actions against her husband. Married in early 1863, William and Cynthia Warren resided in Kentucky with their two children until her departure for Indiana in late 1868. The couple's relationship had always been rocky, and the pair had separated on multiple occasions before her final abandonment. In his petition, William Warren questioned the paternity of at least one of his sons, hinting at possible adultery, though never stating it outright.[26] John F. Poe, less subtle, stated that Cynthia was "too fond of othr men." Poe told the court he had confronted Cynthia about her indelicacy a year before her final departure. She told him "she was a free woman and would do as she pleased."[27] Lenarca McDonald and Cynthia Warren's use of the rhetoric of freedom to make unconventional marital choices suggests the influence of emancipation on marriage and gender roles in the border South.[28] While much of the region's postwar marital pattern echoed antebellum precedent, emancipation did not fail to affect some aspects of border South relationships.

While the bustling border South might expose illicit love affairs to prying eyes, it also provided some protection for women in abusive relationships. In Kentucky and West Virginia, the meeting of urban, rural, and western cultures created a propensity for violence. One couple's story provides a useful example. Elizabeth and Thomas Slattery married in the early

1850s and had seven children together before she sued him for divorce in 1869. By that time, the couple lived in Frankfort in a pair of tenements near the Kentucky River bridge. From 1868 to 1869, Thomas's behavior became increasingly erratic and violent toward his wife. According to Elizabeth, Thomas assaulted her, threatened her life, and even drew a pistol on her.[29]

Elizabeth employed the protection of the community during the relationship, while acting defiantly to stop her husband's attacks. In January 1868, after her husband abused her, she called for two local watchmen to "come and arrest" him. When they arrived, George Goodwin and David Kirkpatrick overheard Thomas call his wife "a damned bitch" and "a damned whore," before he accused her of sleeping with other men and drinking. In response to her tears, Thomas slapped his wife. Elizabeth firmly responded, "Dont you slap me again." This retort was followed quickly by another slap. When Thomas came barreling out to retrieve his gun from next door, Goodwin and Kirkpatrick arrested him.[30]

On another occasion, a neighbor informed Goodwin that Thomas was trying to kill his wife again. When Goodwin arrived on the scene, he saw Thomas run from his store to his home, push a gun through the window, and threaten to shoot. Another night, as he was lighting the streetlamps, Kirkpatrick heard passersby "both white and black" commenting, "Slattery is drunk again and abusing his wife." When he finished his work, he went to the Slattery home and heard Thomas yelling, "Where is your damned watchman now."[31] Clearly the community knew of this couple's marital difficulties and sought to use collective resources to intervene.[32] Yet, Elizabeth was not a passive recipient of their aid. She called for the night watchmen on multiple occasions and angrily resisted her husband's abuse.

Some women used community assistance to protect other women from attack. In June 1864, Frances Martin visited her daughter, Eliza Jane, after she heard rumors that Eliza Jane's husband, William, was beating her. When she arrived at their Wheeling home, she found her daughter in a sorry state. "Her eyes were all blacked and the side of her head bruised, and four finger marks around her neck," Frances told the Ohio County Circuit Court. She added, "Her mouth was also bleeding." William admitted abusing his wife and defiantly told his mother-in-law that he "would do it again; and he didn't consider it any of my business neither."[33] Yet, Frances Martin did consider it her business and sought actively to protect her daughter against her husband's power, calling on the community for help. The following Sunday night, "several men" accompanied her to the Armstrong home to remove Eliza Jane's furniture and personal things.[34] Without their close urban networks, similar to those found by Christine Stansell in New York City, women may not have been able to take such action.[35]

In Frankfort, Louisa Rodgers worked to protect her daughter from sexual slander and herself from financial trouble. Thomas and Sarah Young lived with her parents during their brief marriage. He eventually abandoned her, accusing her of concealing the fact that she was pregnant by another man at the time of their wedding. Her mother, Louisa, vehemently denied the charges and told the court she had confirmed with Thomas that the baby was his before their marriage. While Thomas insisted that he had left the Rodgers home immediately after his wife gave birth to her first child, Louisa Rodgers stated that he had lived with them for years, until about six weeks before the divorce trial and slept there "often enough to have another child for me to maintain." Rodgers clearly resented Thomas's behavior and lamented, "I have been treated as though I had no feelings."[36] Louisa Rodgers asserted her right to respect and authority in her household and expressed frustration with Thomas for taking advantage of her.

Border South women also asserted their rights to divorce, if their marriage failed to live up to expectations.[37] Women filed for two-thirds of the divorces in Ohio County, Franklin County, and Warren County during this period. Divorce was after all, in Norma Basch's words, "a woman's remedy." Women were more likely to seek relief when deserted because of the legal disabilities coverture and marriage placed on them.[38] Yet, the proportion was inverted in Tazewell and Amelia Counties in the postwar era.[39] In addition, many border South women chose to end their relationship first, without waiting for a husband's adultery or abandonment as an excuse. Therefore, the charges in some of the other one-third of these divorce cases reflect women who abandoned their husbands, acted unfaithfully, behaved cruelly, or consumed alcohol and drugs.[40] Some women freely admitted to friends and neighbors that they had abandoned their marriages; their willingness to do so may reflect border South residents' acceptance of marital dissolution and female agency in this action.[41]

For example, John Robinson overheard Amanda Trimble telling someone that she had twice "voluntarily" left her husband and his children and finally driven them off. She defiantly informed her former sister-in-law that she was "glad to get rid" of Ephraim and that "she had never lived happier in her life than she had done since she had been rid of him." Some seemed to accept her decision. One friend told the court that she had heard Amanda "had done a bad business in marrying."[42] Also from Wheeling, Augusta Lindemuth abandoned her husband, Louis, in April 1867, and moved in with her parents in Centre Wheeling. Louis told the court that he asked for her to return but she refused. His neighbor and friend, August Hellenbriche, testified that he also went to take Augusta home and she "said she would'nt do it."[43]

In Franklin County, Martha Taylor embraced the chaos of the war years, donning male clothing and conducting numerous adulterous relationships. In one case, she and another woman, both dressed in Confederate uniforms, dropped in on a woman in Owen County to ask for a drink of whiskey. Others reported that she used this masculine garb to travel through the neighborhood at night and meet her illicit lovers. When questioned by her husband, she defiantly declared that she "loved other men better than she did him."[44] Martha's choice of garb reflects her symbolic decision to reject her husband's control and reclaim her sexual agency and power. She donned a man's clothing and a man's position in the breakdown of her marriage.

One Kentucky woman, Mary Ann Gears, told the court that her husband's failure to support her "forced" her to abandon him. Married at eighteen, "being almost a child," she soon found her marital hopes dashed, when Charles Gears proved to be drunk, obscene, and abusive.[45] Other wives acted in an aggressive and reportedly unfeminine manner, prompting their husbands to seek divorce. Reportedly, James Leasure's wife, Elizabeth, attacked him and consumed large quantities of brandy, whiskey, and laudanum. He stated that, even more appallingly, she "frequently appears on the public streets in a state of intoxication, exposing her person to the public in such a manner as to mortify and wound the feelings" of her husband.[46]

In Warren County, Edmund Scotland told the court that his wife, Julia, did not behave as a proper wife should. Julia refused to wash or mend his clothes or to go to the local market and buy food for their meals. Having done his part by working and providing her money, he fully expected her to uphold her end of the deal. Even more egregiously, however, Julia responded to his attempts to fix these problems with obscenities. This behavior, he stated, was made more "offensive" by her use of tobacco, which she both chewed and smoked. When angry, she would even spit this tobacco on him. Similarly, Kate McNamara allegedly drank constantly during her marriage to Edward. One night, heavily intoxicated, she even drew a gun on him and "snapped it at him."[47]

In Tazewell County, multiple women were accused of abusiveness toward their husbands; this certainly occurred in southern households but was definitely not openly discussed. White southern men had traditionally been defined by their assertive and almost violent masculinity. They were expected to run strict homes in which dependents, whether white or black, fell in line or were severely punished. Accusations of weakness met with violent defenses, such as dueling, caning, or eye-gouging, depending on one's location or class. To admit that a wife was abusive and controlling was to risk unmanning oneself in the community and to reveal a frightening loss of authority in the very place that vested men with that communal power in the first place.

Elderly William Buchanon filed cruelty charges against his wife on two separate occasions. A widower, he married Mary, hoping to find a partner and a marriage based on harmony and love. Mary, who proved ill-tempered and abusive, stated that she did not share in his love. After "frequently receiving at her hands blows & bodily injuries," he moved into another home in the neighborhood. Later, he reported, she told a friend that she would have killed him if he had not left and given her their home. Despite the threat of violence and even death, William still tried to support his wife and children, giving them grain, meat, and wood. When she had used all this, she would take more from him, threatening his life again if he objected. In his first petition, he called her an "unnatural wife," who "compelled" him to "yield submissively to her."[48] Clearly, William saw her assumption of authority, violent or otherwise, as contrary to proper gender norms. However, he was not afraid of admitting that he had submitted passively to his own wife. Perhaps this was because of his age, which he used as his defense. He told the court, "Your orator is too old and infirm and physically unable to protect himself against her violence, even if he were disposed to do so, against a woman."[49]

William's first case went nowhere, languishing on the docket with no response or deponents to support his claims. Most likely, he soon returned to Mary and the cycle of abuse continued. When he filed a new case three years later, he stated that the couple's children had encouraged him to do so and the deciding factor had been Mary's latest round of abuse, which had left him bruised and bloodied. This time he tried to ensure his success by adding a charge of adultery, since enduring a wife's adultery was even more shocking than enduring her abuse. However, few witnesses could provide more evidence than that Mary had sat closely with John Fox, one of her son's friends. One woman swore that Mary stated that "she would sleep with John Fox if it would get her a divorce" but even she could not actually say that that affair actually occurred.[50]

More interestingly, Mary herself responded to William's accusations this time. She refused to allow him to slander her with an accusation of adultery but did not deny the charge of cruelty. The couple agreed, in a statement with dubious legality in a Virginia courtroom, that William could only take evidence on the charge of cruelty.[51] Why did Mary find one charge so much more odious than the other? Clearly, she believed her sexual reputation to be more important than the assumption that she was cruel, unkind, and violent toward her elderly husband. This could reflect a southern community's moral values, or it could have been a conscious choice to maintain one charge in order to obtain a divorce she also desired. Such a choice would have been an interesting indication of contractualism and collusion in this Appalachian community. However, whatever the reason, the contract mattered little in the case's outcome. William Buchanon died only a few months after filing his second petition, and the case devolved into a property dispute among the couple's children.

Other cases in Tazewell County paint a different picture of the dynamics between men and women in the community. When Delila Champ attempted to get a divorce from her abusive husband, John, he quickly responded in an attack on her femininity and a defense of his own actions. During their short marriage, he wrote, Delila had been "insulting & provoking" and had used cruel and obscene language against him. She threatened to poison him and flaunted her feelings for other men. While he denied frequently beating her, he admitted that he might have occasionally used "moderate coercion," but only when provoked. He asserted that a husband had the right to respect and authority in the home and defied the court to reject that. Similarly, in response to his wife's request for custody of their child, he stated flat out that a father's right to a child was superior to the mother's, a fact that was uncertain during this period of transition in domesticity.[52] Still, John Champ believed that he was master of his own small world and, especially in the postwar period, denied the court's authority to usurp it. It appears that he was successful. The case was quickly dismissed.

Women's unconventional behavior is most readily apparent in Ohio County, West Virginia. Compared with the other counties, Ohio County husbands employed a larger range of charges against their wives. While Virginia men in Tazewell, Amelia, and Fauquier Counties stuck to the charges of adultery and abandonment and Franklin and Warren County men added only fraud to that mix, Ohio County husbands charged their wives with adultery, abandonment, cruelty, intemperance, and fraud—sometimes with more than one of these at once. In this volatile and fluid environment, Wheeling women acted in unusual and assertive ways.

Many nineteenth-century women sought divorces because their husbands failed to act as proper providers, but border South divorce cases suggest that women, especially if their husbands failed to support them, often worked outside the home to assist their family, with less social censure.[53] In border South marriages, women contributed financially to the relationship and were commended for it; this reflected the working-class attitudes of many citizens, but also the infiltration of northern middle-class attitudes into cities on the edge of the South.[54]

After her husband abandoned her in December 1860, Elizabeth Goudy supported herself through work. In her 1868 divorce case, witnesses applauded her decision to do so.[55] Another Wheeling woman shared a similar story. Mary Hoffman's husband had never provided a home, so, to care for their two children, she became a seamstress, keeping and "cloth[ing] them by her needle."[56] Catherine Heston was also commended by witnesses for her hard-working behavior after her abandonment. Her husband, a convicted felon who served time for counterfeiting, deserted her and their three children in 1864. Her neighbor, Thomas Bayles, supported her decision to support herself by taking in sewing, calling her an "industrious, prudent woman." Michael Shields stated that Catherine worked whenever she could get something to do. No fewer than three deponents used the word "industrious" to describe Catherine, sometimes multiple times in a deposition.[57]

Henrietta Baily spoke of her work with pride in her petition. Her father had provided her with an excellent education that enabled her to teach after her husband, Gallatin, abandoned her. With her work, she wrote, she felt sure that she could provide for and support her sons.[58] Most Americans at this time believed that a husband should provide economic support for his wife, but white southerners, in particular, were resistant to the idea of a wife earning wages to financially contribute to her family, under any circumstance.[59] Yet, in divorce cases in the border South, women were applauded for stepping into the breadwinner's role. In Henrietta's case, she explicitly took on the masculine role of provider and wanted to carry it on even after her divorce was settled. She had all the necessary skills and desired to be the head of her own household.

Historians have shown that in the nineteenth-century South men and women believed relationships to be a bargain of sorts—men supported, provided for, and protected their wives, who in turn promised to honor, obey, and submit to their husbands.[60] In the border South, some women took it upon themselves to provide for their families. In other cases, assertive working-class women refused to uphold this bargain and defied southern domestic expectations. Samuel Hebrank declared that his wife, Justina, refused to "provide for the house," despite the fact that he "fully provid[ed] her with all the necessaries and comforts of life which one in her station and life demanded."[61] Samuel merely asked that Justina create a warm and welcoming environment—a haven—for him when he returned from the business world.[62] Justina, however, left their home every day from morning until night and did not have dinner prepared when Samuel came home from work at the end of the day.[63] By her refusal to submit to remain in the private sphere, Justina demonstrated her rejection of the domestic role.

Ephraim Trimble's relatives also accused Amanda Trimble of neglecting her domestic duties. According to her former mother-in-law, Amanda "would not cook provisions . . . when it was brought in," even though Ephraim provided "flour by the barrel." Amanda was wantonly wasteful, throwing "beef steak in the yard to spoil and allow[ing] vegetables, peas, and beans to do the same."[64] Amanda's stubborn refusal to act in a proper domestic fashion even forced her husband to cook the meals. Liney and Holland Harrod, a middle-aged couple from Franklin County, Kentucky, had a similar story. Liney accused Holland of abandonment, but he stated that her behavior had made his action necessary. For years, he told the court, Liney had been "dissatisfied & unsettled in her ways." She would "take a notion" not to "perform her domestic duties such as cooking milking &c," leaving Holland and their sons to do it. It was this refusal to perform her wifely duties that led Holland to take Liney to her father's home. Holland believed that Liney had failed to uphold her end of the marital contract by not caring for their home and family.[65]

Tazewell County was a rural community reasserting its southern identity; thus, race may also have played a factor in the hesitation of white Tazewell County men to allow white women to defy their authority. The precarious line between white and black is revealed in a handful of cases in a community that had been only tangentially involved in the antebellum slave economy. In some cases, accusations were subtle. William Staten told the court that one night he had seen Sabra Ann Wimmer in close conversation with a black man in the neighborhood.[66] This charge, although not repeated by any other witness, may, in addition to her husband's accusations of adultery, have been enough to show the court that she was not afraid to flaunt the strict rules of southern life. Similarly, Gabriel Asberry accused his wife of leaving him and living with a black man. Although the paramour's race was not confirmed by Gabriel's witnesses, they did confirm Gemimina's infidelity, and he received a speedy divorce.[67]

Even the few black women in the neighborhood could be attacked for their decision to cross the color line, in defiance of a major social convention. In 1870, Dr. Thomas Painter visited Millie Williams, a black woman, to help deliver her child. Although he failed to remember the sex of the child during her husband's divorce proceedings, he had been "forcibly impressed with the extremely white skin of the child." He had confronted Millie with the fact, although he did not bother to note her response. His only other evidence of an interracial adulterous relationship lay in what he termed the "careless attention given the child." His testimony, a fascinating bundle of racist stereotypes and assumptions, failed to acknowledge the sordid history of race in the South, which could have produced a mixed-race child without Millie's infidelity, and quickly assumed that a black woman was an unfit mother. Yet, based only on his testimony and that of Henry Williams's employer, who merely stated that Henry was black and therefore could not have a "white child," the court divorced the couple.[68] In a southern community in the post-emancipation era, racial lines had to be strictly enforced, and women who crossed these lines strictly punished.

As the stories of these various women demonstrate, there was no universally accepted conception of the proper role of the female residents of the border South, and this role was often contested in streets and homes. Amanda, Hettie, and Barbara Trimble, Mary Hoffman, Elizabeth Leasure, Liney Harrold, and thousands of other women inhabited a region of overlapping cultural, ethnic, racial, economic, and regional borders in which multiple gender ideologies came together. Rarely content to remain quiet, these women publicly challenged their female neighbors, who also had no qualms about defending their behaviors and beliefs. Of course, in a bustling town, secrets were hard to hide. However, the unique combination of urban claustrophobia and a border-like array of identities and attitudes toward marital gender roles may have decreased some women's desire to conceal their behavior. It gave them an avenue through which to challenge badly behaving husbands and, at the same time, to assert their rights to start new relationships and to end old ones. The contending ideological and social views in the border South allowed its citizens the cognitive space to explore new philosophies of marriage, the public and private roles of women, and the bounds of proper behavior. As they interpreted the new desire for mutuality in gender relationships in their own ways, some women grasped the opportunity to act untraditionally and confidently and to make room for their own perception of a woman's place in society and marriage.

Conclusion

A Complicated Legacy

During the hot summer months of the nation's centennial, thirty-three-year-old Semantha Morgan, of Poca, West Virginia, faced a grave peril. Recently married to John Morgan Jr., she was now pregnant with their first child and very much feared the dangers of childbirth. Though she filled her letters to John with love and affection, she also drifted frequently into melancholy and gloom, warning him that she might not be with him much longer. By August, "owing to the uncertainty of life at any time and the peculiar danger" she would soon face, Semantha drew up a will and sent it to John. She admitted that she had few belongings but instructed him to dispose of them carefully to her friends and family. She also demanded that he keep her Bible and "continue to read it, for my sake, and make an effort to believe it." Should their baby survive, Semantha asked that the child be educated by certain teachers and be given the opportunity to cultivate artistic talent. Finally, she gave John permission to remarry if he found a woman who would "make [him] happy." She ended the document simply, "My Dear Husband you have made me very happy. All is well."[1]

Fortunately, Semantha survived her ordeal, and by the summer of 1881, the couple had three sons. John worked hard to support the little family, so hard that he became sick. Upon hearing this news, Semantha wrote to chide him, "What is it to me or these sweet children that you are working and striving to make a little something for us, when you will not be able to enjoy any thing." She urged him to rest and return home, especially since she knew he was lonely without his children. To entice him, she detailed their daily activities (Johnny dragged old chains around the house, Tom was friendly with everyone, and all three behaved "real nice at the table").[2] We can only assume from the large gap in further weekly letters following this request that John quickly returned to his family.

John and Semantha Morgan's correspondence throughout the 1870s and early 1880s reflects many of the trends that had become commonplace in border South marriages by the end of Reconstruction. While not yet his legal or social equal, Semantha wrote to John with a confidence that suggests she expected him to take her opinions and wishes seriously. Faced with the dangers of childbirth, she wrote a will, claiming at least some small bits of personal property as her own and asserting her right to affect her child's life even after her own had ended. Her reassurance that he had made her happy implicitly suggests that this had been a goal of his. As their family grew, Semantha requested that John put his family and the domestic sphere first, a request that she hinted fell easily in line with his own true desires. Ultimately, their correspondence reflects the impact of the philosophies of mutuality and individualism on this successful marriage.

This book explores how Semantha Atkeson Morgan, a woman born in a slaveholding southern state, and John Morgan, a man who served with the Twenty-Second Virginia Regiment of the Confederate army, developed such marital attitudes. The Morgans, whose gentle words of affection seem so unlike those of the volatile Trimbles who opened this book, are nonetheless part of the same story. The Trimbles and the Morgans reflect the learned sensibilities of this unique time and place. Perched between North and South during the crucible of the Civil War, nestled along the bustling Ohio River and the gateway to the American Midwest, transitioning from slavery to freedom, the border South in the mid-nineteenth century was a region in flux. At its heart, two states, Kentucky and West Virginia, exemplified this fluidity. These were states that resisted secession but wearied of the abolitionist impulses of their northern neighbors, states that helped defeat the Confederacy but were reluctant to see the slave system die, states that gave birth to moderates and compromisers as well as to the presidents of both the Union and Confederacy, states whose identities were so ill-defined that their "southernness" remains contested to this day. All of this confusion and contradiction trickled down into hilly farms, into homes above storefronts, into riverboats, into the boardinghouses, and into windy lanes and the rough wooden walls of rural cabins.

Buffeted about by these prevailing winds, border southerners adapted their lives to the turbulence of the times and created lasting marriages built on respect, love, and admiration for one another. Unfolding their letters, now brown and wrinkled, historians can glimpse the negotiations between men and women in this region as they met and tried to determine whether their future partners would share these ideals. Women demurred, struggling to assess young men's intentions. Men parried, trying intense proclamations of love and then settling on promises of friendship and companionship. Marriage, once formed, was no different. Border southerners were not alone in exploring these firmly held Victorian ideals of sentimentality and romanticism, but they proved their commitment to them in their legislative halls and their courtrooms. While many might find divorce cases an odd place to find evidence of these philosophies, the legal system became an ideal arena for border southerners to define and defend their understandings of marriage and gender roles. Divorcing couples questioned the wisdom of remaining married when relationships failed to meet the standard of mutuality and individualism and were unfazed about the broader implications of these divorces. Their ability to achieve a successful separation, many couples even working together to reach that goal, suggests that others in this region agreed.

Even as the war tore the country in two, border southerners remained adaptable. West Virginia men wielded their moderate masculinity as a shield, deflecting the criticism and slights of secessionists. When they created their new state, their laws reflected this moderation and drew from northern and midwestern traditions. Women found new power and purpose in defending their homes on the war-torn home front, and men turned easily to them for support. When the war ended, border southerners' antebellum flexibility enabled them to weather the storm of emancipation and Reconstruction with greater ease than other southerners. Although divorce rates increased in the years immediately following the conflict, it was not nearly as disruptive to society, since many litigants deployed the same language of mutuality, individualism, and contractualism that had made prewar cases successful. Certainly, the region was not a utopia. Its black citizens, after all, found little reason for optimism in the postwar border South. Nonetheless, retrenchment in one area (racial hierarchy) was not accompanied by retrenchment in another (gender hierarchy), and the border South became a progressive outpost in a region that lagged behind the rest of the country in the late nineteenth century.

This book's story ends in the mid-1870s, as Reconstruction waned and the ultimate legacy of the Civil War and black emancipation remained uncertain. In the wake of emancipation, border citizens, displaying their characteristic adaptability, continued to cultivate an identity of moderation, at least in their households. Their retention of mutuality, individualism, and contractualism in their homes suggests that, at least until the close of Reconstruction, these places retained their border characteristics. However, as Reconstruction in the South ended and the postwar racial backlash took a stronger hold, the border identities of Kentucky and West Virginia seemingly began to fade. In her recent study of Civil War memory in the Bluegrass State, Anne Marshall argues that in the years following the war, Kentuckians cemented their new Confederate identities through racial violence, Democratic political dominion, memorialization efforts, and literary and theatrical works.[3] As Kentuckians embraced this new philosophy, did they lose their border identity completely? And if they did, did they lose the progressive attitudes toward marriage that had accompanied it? Perhaps, as the state's citizens splintered into various Unionist, emancipationist, and Confederate strands of historical memory, perceptions of gender fractured as well. Either way, just as this shift obscured Kentucky's Union past from future generations, so too did it hide the state's progressive record regarding marriage and divorce.

Likewise, in West Virginia, long-term political changes and stubborn contemporary narratives disguise unusual trends in the past. In the southern counties of West Virginia, many bemoaned their state's decision to secede, and, following suit with other southern states, "redeemers" swept into power in the decades after the war, threatening the immediate postwar changes in divorce and marriage.[4] In addition, the "southern" identity of West Virginia was soon challenged by a new regional affiliation. Known today as the heart of Appalachia, West Virginia's border identity—like Kentucky's—has been lost, overwhelmed by the power of a late nineteenth-century movement. Travel writers and folklorists who explored the southern Appalachian Mountains at the turn of the century crafted narratives of isolation and backwardness.[5] As historians work to complicate the region's past by overturning these tropes, a glimpse into one state's pre-Appalachian identity as a mid-nineteenth-century border state demonstrates the region's participation in a national web of cultural networks and the implications of this interconnectedness on gender roles in the household.[6]

Such changes lie beyond the scope of this book. Nonetheless, questions remain about how these late nineteenth-century identity crises affected the structure of marriage in these states. In addition, we cannot fully understand the impact of border culture on this region's relationships until we address more deeply how this experience differed for black residents of these states. From the antebellum border South's mix of slavery and freedom to the postwar years of racial turmoil and retrenchment, black border southerners had to navigate a far different social structure than their white counterparts during this era. To what extent did their household gender roles reflect those of the white border South detailed by this book? How, in turn, did their familial structures affect the larger border South culture? Since black border southerners lacked legal access to marriage or divorce for much of this period, it is a challenging subject to investigate but one very much worth the effort. Black border southerners, after all, made up a pivotal part of the cultural mosaic that created this fluid society.

Finally, this work also suggests the power of using the lens of border scholarship to study places that do not fit the typical regional framework. Specifically, I would urge Appalachian historians to consider the ways in which places like Kentucky and West Virginia remained "borders" well into the twentieth century. Despite the efforts of so-called regional experts in the wake of the 2016 election to craft a revitalized narrative of an isolated, white, and rural Appalachia, contemporary Appalachian historians have made great strides in debunking these myths.[7] The history of Appalachia and the region of Appalachia today are filled with stories more complicated, diverse, progressive, and even more radical than many would suspect. Resurrecting moments of progress in the nineteenth century, such as those stories in this book, goes a long way toward disproving the mythology of Appalachia as a backward region. Continuing to emphasize how this region, still an economic, political, racial, and geographical border, has been influenced by this fusion and multiplicity of ideas goes even further. It is my hope that this book helps reconceptualize our understanding of nineteenth-century southern culture, the connections between place and gender hierarchy, and, ultimately, the influence of borderlands and regional identity on American life.

Acknowledgments

While it is a cliché to note that writing a book is a collective rather than individual endeavor, such a sentiment has become commonplace because it remains so true. In one iteration or another, this book has been a part of my life for the last thirteen years. Along the way, friends, family members, mentors, and colleagues have encouraged me, offered me suggestions, read my work, distracted me when I needed a mental break, housed me on research trips, collected cases, and given me the flexibility and support to see this project through. Their inclusion in these acknowledgments is my way of thanking them, but it pales in comparison with the tremendous impact they have had on my life.

Ken Fones-Wolf was my first graduate mentor. He shepherded me through the master's program at West Virginia University, encouraging me to explore the relationship between regional identity and gender roles during the statehood process. Without his help, I could not have written this book or taken my next step—the PhD program at the University of Florida.

At the University of Florida, Bill Link and Matthew Gallman challenged my understanding of the South and my view of regionalism, and they made me a better writer. In research and reading seminars, symposiums, conferences, and workshops with renowned scholars, they provided me with a rich intellectual environment to explore these ideas, to stumble and learn to improve my work, to express myself, and to grow as a scholar. They commented on countless drafts and versions of this work, and I thank them for the time and effort they put into me and into this project. Bill Link especially has been a tremendous mentor, and ultimately, friend. He is that rare find—an advisor who cares for students' well-being both within and beyond the classroom. He gave me opportunities to travel, network with critical scholars, and publish in a fantastic edited collection, and he cheered me on while I navigated the job market. I thank him for his generosity and kindness.

My fellow graduate students at West Virginia University and the University of Florida were my earliest, harshest, and most helpful critics. At WVU, I benefited from the advice and assistance of older graduate students, who never saw me as a mere "M.A." At the University of Florida, intellectual conversations were so absorbing that we could not contain them to the classroom, often continuing them across the street over a pint of beer and a basket of fries. In my years at UF, my friends taught me a lot about history, but they taught me even more about work–life balance, sustaining me through the grueling marathon of graduate school. Although I would truly like to thank them all, I would especially like to thank Angela Diaz, Scott Huffard, Jenn Lyon, Matt Hall, Allen Kent, Timothy Fritz, Aurélia Aubert, Roger Smith, Clay Cooper, Jim Broomall, Erin Zavitz, Johanna Mellis, and Joe Beatty. Most of all, I would like to thank Erin Conlin. We met as prospective students in the spring of 2008, and we have been friends since. She is the master of the pep talk, whether in person or via text, and she is incredibly generous with her time and affection. She has read countless versions of this work, and I appreciate her friendship and her help.

Archivists from around the South assisted me with finding sources. Thank you to all those who helped me at the Kentucky Historical Society, the Filson Historical Society, the Virginia Historical Society, the Library of Virginia, the Southern Historical Collection, and the West Virginia and Regional History Center. I am especially grateful for grants from the Kentucky Historical Society, the Filson Historical Society, and the Virginia Historical Society, which allowed me to complete this work. I also appreciate the efforts of both graduate and undergraduate students who helped research and comment on this work. W. Hal Gorby and Adam Zucconi helped collect cases from the West Virginia and Regional History Center. Christian Ruth and Stefanie King photographed and organized the Warren County court cases from the Kentucky Department of Libraries and Archives. Carly Everhart created the maps for the book, lending her experience in both geography and history to craft a thoughtful product. At Appalachian State, two American women's history classes read through samples of cases from all six counties and lent a fresh eye to the material. Their excitement and inspiration gave me momentum in the final years of the project.

Over the years, I have been fortunate enough to get feedback from a number of scholars at workshops, conferences, and through mentorship programs. I am grateful to them for giving their time and expertise so that I could make this a better project. Michele Gillespie read this work when it was still in its early stages and helped refine my ideas. She commented on later drafts at conferences, and most importantly, she has been a supportive and cheerful mentor at all times. Stephanie Cole, Aaron Astor, Amy Murrell Taylor, Jane Turner Censer, Jeffrey McClurken, Faye Yarbrough, Catherine Clinton, Sean Adams, Louise Newman, Sevan Terzian, Deborah Blackwell, Robin Sager, Jennifer L. Anderson, Jessica Wilkerson, William Davenport Mercer, and many others have commented on parts of this book at one time or another. I thank them for their suggestions. Two anonymous readers for the University Press of Kentucky read my proposal and manuscript and gave thoughtful critiques. As always, these readers have critically improved this work; any mistakes in it are my responsibility alone.

I have been very lucky to have the University Press of Kentucky as a publisher for this book. Anne Dean Dotson, especially, has been an encouraging and enthusiastic editor. She has helped me navigate and learn the publishing process, especially when a critical deadline coincided with the birth of my second child. I am so grateful for her help and support. Natalie O'Neal has also been communicative and responsive, even to the smallest questions. Thank you to the advisory board, the marketing team, the editing department, and the production team for helping create this book.

I was incredibly fortunate to find a home at Appalachian State University after graduate school. My colleagues in the history department have given me countless opportunities to succeed as a scholar and a teacher. They have modeled how to excel as a professor, and they have given me feedback on my work in multiple ways. Without their support and help, I could not have made the tricky maneuver from adjunct to assistant professor in just a few years.

Finally, my family deserves thanks. I have been fortunate to have a large extended family who cares deeply about history and learning. They have listened to me talk about my research for years. When I joined the Hicks family, they generously added history to their family vacations, pointing out museums in the most unexpected places. My sister, Emma, served as a research assistant at one point, but really just deserves thanks for being my first and longest friend.

My parents served as my first role models, bestowing upon me an intensive love of history and learning. They have encouraged me, talked through my ideas, read my work, and were integral to the research process. My father, as an archivist in the West Virginia and Regional History Center, found critical sources and steered me in the right direction from the earliest stages of this project. My mother accessed databases and articles and even, during one particularly hectic summer, served as my research assistant. Their help has been invaluable. More than just intellectual models, though, my parents' relationship—loving, complementary, supportive, and full of mutuality—is one that I have often thought of while I completed this book. Although our society and our regional environment may influence our romantic relationships, often our parents are our first example, and mine gave me a wonderful one. I thank them for that.

My husband, William, is a partner in every sense of the word. My triumphs and successes are also his. Through graduate school, he literally sat beside me while we simultaneously finished our dissertations. He listened to endless hours of frustration, excitement, panic, and confusion. Although I was not always a willing student, he taught me how to use Stata and is responsible for the charts and graphs in this book. In the final stages of the book, he sacrificed his own precious research time to enable me to maximize mine. He is everything I could want: a loving friend, a critical reviewer, and a wonderful cook. Thank you.

And last but never least, I thank my two beautiful sons—Henry and Walter. They are quite simply the most joyous things in my life. Although they are too young to read it, I hope that one day they can learn half as much from my work as I have learned from being their mother.

Notes

Abbreviations

FHS	Filson Historical Society, Louisville, Kentucky
KDLA	Kentucky Department for Libraries and Archives, Frankfort, Kentucky
KHS	Kentucky Historical Society, Frankfort, Kentucky
LVA	Library of Virginia, Richmond, Virginia
NARA	National Archives and Records Administration, Washington, DC
SHC	Southern Historical Collection, Chapel Hill, North Carolina
VHS	Virginia Historical Society, Richmond, Virginia
WVRHC	West Virginia and Regional History Center, Morgantown, West Virginia

Introduction

1. Seventh Census of the United States, 1850, National Archives Microfilm Publication M432, 1,009 rolls, Records of the Bureau of the Census, Record Group 29, National Archives and Records Administration, Washington, DC (hereafter, NARA), accessed through the subscription database Ancestry.com (hereafter, Seventh Census of the United States, 1850); *Trimble, Amanda M. v. Trimble, Ephraim* (1868), Ohio County Circuit Court Records, West Virginia and Regional History Center, Morgantown, West Virginia (hereafter, WVRHC), env. 276 b-5; Ancestry.com, *West Virginia Deaths Index, 1853–1973* (database on-line) (Provo, UT: Ancestry.com Operations, Inc., 2011).

2. *Trimble, Amanda M. v. Trimble, Ephraim* (1868), Ohio County Circuit Court Records, WVRHC, env. 276 b-5.

3. *Williams' Wheeling Directory City Guide and Business Mirror for 1864* (Wheeling, WV: Williams & Co., 1864). Accessed on the subscription database Ancestry.com; *Trimble, Amanda M. v. Trimble, Ephraim* (1868), Ohio County Circuit Court Records, WVRHC, env. 276 b-5; *Ohio, Marriages, 1803–1900* (database on-line) (Provo, UT: Ancestry.com).

4. 1870 US Census, population schedules, NARA microfilm publication M593, 1,761 rolls, NARA, accessed through the subscription database Ancestry.com (hereafter 1870 US Census).

5. NARA; Consolidated Lists of Civil War Draft Registration Records (Provost Marshal General's Bureau; Consolidated Enrollment Lists, 1863–1865);

Record Group: 110, Records of the Provost Marshal General's Bureau (Civil War); Collection Name: Consolidated Enrollment Lists, 1863–1865 (Civil War Union Draft Records); NAI: 4213514; Archive vol.: 2 of 4, accessed through Ancestry.com; *Trimble, Amanda M. v. Trimble, Ephraim* (1868), Ohio County Circuit Court Records, WVRHC, env. 276 b-5.

6. *Trimble, Amanda M. v. Trimble, Ephraim* (1868), Ohio County Circuit Court Records, WVRHC, env. 276 b-5.

7. Ibid.

8. There appears to have been some confusion about Nancy's last name. Sometimes she's called Nancy Sherman, sometimes Shermaid. Either way, I have been unable to find information on her through census records.

9. *Trimble, Amanda M. v. Trimble, Ephraim* (1868), Ohio County Circuit Court Records, WVRHC, env. 276 b-5.

10. Ibid.

11. For more on the river as a boundary and means of escape, see Matthew Salafia, *Slavery's Borderlands: Freedom and Bondage along the Ohio River* (Philadelphia: University of Pennsylvania Press, 2013), 2–9.

12. Amy Murrell Taylor, *The Divided Family in Civil War America* (Chapel Hill: University of North Carolina Press, 2005), 3; Aaron Astor, *Rebels on the Border: Civil War, Emancipation, and the Reconstruction of Kentucky and Missouri* (Baton Rouge, Louisiana State University Press, 2012), 3, 8. Astor calls Kentucky a "western replication" of what Barbara Fields refers to as the "middle ground." Barbara Jeanne Fields, *Slavery and Freedom on the Middle Ground: Maryland during the Nineteenth Century* (New Haven: Yale University Press, 1985). See also Stephen Berry, *House of Abraham: Lincoln and the Todds, a Family Divided by War* (New York: Houghton Mifflin, 2007), 67.

13. Diane Mutti Burke was one of the first to explore households in the region in her recent work, *On Slavery's Border: Missouri's Small Slaveholding Households, 1815–1865* (Athens: University of Georgia Press, 2010). Her purpose is to demonstrate "how small-scale slavery affected the families and communities of both slaves and owners, as well as the many ways their lives intersected." Her work demands that other communities in the border area receive the same thoughtful treatment and that historians continue to explore border households as their relationship with slavery faltered after the Civil War. Burke, *On Slavery's Border*, 5–6. See also Bridget Ford, *Bonds of Union: Religion, Race, and Politics in a Civil War Borderland* (Chapel Hill: University of North Carolina Press, 2016), xiv, xii; Christopher Phillips, *The Rivers Ran Backward: The Civil War and the Remaking of the American Middle Border* (New York: Oxford University Press, 2016), 21. His work reveals how this unified western regional identity fractured during the Civil War, with the states below the river becoming more "southern" in their identity after the war and the states above the river becoming more "northern." These conclusions echo those of Anne Marshall and Aaron Astor, whose work on Kentucky and Missouri demonstrates how residents of these states became "belated Confederates"

after the war's conclusion. Marshall, *Creating a Confederate Kentucky: The Lost Cause and Civil War Memory in a Border State* (Chapel Hill: University of North Carolina Press, 2010); Astor, *Rebels on the Border*, 145.

14. Contractualism was an ideology that reflected a belief in "self-ownership, volition, and reciprocal exchange among formally equal individuals." Amy Dru Stanley, *From Bondage to Contract: Wage, Labor, Marriage, and the Market in the Age of Slave Emancipation* (Cambridge: Cambridge University Press, 1998), np, x, xii, 10, 33.

15. West Virginia officially became a state on June 20, 1863. When discussing citizens' antebellum attitudes, I use the term "western Virginia" to refer to those counties which became part of the future state. "Eastern Virginia" or just "Virginia" should be understood as those counties that remained in Virginia after the war. I use "West Virginia" to describe the state after 1863. In places of uncertainty, I default to "West Virginia."

16. Scott Michaelsen and David E. Johnson, "Border Secrets: An Introduction," in *Border Theory: The Limits of Cultural Politics* (Minneapolis: University of Minnesota Press, 1997); Benedict R. Anderson, *Imagined Communities: Reflections on the Origin and Spread of Nationalism* (London: Verso, 1983), 6–7, 53; Peter Sahlins, *Boundaries: The Making of France and Spain in the Pyrenees* (Berkeley: University of California Press, 1989); Andres Resendez, *Changing National Identities at the Frontier: Texas and New Mexico, 1800–1850* (New York: Cambridge University Press, 2006), 169.

17. Undated clipping from *Louisville Courier-Journal*, George W. Johnson Papers, 1850–1920, Kentucky Historical Society, Frankfort, Kentucky (hereafter, KHS), box 1, folder 6; Edward A. Bennett to Judith Bellestine, June 1841, Edward A. Bennett Papers, Filson Historical Society, Louisville, Kentucky (hereafter, FHS); "Preamble and resolutions containing the objections of North Western Virginia to the withdrawal of Virginia from the Union and its adoption of the provisional Government of the Confederate States," in John J. Davis Papers, WVRHC, box 4; *Wheeling Intelligencer*, January 25, 1861.

18. Kenneth Fones-Wolf and Ronald L. Lewis, "Introduction: Networks Large and Small," in *Transnational West Virginia: Ethnic Communities and Economic Change, 1840–1940* (Morgantown: West Virginia University Press, 2003), ix; David Hackett Fischer and James C. Kelly, *Bound Away: Virginia and the Westward Movement* (Charlottesville: University of Virginia Press, 2000).

19. Anne Marshall has argued that the border states "lay at both a geographical and an ideological crossroads." Marshall, *Creating a Confederate Kentucky*, 1. Other scholars address border southerners' increasing industrialization and urbanization, their decreasing attachment to slavery, and their reluctance to secede, but few show how this affected ideas about gender (except during bloody Civil War guerrilla conflict). Fields, *Slavery and Freedom on the Middle Ground*; Midori Takagi, *"Rearing Wolves to Our Own Destruction": Slavery in Richmond, Virginia, 1782-1865* (Charlottesville: University of Virginia Press, 1999); William W.

Freehling, *The South vs. the South: How Anti-Confederate Southerners Shaped the Course of the Civil War* (Oxford: Oxford University Press, 2001); Kristen Leonore Streater, "She-Rebels on the Border: Gender and Politics in Civil War Kentucky" (PhD diss., University of Kentucky, 2001).

While individual men and women may have deviated from the regional norms, this does not mean that a regional ideal did not exist, which affected the attitudes or aspirations of a large swath of the population. In her pivotal work on white and black women in the slaveholding South, Elizabeth Fox-Genovese argues that although nonslaveholding women were the majority, slaveholding ideals still shaped their lives, as well as the lives of the elite. Fox-Genovese, *Within the Plantation Household: Black and White Women of the Old South* (Chapel Hill: University of North Carolina Press, 1988), 47.

20. Burke, *On Slavery's Border*, 58.

21. For an excellent new work on enslaved and free black marriage, see Tera Hunter, *Bound in Wedlock: Slave and Free Black Marriage in the Nineteenth Century* (Cambridge: Harvard University Press, 2017).

22. Naturally, as Suzanne Lebsock states, "Companionate marriage only describes the general direction in which marriages were moving; it was an ideal that influenced behavior, but as with all ideals, it was often difficult for real people to achieve." Lebsock, *The Free Women of Petersburg: Status and Culture in a Southern Town, 1784–1860* (New York: W.W. Norton, 1984), 17. See also Stephanie Coontz, *Marriage, a History* (New York: Viking, 2005), 5.

23. Many scholars, such as Norma Basch and Robert Griswold, argue that this change came about during the early to mid-nineteenth century. Others, such as Nancy Cott, push its beginnings back to the late eighteenth century. In a recent article, Rebecca L. Davis contends that truly modern, companionate marriages did not arise until the tumultuous 1920s. Despite the disagreement, however, historians tend to agree that the late eighteenth and early nineteenth century was a pivotal turning point. Basch, *Framing American Divorce: From the Revolutionary Generation to the Victorians* (Berkeley: University of California Press, 1999), 99–100; Griswold, *Family and Divorce in California, 1850–1890: Victorian Illusions and Everyday Realities* (Albany: State University of New York Press, 1982), 4–5; Cott, "Divorce and the Changing Status of Women in Eighteenth-Century Massachusetts," *William and Mary Quarterly* 33, no. 2 (1976): 593, 613; Davis, "'Not Marriage at All, but Simple Harlotry': The Companionate Marriage Controversy," *Journal of American History* 94, no. 4 (2008): 1137–1138. Coontz argues that in the eighteenth century, people began to advocate love as the basis of marriage, and this idea was "sentimentaliz[ed]" in the nineteenth century and "sexualiz[ed]" in the twentieth. Coontz, *Marriage, a History*, 4–5. See also Lawrence Stone, *The Family, Sex, and Marriage in England, 1500–1800* (New York: Harper & Row, 1979).

24. According to Craig Thompson Friend and Anya Jabour, "While there is near-universal agreement among scholars that antebellum southern families were 'modern' insofar as they adopted the nuclear family ideal, families in the Old

South remained 'traditional' in their adherence to patriarchal authority." Friend and Jabour, "Introduction: Families, Values, and Southern History," in *Family Values in the Old South* (Gainesville: University of Florida Press, 2010), 6. For further discussion of southern attitudes, see Jane Turner Censer, *The Reconstruction of White Southern Womanhood, 1865–1895* (Baton Rouge: Louisiana State University Press, 2003), 252; Lebsock, *Free Women of Petersburg*, 18.

25. For example, Brenda Stevenson argues that couples in Loudoun County, Virginia, adhered to a companionate ideal, though she admits that it was one that emphasized gender-related differences and wives' ultimate subordination to men as the key to happiness. Stevenson, *Life in Black and White: Family and Community in the Slave South* (New York: Oxford University Press, 1997), 41–43, 47–48. See also Jan Lewis, *The Pursuit of Happiness: Family and Values in Jefferson's Virginia* (Cambridge: Cambridge University Press, 1983).

26. Nina Silber, *Gender and the Sectional Conflict* (Chapel Hill: University of North Carolina Press, 2008), xv. In addition, during this period, regional factors such as industrialization, slavery, immigration, and urbanization also affected the development of gender roles, both within and outside the home. With the birth of the New England–based industrial revolution in the early 1800s, economic roles for men moved increasingly into the public sphere, leaving women in control of the domestic realm. In the South, a rigidly hierarchical slave system led to a more structured and patriarchal household gender ideology, one based on the dependence of both slaves and white women. See Nancy Cott, *The Bonds of Womanhood: "Woman's Sphere" in New England, 1780–1835* (New Haven: Yale University Press, 1977), 19–27; Mary Ryan, *Cradle of the Middle Class: The Family in Oneida County, New York, 1790–1865* (Cambridge: Cambridge University Press, 1981); Stephanie McCurry, *Masters of Small Worlds: Yeoman Households, Gender Relations, and the Political Culture of the Antebellum South Carolina Low Country* (New York: Oxford University Press, 1995), 215–225; Anne Firor Scott, *The Southern Lady: From Pedestal to Politics, 1830–1930* (Chicago: University of Chicago Press, 1970); Fox-Genovese, *Within the Plantation Household*; Catherine Clinton, *Planation Mistress: Woman's World in the Old South* (New York: Pantheon, 1982).

27. Victoria Bynum, "Reshaping the Bonds of Womanhood: Divorce in Reconstruction North Carolina," in *Divided Houses: Gender and the Civil War*, ed. Catherine Clinton and Nina Silber (New York: Oxford University Press, 1992), 322.

28. Border/upper South residents did have a less rigid connection to the slave system; still, they remained firmly committed to the system in many ways. In addition, though their smaller slaveholding system may have allowed them the mental flexibility to accept changes in marital roles, their society was still ultimately built on the institution and its role in constructing white femininity and masculinity.

29. Basch, *Framing American Divorce*, 1–4, 100–102.

30. Eric Foner, *Free Soil, Free Labor, Free Men: The Ideology of the Republican Party before the Civil War* (New York: Oxford University Press, 1871), 260–280.

31. Phillips, *The Rivers Ran Backward*, xvii; Ford, *Bonds of Union*, xi–xv; Astor, *Rebels on the Border*, 3–7.

32. Ira Berlin, *Many Thousands Gone: The First Two Centuries of Slavery in North America* (Cambridge, MA: Harvard University Press, 1998), 7–8, 256.

33. Peter W. Bardaglio, *Reconstructing the Household: Families, Sex, and the Law in the Nineteenth-Century South* (Chapel Hill: University of North Carolina Press, 1995), xii. Other scholars make a similar argument about marriage's relationship to the "social order." See Basch, *Framing American Divorce*, 3; Edwards, "The Politics of Marriage and Households in North Carolina during Reconstruction," in *Jumpin' Jim Crow: Southern Politics from Civil War to Civil Rights*, ed. Jane Dailey, Glenda Elizabeth Gilmore, and Bryant Simon (Princeton: Princeton University Press, 2000), 7–27. Over the past three decades, many scholars have explored the development of antebellum American domestic law, and in more recent years, this attention has also extended below the Mason–Dixon Line. Still, rarely do scholars explore the impact of border identity upon the upper South's adjudication and acceptance of divorce. The newest broad exploration of divorce in the antebellum South is Loren Schweninger, *Families in Crisis in the Old South: Divorce, Slavery, and the Law* (Chapel Hill: University of North Carolina Press, 2012). Other scholars have done in-depth explorations of divorce in Texas and North Carolina, but the most extensive work on the border South remains Richard Chused's 1994 book on divorce in early Maryland and Thomas Buckley's 2001 monograph on divorce in early Virginia. On Texas divorce, see Angela Boswell, *Her Act and Deed: Women's Lives in a Rural Southern County, 1837–1873* (College Station: Texas A&M University Press, 2001). On North Carolina divorce, see David Silkenat, *Moments of Despair: Suicide, Divorce and Debt in Civil War Era North Carolina* (Chapel Hill: University of North Carolina Press, 2011). On legislative divorce see Thomas E. Buckley, *The Great Catastrophe of My Life: Divorce in the Old Dominion* (Chapel Hill: University of North Carolina Press, 2001); Richard H. Chused, *Private Acts in Public Places: A Social History of Divorce in the Formative Era of American Family Law* (Philadelphia: University of Pennsylvania Press, 1994); Lebsock, *Free Women of Petersburg*; Stevenson, *Life in Black and White*; and Bertram Wyatt-Brown, *Southern Honor: Ethics and Behavior in the Old South* (New York: Oxford University Press, 1982). Two article-length works are Jane Turner Censer's classic "'Smiling through her Tears': Ante-Bellum Southern Women and Divorce," *American Journal of Legal History* 25 (January 1982):114–134 and Honor Sachs, "The Myth of the Abandoned Wife: Married Women's Agency and the Legal Narrative of Gender in Eighteenth-Century Kentucky," *Ohio Valley History* 3, no. 4 (Winter 2003): 3–20. In her recent book, Diane Mutti Burke addresses divorce in Missouri, but only briefly. Burke, *On Slavery's Border*, 66–68, 225. Perhaps the closest to my own work is Keith C. Barton, "'Good Cooks and Washers': Slave Hiring, Domestic Labor, and the Market in Bourbon County, Kentucky," *Journal of American History* 84, no. 2 (September 1997): 436–460, but divorce makes up only a small part of his excellent analysis on the formation of domestic economic roles in antebellum Kentucky households.

34. According to Bardaglio, individualism and contractualism infiltrated southern culture during the 1850s. This process happened more quickly in the border states, where moderation and a weaker attachment to slavery, combined with geographical proximity, created fertile ground for such concepts. Bardaglio, *Reconstructing the Household*, xiv. For a discussion of gender and issues of contract, see Stanley, *From Bondage to Contract*.

35. Cott, "Divorce and the Changing Status of Women," 586.

36. Yvonne Pitts, *Family, Law, and Inheritance in America: A Social and Legal History of Nineteenth-Century Kentucky* (New York: Cambridge University Press, 2013), 21.

37. I analyze a total of 328 cases over these six counties. During this era, there were 66 divorce cases in Ohio County, 20 in Fauquier County, 123 in Franklin County, 49 in Warren County, 61 in Tazewell County, and 9 in Amelia County. I chose these dates because of the availability of records, both in the archives and in terms of judicial divorce. Statistics compiled from those cases were found at the Library of Virginia, accessed through the online Chancery Court Records Index; in circuit court cases on microfilm at WVRHC; and in original copies of the circuit court records at the Kentucky Department for Libraries and Archives, Frankfort, Kentucky (hereafter, KDLA). All statistics should be understood as the number of cases of those found, since numerous natural and man-made disasters may account for cases missing or destroyed.

38. In 1800, Franklin County was home to thirteen hundred slaves and, by 1860, over three thousand. About 27 percent of Franklin County's population was enslaved by the eve of the war. Of slaves, 47 percent were male and 53 percent female. About 21 percent of Kentucky's total population was enslaved in 1850. The number had decreased to about 20 percent in 1860. Census of the United States, 1800, 1850, 1860. See also Astor, *Rebels on the Border*, 8–13.

39. Marshall, *Creating a Confederate Kentucky*, 11–15.

40. Roughly two hundred square miles in 1800, Franklin County contained scarcely five thousand residents; by 1860, its population had more than doubled in size to over twelve thousand residents. Census of the United States, 1800, 1860.

41. Lowell H. Harrison and James C. Klotter, *A New History of Kentucky* (Lexington, University of Kentucky Press, 1997), 199.

42. Lewis Collins, *Collins' Historical Sketches of Kentucky: History of Kentucky, vol. 2* (Covington, KY: Collins & Co., 1882), 736–738.

43. Census of the United States, 1860.

44. McKenzie Martin, "Shake Rag." Kentucky Historical Society (website), accessed January 31, 2019, https://explorekyhistory.ky.gov/items/show/380.

45. Harrison and Klotter, *A New History of Kentucky*, 191–194.

46. Over two thousand Ohio County residents worked in dozens of manufacturing establishments; 10 percent of them were women. Barbara J. Howe, "Patient Laborers: Women at Work in the Formal Economy of West(ern) Virginia," in *Neither Lady nor Slave: Working Women in the Old South*, ed. Susanna Delfino and

Michele Gillespie (Chapel Hill: University of North Carolina, 2002), 121–124; Ken Fones-Wolf, "Caught between Revolutions: Wheeling Germans in the Civil War Era," in *Transnational West Virginia: Ethnic Communities and Economic Change, 1840–1940*, ed. Ken Fones-Wolf and Ronald L. Lewis (Morgantown: West Virginia University Press, 2003), 19–40.

47. Almost 60 percent of Ohio County's black residents were free in 1850. This number had slightly decreased to 56 percent in 1860. Census of the United States, 1850, 1860.

48. Ohio County's slave population actually shrank from 1800 to 1860, falling to a mere one hundred by Lincoln's election. Half of Ohio County's slaveholders owned only one slave. In addition, 60 percent of those enslaved were women. Census of the United States, 1800, 1860.

49. During the six decades before the Civil War, Ohio County's population quadrupled, from less than five thousand in 1800 to over twenty-two thousand in 1860. Census of the United States, 1800, 1860.

50. Ralph Mann, "Diversity in the Antebellum Appalachian South: Four Farm Communities in Tazewell County, Virginia," in *Appalachia in the Making: The Mountain South in the Nineteenth Century*, ed. Mary Beth Pudup, Dwight B. Billings, and Altina L. Waller (Chapel Hill: University of North Carolina Press, 1995), 132–133.

51. Census of the United States, 1860.

52. Mann, "Diversity in the Antebellum Appalachian South," 132–135.

53. In 1800, 21,329 residents called the county home; the number had increased by less than four hundred by 1860. Census of the United States, 1800, 1860.

54. Kathi Ann Brown, Walter Nicklin, and John T. Toler, *250 Years in Fauquier County: A Virginia Story* (Fairfax, VA: George Mason University Press, 2008), 2–4, 57–65.

55. Francis Fedric, *Slave Life in Virginia and Kentucky; or, Fifty Years of Slavery in the Southern States of America* (London: Wertheim, Macintosh, and Hunt, 1863), 7–8.

56. Slightly more than 50 percent of those enslaved were women. Virginia's total slave population was a little less than one-third of its total population. Fauquier County had over nine hundred farms. In 1860, only 15 percent of Fauquier County's farms were smaller than fifty acres. In fact, an equal number were over five hundred acres. The majority of farms (565 out of a total of 966) were between 100 and 500 acres. Of Virginia's more than eighty-six thousand farms, about 32 percent were smaller than fifty acres, half more than one hundred acres. Census of the United States, 1800, 1860.

57. Brown, Nicklin, and Toler, *250 Years in Fauquier County*, 73–74.

58. During one year, over 60 percent of those enslaved in the county were African. Philip D. Morgan and Michael L. Nicholls, "Slaves in Piedmont Virginia, 1720–1790," *William and Mary Quarterly* 46, no. 2 (April 1989): 217–218.

59. Kathleen Halverson Hadfield, ed., *Historical Notes on Amelia County, Virginia* (Amelia, VA: Amelia County Historical Committee, 1982). The railroad

connections of Tazewell, Fauquier, and Amelia Counties cemented their ties with other parts of the Old Dominion and southern states; in contrast, Ohio County had trade connections with the West, mid-Atlantic, and Northeast through the Ohio River and the Baltimore and Ohio Railroad.

60. Laura Edwards, *Gendered Strife and Confusion: The Political Culture of Reconstruction* (Urbana: University of Illinois Press, 1997), 18.

1. To Form an Enviable Marriage

1. Ellen Green to Hector Green, November 8, 1833, Green Family Papers, FHS, folder 12. For an analysis of northern middle-class domesticity, see Cott, *The Bonds of Womanhood*, 64–100.

2. As much as possible, I tried to find border South residents who lived adult lives between the early 1830s and late 1870s. This obviously means there is a wide disparity in ages, and when possible, I have tried to note the ages of the subjects in the text. Regionally, the manuscripts cover nearly all areas of Kentucky and Virginia, with the exception of the contemporary Appalachian region, which has far fewer of these types of sources than the rest of the state. The manuscripts tend to skew toward the elite or middle-class residents of Kentucky and Virginia, but the circuit court cases seem to reflect a larger portion of the working class. Combining both, I hope to give a broader view of antebellum marital roles. When the sources have given me information about enslaved or free black relationships, I have included it, but more analysis using these sources needs to be done.

3. Burke, *On Slavery's Border*, 58. Stephen Berry calls Kentucky "thoroughly Southern in its social customs, increasingly Northern in its economic interests . . . a unique hybrid of the two regions." While I agree with Berry that Kentucky displayed "hybrid" tendencies, I would argue that a gendered analysis of marriage demonstrates that Kentucky was not as "thoroughly Southern" as scholars have thought. Berry, *House of Abraham*, 67.

4. McCurry, *Masters of Small Worlds*, 239–278.

5. As defined by Barbara Welter in her foundational article, "The Cult of True Womanhood: 1820–1860," *American Quarterly* 18:2 (Summer 1966): 151–174.

6. Cott, *The Bonds of Womanhood*, 63–65; Jeanne Boydston, *Home and Work: Housework, Wages, and the Ideology of Labor in the Early Republic* (New York: Oxford University Press, 1990), 56–61; Fox-Genovese, *Within the Plantation Household*, 202.

7. Stephanie Coontz has an excellent discussion of companionate marriage's development in a transatlantic context. Coontz, *Marriage, a History*. See also Stone, *The Family, Sex and Marriage in England*.

8. Lebsock, *Free Women of Petersburg*, 17, 32–35.

9. Nancy Cott, *Public Vows: A History of Marriage and the Nation* (Cambridge, MA: Harvard University Press, 2000), 11–12.

10. McCurry, *Masters of Small Worlds*, 228–229.

11. Kentucky was more of a "society with slaves" than a "slave society." Berlin, *Many Thousands Gone*, 7–8; Burke, *On Slavery's Border*, 1–7.

12. Stevenson, *Life in Black and White*, 51–58.

13. Edward A. Bennett to Judith Bellestine, June 1841, Edward A. Bennett Papers, FHS.

14. Willa Johnson to Ann Johnson, September 28, 1860, George W. Johnson Papers, KHS, box 1, folder 8.

15. Will Coburn to Phoebe M. Coburn Daugherty, August 4, 1836, Phoebe Wood Coburn Daugherty Papers, FHS, folder 1.

16. E. Anthony Rotundo, *American Manhood: Transformations in Masculinity from the Revolution to the Modern Era* (New York: Basic Books, 1993), 114–115.

17. G. B. Miller to Barnabas Lee, May 16, 1844, Barnabas Lee Papers, FHS.

18. Ellen K. Rothman, *Hands and Hearts: A History of Courtship in America* (Cambridge, MA: Harvard University Press, 1987), 157–159.

19. Susan P. Bullitt Dixon to Helen Bullitt, 1853, Bullitt-Chenoweth Family Papers, FHS, folder 5.

20. According to Stephanie Coontz, in the seventeenth and eighteenth centuries, people generally believed that love developed over time with an appropriate mate. Coontz, *Marriage, a History*, 178.

21. A. C. Williams to Frances, January 15, 1854, A. C. Williams Letters, FHS.

22. John Tosh makes a convincing case for the connection between education and companionate marriage. Tosh, *A Man's Place: Masculinity and the Middle-Class Home in Victorian England* (New Haven: Yale University Press, 1999), 66–67.

23. Stephen Berry, *All That Makes a Man: Love and Ambition in the Civil War South* (Chapel Hill: University of North Carolina, 1992), 95. For an excellent analysis of how female education shaped women's public roles, see Mary Kelley, *Learning to Stand and Speak: Women, Education, and Public Life in America's Republic* (Chapel Hill: University of North Carolina Press, 2006). Jane Turner Censer finds that, as for Cott's northern women, the increasing number of public and private schools in the Reconstruction South helped to increase the cultural value of women's intellectual engagement. Censer, *Reconstruction of White Southern Womanhood*, 153. According to Christie Anne Farnham, in the antebellum South, "A college education became emblematic of class, a means to a type of refinement that labeled one a lady worthy of protection, admiration, and chivalrous attention." Farnham, *The Education of the Southern Belle: Higher Education and Student Socialization in the Antebellum South* (New York: New York University Press, 1994), 3. See also Cara Anzilotti, *In the Affairs of the World: Women, Patriarchy, and Power in Colonial South Carolina* (Westport, CT: Greenwood, 2002), 45.

24. Charles Morehead, *An Address Delivered on the Second Anniversary of Van Doren's Collegiate Institute for Young Ladies, in the City of Lexington, Kentucky, on the Last Thursday in July, 1833, by Charles Morehead, Esq.* (Lexington, KY: Wm. M. Todd and Thos. T. Skillman, 1833). According to Jonathan Daniel Wells, middle-class southerners positively compared the role of women in nineteenth-century

American with their earlier "unchristian" place, bragging that they especially valued women as "teachers, mothers, and wives." Wells, *The Origins of the Southern Middle Class: 1800–1861* (Chapel Hill: University of North Carolina Press, 2004), 77.

25. Morehead, *An Address Delivered on the Second Anniversary.*

26. Morehead's philosophy about Republican Motherhood is similar to ideas that Kerber found in a largely New England–based sample of early American women. Linda K. Kerber, *Women of the Republic: Intellect and Ideology in Revolutionary America* (Chapel Hill: University of North Carolina Press, 1980), 11.

27. Sarah L. Hyde, *Schooling in the Antebellum South: The Rise of Public and Private Education in Louisiana, Mississippi, and Alabama* (Baton Rouge: Louisiana State University Press, 2016), 1–6.

28. Z. G. Offutt to Sallie Offutt, January 25, 1838, Moxley-Offutt Family Papers, FHS, folder 1.

29. Albana C. Carson's Composition for the Examination of 1851, Science Hill Academy, Shelbyville, KY, Albana C. Carson Papers, FHS.

30. Hubbard, who had moved to western Virginia when he was four, served in the Virginia legislature from 1852 to 1854, and was a member of the Virginia secession convention. He would eventually serve in the West Virginia state senate and the US House of Representatives. Chester D. Hubbard to Henry Hubbard, April 30, 1840, Hubbard Family Papers, WVRHC, microfilm, reel 1. George W. Atkinson and Alvaro F. Gibbens, *Prominent Men of West Virginia: Biographical Sketches of Representative Men in Every Honorable Vocation, including Politics, the Law, Theology, Medicine, Education, Finance, Journalism, Trade, Commerce and Agriculture* (Wheeling, WV: W.L. Callin, 1890), 258–259; William P. Willey, *An Inside View of the Formation of the State of West Virginia* (Wheeling, WV: Thew News Pub. Co., 1901), 242–245.

31. Waitman T. Willey, another key western Virginia politician, was a trustee of the Morgantown Female Academy. Henry Dering to Waitman T. Willey, June 9, 1851, Waitman T. Willey Papers, WVRHC, box 1.

32. Sarah Hubbard to Hannah List, January 30, 1845, Hubbard Family Papers, WVRHC, microfilm, reel 1.

33. Undated speech in Hubbard Family Papers, WVRHC, box 1.

34. Salathiel Voris to Mary Woolridge, July 15, 1857, Mary Woolridge Voris Papers, FHS, folder 2.

35. All letters are from the Mary Woolridge Voris Papers, FHS: Salathiel Voris to Mary Woolridge, September 8, 1857, folder 2; Salathiel Voris to Mary Woolridge, September 25, 1857, folder 2; Salathiel Voris to Mary Woolridge, September 1859, folder 6.

36. All letters are from the Mary Woolridge Voris Papers, FHS: Salathiel Voris to Mary Woolridge, September 15, 1857, folder 2; Salathiel Voris to Mary Woolridge, March 24, 1858, folder 3; Salathiel Voris to Mary Woolridge, June 5, 1858, folder 3; Salathiel Voris to Mary Woolridge, July 17, 1858, folder 3.

37. All letters are from the Mary Woolridge Voris Papers, FHS: Salathiel Voris to Mary Woolridge, August 1858, folder 3; Salathiel Voris to Mary Woolridge, January 1, 1859, folder 5; Salathiel Voris to Mary Woolridge, August 1859, folder 6; Salathiel Voris to Mary Woolridge, undated, folder 6; Salathiel Voris to Mary Woolridge, September 1859, folder 7; Salathiel Voris to Mary Woolridge, February 2, 1860, folder 8.

38. Cott, *Bonds of Womanhood*, 80–81.

39. Rotundo, *American Manhood*, 116–18. On the other hand, in the antebellum white southern engagements documented by Brenda Stevenson communal approval and familial involvement were much more important. Stevenson, *Life in Black and White*, 60–62.

40. Smith-Rosenberg, "The Female World of Love and Ritual: Relations between Women in Nineteenth-Century America," *Signs* 1, no. 1 (Autumn 1975): 9–14.

41. Cott, *Bonds of Womanhood*, 63–64, 98. For a look at the southern literary scene, see Wells, *Origins of the Southern Middle Class*, 116–132.

42. For an excellent look at one of the foundational authors of the domesticity literature, see Kathryn Sklar, *Catherine Beecher: A Study in American Domesticity* (New Haven: Yale University Press, 1973). See also Mary Ryan, *The Empire of the Mother: American Writing about Domesticity, 1830–1860* (New York: Routledge, 1985); Sarah A. Levitt, *From Catherine Beecher to Martha Stewart: A Cultural History of Domestic Advice* (Chapel Hill: University of North Carolina Press, 2002). On advice manuals particularly, see C. Dallett Hemphill, *Bowing to Necessities: A History of Manners, 1620–1860* (New York: Oxford University Press, 2002).

43. Daniel Wise, *Bridal Greetings: A Marriage Gift, in Which the Mutual Duties of Husband and Wife are Familiarly Illustrated and Enforced* (New York: Carlton & Phillips, 1856), 3, 25.

44. Wise, *Bridal Greetings*, 67–69, 86–91, 93.

45. Ibid., 104–107.

46. James Bean, *The Christian Minister's Affectionate Advice to a Married Couple* (New York: American Tract Society, 1840), 3, 5–6, 15.

47. Charles H. Ambler, *The Makers of West Virginia and Their Work* (Huntington, WV: Gentry Brothers, 1942), 101–102. Van Winkle married Juliet Rathbone in 1831, and the marriage was generally described as a happy one. He was distraught at her death just nine years later, and he never remarried. In his diary, he described her as "literally my better half." Peter Van Winkle Diary, July 21, 1844 in Peter Van Winkle Papers, WVRHC, box 2; Atkinson and Gibbens, *Prominent Men of West Virginia*, 162.

48. Peter Van Winkle, "Position and Relation of the Household and its Members," handwritten manuscript in Van Winkle Papers, WVRHC, box 1.

49. William Thomas McElroy Papers, diary, FHS, folder 10.

50. Cott, *Bonds of Womanhood*, 64–74; Fox-Genovese, *Within the Plantation Household*, 192–195.

51. Barton, "'Good Cooks and Washers,'" 450–451.

52. Boydston, *Home and Work*, 144–149.

53. *Glenn v. Glenn* (1853), Franklin County Circuit Court Records, KDLA, box 111, no. 825.

54. *Christiana Merritt v. Richard Merritt* (1854), Franklin County Circuit Court Records, KDLA, box 112, no. 846.

55. *Lutheran Buckley v. Michael Buckley* (1852), Franklin County Circuit Court Records, KDLA, no. 798.

56. *Robinson, Jas. H. v. Robinson, Mary* (1850), Ohio County Circuit Court Records, WVRHC, env. 196 c-9.

57. *Maria E. English v. Morris English* (1853), Franklin County Circuit Court Records, KDLA, no. 907. Morris, like Michael Buckley in the above case, was born in Ireland.

58. Ibid.

59. *Jane Vawter v. H. Vawter* (1846), Franklin County Circuit Court Records, KDLA, no. 751. The Vawters were not slave owners.

60. Ibid.

61. *William H. Howard v. Catherine Howard* (1854), Warren County Circuit Court Records, KDLA, no. 2212.

62. *Catharine Lynch v. John Lynch* (1855), Franklin County Circuit Court Records, KDLA, no. 865. John told the court that Catharine had lived with him only a few weeks, long enough to accomplish her goal in marrying him—obtaining all his money (seventy-five dollars). Since then, she had had an affair with Michael Clancy, traveling with him throughout Kentucky and Ohio.

63. Salathiel Voris to Mary Woolridge, July 15, 1857, Mary Woolridge Voris Papers, FHS, folder 2.

64. *Sarah J. Boyd v. Hiram Boyd* (1857), Warren County Circuit Court Records, KDLA, no. 2385.

65. Boswell, *Her Act and Deed*, 51–52.

66. *Martha F. Hicatt v. James J. Hicatt* (1854), Franklin County Circuit Court Records, KDLA, no. 845.

67. *Mary Fitzgerald v. Patrick Fitzgerald* (1853), Franklin County Circuit Records, KDLA, no. 825.

68. *Henry Snelling v. E. Snelling* (1853), Franklin County Circuit Court Records, KDLA, no. 827. See also *Joshua Martin v. Margaret E. Martin* (1859), Warren County Circuit Court Records, KDLA, no. 2548.

69. Interestingly, it appears that the friend to whom he addressed the letter was the same person who "joined" Margaret Bole as her next friend in suing for divorce. *Bole, Margaret, by her next friend Jimeson, Wm. W. v. Bole, Wm.* (1855), Ohio County Circuit Court Records, WVRHC, env. 208 b-4.

70. Ibid.

71. Barton, "'Good Cooks and Washers,'" 455. According to Angela Boswell, this ideal held sway in the South, too, especially for plantation households, in

which women were expected to manage slave labor and were protected from doing heavy lifting themselves. Boswell, *Her Act and Deed*, 4.

72. Barton, "'Good Cooks and Washers,'" 448; Susan Strasser, *Never Done: A History of American Housework* (New York: Pantheon, 1982), 182–190; Linda K. Kerber, "Separate Spheres, Female Worlds, Woman's Place: The Rhetoric of Women's History," *Journal of American History* 75, no. 1 (June 1988): 9–39; Boydston, *Home and Work*, 144.

73. Barton's article addresses many of these issues, through the lens of slave hiring. He argues that women in Bourbon County, Kentucky, adapted their slave society to a more northern ideal of domesticity. These women, for example, hired slave women to take over the more arduous tasks of the home, which gave them social standing and freed them for more specialized tasks. Barton states that husbands did not expect their wives to labor extensively in the household, and in fact, "not once in any of the forty-one cases did a woman point to her role in household production as a defense of her character as a wife; every mention of material production by a woman was used as an indictment of her husband." Barton, "'Good Cooks and Washers,'" 450–451. I argue that class complicates these findings. For more on border South women and enslaved/hired help, see Stephanie Cole, "Servants and Slaves in Louisville: Race, Ethnicity, and Household Labor in an Antebellum Border City," *Ohio Valley History* 11:1 (Spring 2011): 3–25.

74. Arlette Farge argues that in the poorer rungs of eighteenth-century Paris, "both partners had to work together of necessity and a considerable part of their relationship was bound up in their mutual commitment to their economic survival." Farge, *Fragile Lives: Violence, Power and Solidarity in Eighteenth-Century Paris* (Cambridge, MA: Harvard University Press, 1993), 21–23.

75. Ellen Green to Hector Green, January 3, 1834, Green Family Papers, FHS, folder 13. In another letter, she referred to her opinions as "yankee notions," and she was initially from Massachusetts. Her views, though, reflect the influence of new residents on border South residents.

76. Elizabeth Willey to Waitman T. Willey, June 26, 1870, Waitman T. Willey Papers, WVRHC, box 4.

77. *Priscilla Potts v. Jonathan Potts* (1855), Warren County Circuit Court Records, KDLA, no. 2375.

78. *Avery Williams v. E.R. Williams* (1856), Warren County Circuit Court Records, KDLA, no. 2355; *Polly Hancock v. Isiah Hancock* (1857), Warren County Circuit Court Records, KDLA, no. 2397; *Elizabeth Lancaster v. Zachariah Lancaster* (1858), Warren County Circuit Court Records, KDLA, no. 2582.

79. Amy Greenberg, *Manifest Manhood and Antebellum American Empire* (New York: Cambridge University Press, 2005), 11–13; Bruce E. Stewart, "Select Men of Sober and Industrious Habits: Alcohol Reform and Social Conflict in Antebellum Appalachia," *Journal of Southern History* 73, no. 2 (May 2007): 290–293.

80. In his analysis of Victorian England, John Tosh argues that those historians who believe in the dichotomy of the public and private spheres and those who

seek to complicate it both overlook the role of men in the home. Women's historians who challenge the doctrine of separate spheres tend to insist that the line between private and public for women was more blurred than previously believed. Few have made the opposite argument—that men were not merely creatures of the world but that they shaped a considerable portion of their identity around the home. Tosh, *A Man's Place*, 1–4. E. Anthony Rotundo argues that men often had to make a choice between the home or the world because they perceived a stronger dichotomy between masculinity and domesticity at this time. Rotundo, *American Manhood*, 165.

81. Bean, *Christian Minister's Advice*, 9.

82. G. B. Miller to Barnabas Lee, May 16, 1844, Barnabas Lee Papers, FHS.

83. George Robertson, *An Outline of the Life of George Robertson, Written by Himself* (Lexington, KY: Transylvania Printing & Publishing Co., 1876), 31, 115, 133. Robertson, raised and educated in Kentucky, attended Transylvania University in Lexington before studying the law briefly with Chief Justice Boyle in Lancaster, Kentucky. He served in Congress and was a Kentucky Court of Appeals justice.

84. George Robertson Manuscript, KHS; Robertson, *An Outline of the Life of George Robertson*, 171. This does not mean he defined himself solely in this way or that he lessened his wife's role there. To Robertson, his wife was "queen of the house" and was properly devoted to "home and fond of domestic cares." Separate spheres remained, even when the husband prided himself on his attention to home life.

85. Undated note, George W. Johnson Papers, KHS, box 1, folder 6.

86. Coontz, *Marriage, a History*, 182.

87. Ellen Bodley to William J. Bodley, December 22, 1849, Bodley Family Papers, FHS. For a discussion on decision-making in nineteenth-century relationships, see Rotundo, *American Manhood*, 136–139.

88. Tosh, *A Man's Place*, 56–57; Cott, *Bonds of Womanhood*, 64–66.

89. Salathiel Voris to Mary Woolridge, September 25, 1857, Mary Woolridge Voris Papers, FHS, folder 2; Salathiel Voris to Mary Woolridge, January 1, 1859, Mary Woolridge Voris Papers, FHS, folder 5.

90. *Robinson, Rebecca v. Robinson, John J.* (1871), Ohio County Circuit Court Records, WVRHC, env. 288 b-4.

91. *Boyd, Sarah J. v. Boyd, Hyram* (1857), Warren County Circuit Court Records, KDLA, no. 2385.

92. Shawn Johansen, *Family Men: Middle-Class Fatherhood in Early Industrializing America* (New York: Routledge, 2001), 1–3.

93. Tosh, *A Man's Place*, 39.

94. Mildred Bullitt, October 27, 1854, Bullitt-Chenoweth Family Papers, FHS, folder 5.

95. S. T. January to Clementine Machir, December 1, 1835, Wall-Machir Family Papers, FHS.

96. Lucinda Barbour Helm to her daughter, Helm Family Papers, FHS.

97. Johansen, *Family Men*, 65.

98. John Wall to Clementina Wall, August 22, 1852, Wall-Machir Family Papers, FHS.

99. Susan Scrogin to "Mr. Shoaff," January 16, 1860, Scrogin/Haviland Collection, KHS, box 1, folder 5.

100. Henry Haviland to Susan Scrogin, March 6, 1857, Scrogin/Haviland Collection, KHS, box 1, folder 4.

101. Henry Haviland to Susan Scrogin, February 17, 1861, Scrogin/Haviland Collection, KHS, box 1, folder 6.

102. Susan Scrogin to Henry Haviland, January 24, 1861, Scrogin/Haviland Collection, KHS, box 1, folder 6.

103. Ford, *Bonds of Union*, xvii.

104. Francis H. Pierpont to Julia Pierpont, undated letter, Francis H. Pierpont Papers, WVRHC, box 1.

2. No More, Together

1. *Simpson v. Simpson*, 34 Kentucky Court of Appeals 140 (1836).

2. Ibid.

3. Mary Somerville Jones, *An Historical Geography of the Changing Divorce Law in the United States* (New York: Garland, 1987), 17–18, 20; Stanley, *From Bondage to Contract*, xii–xiii, 18, 24, 175–177; Norma Basch, *In the Eyes of the Law: Women, Marriage, and Property in Nineteenth-Century New York* (Ithaca, NY: Cornell University Press, 1982), 71.

4. Jones, *An Historical Geography*, 18, 24, 175; Basch, *In the Eyes of the Law*, 71; Bardaglio, *Reconstructing the Household*, xii–xiv; Buckley, *Great Catastrophe of My Life*, 17; Cornelia Hughes Dayton, *Women before the Bar: Gender, Law, and Society in Connecticut, 1639–1789* (Chapel Hill: University of North Carolina Press, 1995). See also Cott, "Divorce and the Changing Status of Women in Eighteenth-Century Massachusetts," 589. According to Cott, "Opposing canon law, Puritan divorce theory held that marriage was a civil contract which could and should be dissolved for such breaches as adultery, long absence, or irremediable cruelty." See also Schweninger, *Families in Crisis in the Old South*, 1–5.

5. Basch, *Framing American Divorce*, 24, 29; Buckley, *Great Catastrophe of My Life*, 51. On alterations to women's legal rights with the Revolution, see Linda K. Kerber, *No Constitutional Right to Be Ladies: Women and the Obligations of Citizenship* (New York: Hill and Wang, 1998), 3–46. Historians continue to debate the effect of the change from legislative to judicial divorce. While some have seen it as a sign of liberalization, others, like Buckley, argue that it was not an attempt to make divorce easier to obtain. He argues that when Virginia eventually allowed for judicial divorce (in 1851) that it was on limited grounds and that the state was still committed to "marriage as foundational to [its] society." Buckley, *Great*

Catastrophe of My Life, 8–9. On the other hand, Norma Basch states that the "exclusive legislative administration of divorce severely restricted the total number of divorces," especially because it relied on the assumption that divorce was rare enough that legislative intervention was feasible and efficient. Basch, *Framing American Divorce*, 51, 57.

6. Basch, *Framing American Divorce*, 9; Lawrence B. Goodheart, Neil Hanks, and Elizabeth Johnson, "'An Act for the Relief of Females . . .': Divorce and the Changing Legal Status of Women in Tennessee, 1796–1860, Part 1," *Tennessee Historical Quarterly* 44, no. 3 (Fall 1985): 3.

7. Hendrik Hartog, *Man and Wife in America: A History* (Cambridge: Harvard University Press, 2000), 63–64; Basch, *Framing American Divorce*, 3.

8. Bardaglio, *Reconstructing the Household*, 5. Likewise, Norma Basch has stated that historians should not ignore the impact of slavery on southern divorce. Basch, *Framing American Divorce*, 48.

9. Here are a few examples of southern states' interpretations of divorce statutes: North Carolina allowed for judicial divorce in 1835, over fifteen years earlier than Virginia, but continued to maintain harsh restrictions against absolute divorce. Virginia itself did not allow for legislative divorce before 1833. Georgia combined legislative and judicial divorce, doubling the requirements for divorce, until 1833. South Carolina, of course, did not allow for divorce at all during the antebellum era. Buckley, *Great Catastrophe of My Life*, 51.

10. McCurry, *Masters of Small Worlds*, 86–91.

11. Jones, *An Historical Geography*, 17–18, 20; Stanley, *From Bondage to Contract*, xii–xiii, 18, 24, 175–177; Basch, *In the Eyes of the Law*, 71.

12. Michael Grossberg argues that these innovations challenged power relations within the household, decreased "paternal authority," and increased the state's involvement in family life—creating a new judicial patriarchy. Yet, his analysis, though revealing, is exceedingly broad and makes few distinctions between regional interpretations of these changes. Other scholars have sought to determine whether such disparities existed and, if so, to discover their pattern and cause. See Michael Grossberg, *Governing the Hearth: Law and the Family in Nineteenth-Century America* (Chapel Hill: University of North Carolina Press, 1985), ix, xi–xii, 7–9. For a discussion of gender and issues of contract, see Stanley, *From Bondage to Contract*; for a discussion of the free labor North, see Foner, *Free Soil, Free Labor, Free Men*; for a description of the development of marriage, see Cott, *Public Vows*, 56–76; for an article on the correlation among companionate marriage, divorce, and manhood, see Robert L. Griswold, "Divorce and the Legal Redefinition of Victorian Manhood," in *Meanings for Manhood: Construction of Masculinity in Victorian America*, ed. Mark Carnes and Clyde Griffin (Chicago: University of Chicago Press, 1990), 205–211.

13. Amanda Ray, "The Impact of Statehood and Republican Politics on Women's Legal Rights in West Virginia, 1863–1872" (master's thesis, West Virginia University, 2001), 15; Joan Hoff, *Law, Gender, and Injustice: A Legal History of*

U.S. Women (New York: New York University Press, 1991), 119. See also William Blackstone, *Commentaries on the Laws of England*, ed. W. G. Hammond (San Francisco, 1898); Mary Ritter Beard, *Women as a Force in History* (New York: Macmillan, 1946); Carole Shammas, "Re-Assessing the Married Women's Property Acts," *Journal of Women's History* 6, no. 1 (Spring 1994): 9–30; Elizabeth Bowles Warbasse, *The Changing Legal Rights of Married Women: 1800–1861* (New York: Garland, 1987); Marylynn Salmon, *Women and the Law of Property in Early America* (Chapel Hill: University of North Carolina Press, 1986).

14. Elizabeth Cady Stanton, "The Need of Liberal Divorce Laws," *North American Review* 139 (September 1884): 242–243.

15. "Baron and feme" translates to "lord and woman."

16. Tapping Reeve, *The Law of Baron and Femme, of Parent and Child, Guardian and Ward, Master and Servant, and of the Powers of the Courts of Chancery; with an Essay on the Terms Heir, Heirs, Heirs of the Body* (Albany, NY: William Gould, 1862), 1–226.

17. Basch, *Framing American Divorce*, 9–10, 48–49. For a similar argument, see Censer, "'Smiling through her Tears,'" 26; Schweninger, *Families in Crisis in the Old South*, 6.

18. Bardaglio, *Reconstructing the Southern Household*, xiv, xvii.

19. During the years 1850–1861, residents initiated forty-eight cases in Franklin County, Kentucky; twenty-two cases in Warren County, Kentucky; thirteen in Ohio County, Virginia; twenty-one in Tazewell County, Virginia; eight in Fauquier County, Virginia; and two in Amelia County, Virginia.

20. *Altpeter, Frederick v. Altpeter, Catharine* (1863) in Ohio County Circuit Court Records, WVRHC, env. 235 b-7.

21. *Smith, Elizabeth—by her next friend Shields, Wm., v. Smith, Jos.* (1864), Ohio County Circuit Court Records, WVRHC, env. 257 b-6. Plaintiffs also swore out an affidavit, attesting to their spouse's nonresidence.

22. *Revised Statutes, Kentucky, vol. 2* (1852), chap. 47, art. iii, sec. iii.

23. Buckley, *Great Catastrophe of My Life*, 6; A. Cheree Carlson, *The Crimes of Womanhood: Defining Femininity in a Court of Law* (Urbana: University of Illinois Press, 2009), 1; Mary Frances Berry, *The Pig Farmer's Daughter and Other Tales of American Justice: Episodes of Racism and Sexism in the Courts from 1865 to the Present* (New York: Knopf, 1999); Schweninger, *Families in Crisis in the Old South*, 15–16.

24. *Revised Statutes, Kentucky, vol. 2* (1852), chap. 47, art. iii, sec. i.

25. *Menefee, Susan C. v. Menefee, Banks S.* (1854), Fauquier Count Circuit Court Records, Library of Virginia, Richmond, Virginia (hereafter, LVA), no. 1854-054.

26. Barbara Alpern Engel, *Breaking the Ties That Bound: The Politics of Marital Strife in Late Imperial Russia* (Ithaca, NY: Cornell University Press, 2011), 10–11.

27. See Censer, "'Smiling through Her Tears,'" 27–34, for a detailed analysis of the various southern statutes. According to Lawrence M. Friedman, "It is . . . likely

that southern and border states granted fewer divorces than the northern states." Friedman, "Rights of Passage: Divorce Law in Historical Perspective," *Oregon Law Review* 63 (1984): 652. My findings complicate this statement.

28. *Revised Statutes, Kentucky, vol. 2* (1852), chap. 47, art. iii, sec. i, xi. Clearly Kentuckians worried about the rise of religious groups, such as the Shakers, because numerous clauses in their state code allowed divorce in cases in which a spouse had "unit[ed] with any religious society whose creed and rules require a renunciation of the marriage covenant, or forbid husband and wife from cohabiting." Often, the Shakers were mentioned by name.

29. *Revised Statutes, Kentucky, vol. 2* (1852), chap. 47, art. iii, sec. i. In Kentucky, a successful plaintiff could remarry after one year; the defendant had to wait five years. *Revised Statutes, Kentucky, vol. 2* (1852), chap. 47, art. iii, sec. ii.

30. In this chapter, both absolute divorce and divorce from bed and board will be considered a "successful" divorce, since plaintiffs often asked only for divorce from bed and board. Therefore, success is measured by whether the charging spouse received some measure of relief. Chused, *Private Acts in Public Places*, 56–69.

31. *Revised Statutes, Kentucky, vol. 2* (1852), chap. 47, art. iii, sec. vi. New York, for example, allowed for full divorce only in cases of adultery and relegated all other charges to divorce *a mensa et thoro*.

32. According to Virginia law, a divorce from bed and board meant that the parties were "perpetually separated and protected in their persons and property." It would act much as a regular decree for divorce, except that neither party could remarry. As in Kentucky (and most states), petitioners could receive a divorce for their partner's adultery only if they had not lived with that person after knowing about said adultery. *Code of Virginia* (1849), title 31, chap. cix, sec. 6–7, 11, 13–14.

33. James Ann Pearce to Sarah Vick, December 30, 1848, Bodley Family Papers, FHS.

34. The 1851 Kentucky House of Representatives had 95 members. Of those, I could only find definitive evidence of slaveholding or a lack of slaveholding for 66. Of those, 89.4 percent, or 59 members, owned slaves. Of all members, no more than 92.6 percent owned slaves and no fewer than 62.1 percent. The 1848 Virginia General Assembly had 137 members. Of those, I could only find definitive evidence of slaveholding or a lack of slaveholding for 99. Of those, 92.9 percent, or 92 members, owned slaves. Of all members, no more than 94.9 percent owned slaves and no fewer than 67.2 percent. Census of the United States, 1840, 1850, 1860. Slave Schedules, Census of the United States, 1850, 1860. Cynthia Miller Leonard, ed., *The General Assembly of Virginia, July 30, 1619–January 11, 1978: A Bicentennial Register of Members* (Richmond: Virginia State Library, 1978).

35. All percentages are a sample of those whose backgrounds could be determined. The second bill passed by a margin of 38 to 34. Of those who supported it, 88.9 percent were slaveholders; of those who opposed it, 92 percent were. *Journal of the Kentucky House of Representatives*, 1849, 98–99, 472–473.

36. Richard Wires, *The Divorce Issue and Reform in Nineteenth-Century Indiana* (Muncie, IN: Ball State University, 1967).

37. This would also align with Basch's and Censer's argument that newer southern states or more western states liberalized their divorce laws first. Basch, *Framing American Divorce*, 9–10; Censer, "'Smiling through Her Tears,'" 26.

38. This conclusion is based on an analysis of any instance of someone charging one of the following: adultery, intemperance, jail, cruelty, and abandonment. Often, litigants charged more than one, but the important factor here is how often adultery was one of those charges because it was the charge most likely to tip the scale in a plaintiff's favor.

39. Bardaglio, *Reconstructing the Southern Household*, xiv. For a discussion of gender and issues of contract, see Stanley, *From Bondage to Contract.*

40. According to Bertram Wyatt-Brown, southern divorce cases show a striking amount of "male favoritism." Whereas northern women could expect a fair chance of success, southern women "had to be pessimistic." Wyatt-Brown, *Southern Honor*, 244–245.

41. *Civil Code of the State of Louisiana* (1853), title v, chap. i, art. 136-7.

42. In Tazewell County, women filed only 10 percent of the cases, and in Warren County, women filed for 36 percent. In Amelia County, 100 percent of the cases (only two in total) were filed by women.

43. Norma Basch, "Relief in the Premises: Divorce as a Woman's Remedy in New York and Indiana, 1815–1870," *Law and History Review* 8, no. 1 (Spring 1990): 1–24.

44. In her article on Massachusetts, Nancy Cott ties rising numbers of divorce petitions by women and an increasing divorce rate to greater "self-assertion" and independence on the part of women. Moreover, the "changing treatment of their petitions implies that wives' objections were being regarded more seriously—that their status within the family had risen in the eyes of authorities." Cott, "Divorce and the Changing Status of Women," 593–594, 605, 613.

45. Jones, *An Historical Geography*, 53; Hartog, *Man and Wife in America*, 70; Censer, "'Smiling through her Tears,'" 37.

46. *George Williams v. Elizabeth Williams*, 3 Kentucky Court of Appeals 363 (1869); Hartog, *Man and Wife in America*, 57, 80–82. However, Tapping Reeve defended wives' ability and right to enter into separation agreements as early as 1816. Reeve, *Law of Baron and Femme*, 178–179.

47. Hartog, *Man and Wife in America*, 85.

48. *Revised Statutes, Kentucky, vol. 2* (1852), chap. 47, art. iii, sec. i.

49. Sachs, "The Myth of the Abandoned Wife," 6–8, 12.

50. Hartog, *Man and Wife in America*, 79; *Simpson v. Simpson*, 34 Kentucky Court of Appeals 140 (1836).

51. Local court cases often feature a variety of spellings of people's names. In this case, the last name of the litigants is alternately spelling "Carell," "Carroll," and "Carral." Whether this is due to poor handwriting or poor spelling is difficult

to determine, but in most cases, when differences occur, I have chosen the most commonly used spelling or the one chosen by the archivists at each location.

52. *Carrall v. Carrall*, (1842), Franklin County Circuit Court Records, KDLA, no. 661.

53. Ibid.

54. Laura Edwards, *The People and Their Peace: Legal Culture and the Transformation of Inequality in the Post-Revolutionary South* (Chapel Hill: University of North Carolina Press, 2009), 3–10.

55. *McKee v. McKee* (1856), Franklin County Circuit Court Records, KDLA, no. 893.

56. Ibid.

57. *Smith, James P. v. Smith, Mary alias Holloway* (1861), Warren County Circuit Court Records, KDLA, no. 2683.

58. *Wells, Christina by her next friend, James Alexander v. Wells, Levi* (1857), Ohio County Circuit Court, WVRHC, env. 216 b-6.

59. In 1860, they lived together with two children, William (age four) and Mary (age two). George Charles served as a private in the Thirty-Ninth Kentucky Infantry and was captured by the Confederates in late 1862 before being killed "by the Rebels" on January 1, 1863. Just five months later, his community would officially become part of the new Union state of West Virginia. *Charles, George W. v. Charles, Leah* (1859), Tazewell County Circuit Court, LVA, 1859-002; Year: 1860; Census Place: District 13, McDowell, Virginia; Roll: M653_1362; Page: 108; Family History Library Film: 805362; Compiled Service Records of Soldiers Who Fought in Volunteer Organizations during the American Civil War, compiled 1890–1912, documenting the period 1861–1866, NARA, publ. no. M397, roll 0422.

60. This is unusual. According to Angela Boswell, in Texas, men who accused their wives of adultery were likely to meet with success, but these were also the most contested cases. Boswell, *Her Act and Deed*, 76.

61. Silkenat, *Moments of Despair*, 79–80.

62. They had the highest rate other than Amelia County, which was exceptional for reasons stated earlier in the chapter.

63. *Robinett, Addison v. Robinett, Polly* (1852), Tazewell County Circuit Court, LVA, 1852-005; *Rose, Solomon v. Rose, Mary* (1854), Tazewell County Circuit Court, LVA, 1854-021; *Deal, Susan v. Deal, Richard* (1858), Tazewell County Circuit Court, LVA, 1858-007; *Charles, George W. v. Charles, Leah* (1859), Tazewell County Circuit Court, LVA, 1859-002; *Payne, Simeon v. Payne, Jane* (1859), Tazewell County Circuit Court, LVA, 1859-008.

64. *Boyd, Sarah J. v. Boyd, Hyram* (1857), Warren County Circuit Court Records, KDLA, no. 2385.

65. When defendants chose to respond to a divorce petition by filing their own requests for divorce, often with separate charges against their spouses, the court labeled these "cross petitions," including them within the same file. The court

could then choose to grant either the original petitioner a divorce (forcing the defendant to pay court costs) or the cross petitioner a divorce (forcing the original plaintiff to pay court costs).

66. *Glenn v. Glenn* (1853), Franklin County Circuit Court Records, KDLA, no. 529; *Henry Snelling v. E. Snelling* (1853), Franklin County Circuit Court Records, KDLA, no. 827; *Morgan, Jonathan v. Morgan, Nancy* (1854), Warren County Circuit Court Records, KDLA, no. 2186; *Martin, Joshua v. Martin, Margaret E.* (1859), Warren County Circuit Court Records, KDLA, no. 2548. Other than social sanction, respondents might attempt to file their own divorce petitions or counter the other partner's claims in order to avoid paying the costs of the suit (usually assigned to the offending spouse) or alimony (only in the case of male defendants).

67. *Kinslow, John P. v. Kinslow, Eliza Jane* (1852), Warren County Circuit Court Records, KDLA, no. 2024.

68. *Wilkinson, Melinda Frances v. Wilkinson, Thomas B.* (1853), Warren County Circuit Court Records, KDLA, no. 2122; *Boyd, Sarah J. v. Boyd, Hyram* (1857), Warren County Circuit Court Records, KDLA, no. 2385.

69. *Menefee, Susan C. v. Menefee, Banks S.* (1854), Fauquier County Circuit Court Records, LVA, no. 1854-054.

70. Ibid.

71. Ibid.

72. Berlin, *Many Thousands Gone*, 7–8.

3. To Honor and Obey

1. *Deaton, Lucinda v. Deaton, Alfred* (1860), Amelia County Circuit Court Records, LVA, 1860-001.

2. Census of the United States, 1860.

3. *Deaton, Lucinda v. Deaton, Alfred* (1860), Amelia County Circuit Court Records, LVA, 1860-001.

4. They also still lived together in 1870, according to the census. 1850, Amelia, Virginia; roll M432_933; p. 37A; image 77, Seventh Census of the United States, 1850; NARA microfilm publ. M432, 1,009 rolls; Records of the Bureau of the Census, Record Group 29; NARA; 1860, District 1, Amelia, Virginia; roll M653_1332; p. 160; Family History Library Film 805332; 1860 US Census, population schedule, NARA microfilm publ. M653, 1,438 rolls, Washington, DC, NARA, n.d.; 1870, Leigh, Amelia, Virginia; roll M593_1633; p. 378A; image 328923; Family History Library Film 553132, 1870 US census, population schedules, NARA microfilm publ. M593, 1,761 rolls, Washington, DC: NARA, n.d.

5. Buckley, *Great Catastrophe of My Life*, 3.

6. All data assessed came from a survey of circuit court cases from 1850 to 1861, using the Library of Virginia Chancery Court Records Index. Accessed February 2, 2017. http://www.virginiamemory.com/collections/chancery/.

7. *Cole, Frances v. Cole, Thomas* (1859), Amelia County Circuit Court Records, LVA, 1859-002.

8. Berlin, *Many Thousands Gone*, 7–8; Burke, *On Slavery's Border*, 1–7.

9. *The Etiquette of Courtship and Matrimony: With a Complete Guide to the Forms of a Wedding* (London: George Routledge & Sons, 1852), 8, 11–14, 18–21, 32. Found in the Louthan Family Papers, Virginia Historical Society, Richmond, Virginia (hereafter, VHS).

10. *The Etiquette of Courtship and Matrimony*, 88–92.

11. To Maria Curtis, unknown date, Taliaferro Family Papers, VHS, sec. 10. Rotundo, *American Manhood*, 138.

12. McCurry, *Masters of Small Worlds*, 215–225; Bardaglio, *Reconstructing the Household*, 24, 27. Bardaglio argues that men were dominant over their household dependents—women, children, and enslaved people. Each person had a place and each owed their ultimate allegiance and obedience to him.

13. Lebsock, *Free Women of Petersburg*, 18. Brenda Stevenson has documented similar trends in her work on antebellum Loudoun County, Virginia. Stevenson, *Life in Black and White*, 73–94.

14. Stevenson, *Life in Black and White*, 74.

15. From two undated letters, Carter Harrison to Alice Williams, Harrison Family Papers, VHS, sec. 15. Again, she was a possession—something to be won, as Stephen Berry says. Berry, *All That Makes a Man*, 86.

16. Undated letter, Carter Harrison to Alice Williams, Harrison Family Papers, VHS, sec. 15.

17. Undated letter, Carter Harrison to Alice Harrison, Harrison Family Papers, VHS, sec. 15; Carter Harrison to Alice Harrison, September 16, 1854, Harrison Family Papers, VHS, sec. 15.

18. Ibid.

19. Carter Harrison to Alice Harrison, October 31, 1857, Harrison Family Papers, VHS, sec. 15.

20. Griswold, *Family and Divorce in California*, 49–50.

21. As Peter Bardaglio states, "The patriarchal impulse to impose domestic order found itself increasingly at odds with the growing influence of romantic love," leading to conflict in southern families "between authority and autonomy." Bardaglio, *Reconstructing the Southern Household*, 26.

22. *Menefee, Susan C. v. Menefee, Banks S.* (1854), Fauquier County Circuit Court Records, LVA, no. 1854-054.

23. *Jackson, Elizabeth B. v. Jackson, John F.* (1852), Fauquier County Circuit Court Records, LVA, no. 1852-002.

24. In addition, Elizabeth had sued John for divorce a few years prior, a case that eventually went to the Virginia Supreme Court of Appeals, which ruled in his favor. In that case, she had asked for divorce *a mensa et thoro*. In 1849, she asked for a divorce *a vinculo matrimonii*. *Jackson, Elizabeth B. v. Jackson, John F.* (1852), Fauquier County Circuit Court Records, LVA, no. 1852-002.

25. *Jackson, Elizabeth B. v. Jackson, John F.* (1852), Fauquier County Circuit Court Records, LVA, no. 1852-002.

26. Ibid.

27. Ibid.

28. Ibid. According to Bardaglio, antebellum divorce cases and reforms only served to bolster "patriarchal dominance" and increase the dependence of the wife on her husband. In addition, the state was reluctant to intervene in these relationships, favoring a husband's authority. By asking the state to avoid sanctioning his wife's behavior, John Jackson gestured at these trends. Bardaglio, *Reconstructing the Household*, 34–35.

29. Schweninger, *Families in Crisis in the Old South*, 66. Schweninger argues that many southern women did not employ this device and that that fact suggests that women "were not considered as 'covered' by their husbands in the law." This does not apply in Virginia, however.

30. *Menefee, Susan C. v. Menefee, Banks S.* (1854), Fauquier Count Circuit Court Records, LVA, no. 1854-054.

31. Not a single woman in Franklin County, Kentucky, and only one woman in Warren County, Kentucky, sued by her next friend, while every single woman in Fauquier and Amelia County, Virginia, did.

32. In response to his wife's original petition in 1854, Thomas Rogers refused to even comment at first and stated that she appeared "to be a *feme covert*" and "hath exhibited her said Bill without any person being therein named her next friend." Elizabeth, his wife, immediately filed an amended bill with Thomas Owen as her next friend. *Rogers, Elizabeth A. v. Rogers, Thomas* (1854), Ohio County Circuit Court Records, WVRHC, env. 206 b-1.

33. Wyatt-Brown, *Southern Honor*, 281. He also argues that the "general level of violence" in the South may have increased the number of domestic assaults. See also Schweninger, *Families in Crisis in the Old South*, 51–52.

34. *Ramey, Mary Jane v. Ramey, Isaac* (1856), Fauquier County Circuit Court Records, LVA, no. 1856-038.

35. Quoted in Bardaglio, *Reconstructing the Household*, 34.

36. Wyatt-Brown, *Southern Honor*. See also Dickson D. Bruce, *Violence and Culture in the Antebellum South* (Austin: University of Texas Press, 1979).

37. *Jackson, Elizabeth B. v. Jackson, John F. (*1852), Fauquier County Circuit Court Records, LVA, no. 1852-002.

38. *Menefee, Susan C. v. Menefee, Banks S.* (1854), Fauquier Count Circuit Court Records, LVA, no. 1854-054. Susan Menefee's violent passions and actions share numerous similarities with those uncovered by Thavolia Glymph in the rest of the plantation South. Glymph, *Out of the House of Bondage: The Transformation of the Plantation Household* (New York: Cambridge University Press, 2008), 18–31.

39. *Wingo, Harriet T. v. Wingo, John* (1857), Amelia County Circuit Court Records, LVA, no. 1857-001.

40. *Statutes at Large of Virginia, From October Session 1792, to December Session 1806, Inclusive, in Three Volumes*, vol. 1 (Richmond: Samuel Shepherd, 1835), 133–135; Peggy Pascoe, *What Comes Naturally: Miscegenation Law and the Making of Race in America* (New York: Oxford University Press, 2019), 270–284.

41. Glenda Riley, "Legislative Divorce in Virginia, 1803–1850" *Journal of the Early Republic* 11, no. 1 (Spring 1991): 57; Joshua Rothman, "'To Be Freed from Thate Curs and Let at Liberty': Interracial Adultery and Divorce in Antebellum Virginia," *Virginia Magazine of History and Biography* 106 (Autumn 1998): 447–448. See also Thomas E. Buckley, "'Placed in the Power of Violence': The Divorce Petition of Evelina Gregory Roane, 1824," *Virginia Magazine of History and Biography* 100, no. 1 (January 1992): 36; Joshua D. Rothman, *Notorious in the Neighborhood: Sex and Families across the Color Line in Virginia, 1787–1861* (Chapel Hill: University of North Carolina Press, 2003); Martha Hodes, *White Women, Black Men: Illicit Sex in the Nineteenth-Century South* (New Haven: Yale University Press, 1997).

42. He also demonstrates that a husband's interracial infidelity did not noticeably improve a white woman's chances of receiving a divorce. Rothman, "'To Be Freed from Thate Curs,'" 448.

43. *Hawkins, Mary v. Hawkins, John* (1802), Louisa County Court Records, LVA, no. 1802-016.

44. Schweninger, *Families in Crisis in the Old South*, 18–22.

45. *Patterson, Maria F. v. Patterson, John W.* (1856) Fauquier County Court Records, LVA, no. 1856-020. For more on domestic violence in the antebellum era, see Robin Sager, *Marital Cruelty in Antebellum America* (Baton Rouge: Louisiana State University Press, 2016).

46. According to the 1850 Census, John Patterson owned twenty-two slaves. Maria's pleas proved in vain; in 1860, she was still living with her husband on their farm, worth twenty thousand dollars. Census of the United States, 1840, 1850, 1860.

47. *Bole, Margaret, by her next friend Jimeson, Wm. W. v. Bole, Wm.* (1855), Ohio County Circuit Court Records, WVRHC, env. 208 b-4.

48. Ibid.

49. Southern cultural ideals, such as honor, might also discourage the public airing of one's marital grievances through a court trial and, thus, decrease the number of formal divorces. Bardaglio, *Reconstructing the Household*, xii, 5. See also Wyatt-Brown, *Southern Honor*. James W. Ely Jr. and David J. Bodenhamer argue a similar point, stating that for a region constantly obsessed with maintaining racial order, any legal innovations could seem threatening. Ely Jr. and Bodenhamer, "Regionalism and the Legal History of the South," in *Ambivalent Legacy: A Legal History of the South*, ed. Bodenhamer and Ely Jr. (Jackson: University Press of Mississippi, 1984), 4, 7.

50. Bynum, "Reshaping the Bonds of Womanhood," 322. In addition, Brenda Stevenson has argued that white couples who sought divorce risked imperiling the

racial narrative that said white marriages were committed, monogamous, and lifelong, while black relationships were promiscuous, fluid, and immoral. Stevenson, *Life in Black and White,* 141.

51. Silkenat, *Moments of Despair*, 82–83.

52. *Bayliss, Martha C.G. (by Wm. R. Haynie her next friend) v. Bayliss, Marshall* (1852), Fauquier County Circuit Court Records, LVA, no. 1852-049.

53. *Patterson, Maria F. v. Patterson, John W.* (1856) Fauquier County Court Records, LVA, no. 1856-020.

54. *Jackson, Elizabeth B. v. Jackson, John F. (*1852), Fauquier County Circuit Court Records, LVA, no. 1852-002.

55. *Patterson, Maria F. v. Patterson, John W.* (1856) Fauquier County Court Records, LVA, no. 1856-020.

56. Ibid.

57. *Menefee, Susan C. v. Menefee, Banks S.* (1854), Fauquier Count Circuit Court Records, LVA, no. 1854-054.

58. Peter Bardaglio, for example, downplays the role of the Civil War in creating legal discontinuity, stating that often "important alterations in slavery, married women's property rights, divorce, and child-custody law did take place, especially in the 1850s, largely as a result of ideas such as individualism and contractualism beginning to penetrate southern culture." Bardaglio, *Reconstructing the Household*, xiv.

59. *America Palsgrove v. Benjamin J. Palsgrove* (1861), Franklin County Circuit Court Records, KDLA, no. 955.

60. *Nancy Hulett v. Joseph Hulett* (1860), Franklin County Circuit Court Records, KDLA, no. 950.

4. Irreconcilable Differences

1. George W. Johnson to Ann Johnson, October 20, 1861, George W. Johnson Papers, KHS, box 1, folder 5.

2. J. S. Jackson to Ann Johnson, April 14, 1862, George W. Johnson Papers, KHS, box 1, folder 6.

3. Aaron Sheehan-Dean, *Why Confederates Fought: Family and Nation in Civil War Virginia* (Chapel Hill: University of North Carolina Press, 2007), 4–5. For more on the Virginia conflict, see William Blair, *Virginia's Private War: Feeding Body and Soul in the Confederacy, 1861–1865* (New York: Oxford University Press, 1998).

4. Historians have long debated the lasting impact of southern white women's expanded household roles during the war. While some argue that women's newfound independence led them to push for an expansion of both their public and private roles in the postbellum years, others believe that the hardships of the wartime years, combined with emancipation, led many women to reclaim their positions in the patriarchal household and work to reestablish these antebellum households. For examples of the former, see Scott, *The Southern Lady* and Censer, *Reconstruction of White Southern Womanhood.* For examples of the latter, see

LeeAnn Whites, *The Civil War as Crisis in Gender: Augusta, Georgia, 1860–1890* (Athens: University of Georgia Press, 1995) and Drew Gilpin Faust, *Mothers of Invention: Women of the Slaveholding South in the American Civil War* (Chapel Hill: University of North Carolina Press, 1996). Fewer scholars have addressed how the war affected male attitudes toward domestic life, but most have shown how, for southerners especially, fighting for the Confederacy became intertwined with defending their homes and families, which elevated the role of the private sphere in their minds. For an excellent example, see Sheehan-Dean, *Why Confederates Fought.*

5. McCurry, *Confederate Reckoning*, 11–13, 26–30; Sheehan-Dean, *Why Confederates Fought*, 14–16, 25; William A. Link, *Roots of Secession: Slavery and Politics in Antebellum Virginia* (Chapel Hill: University of North Carolina Press, 2003), 215–232.

6. Journal of Ellen Kenton McGaughey Wallace, January 4, 1861, January 10, 1861, February 10, 1861, Wallace-Starling Diaries and Papers, transcribed by James T. Killebrew, KHS.

7. *Lexington Kentucky Statesman*, November 13, 1860, as reported in Dwight Lowell Dumond, ed. *Southern Editorials on Secession* (1931; repr., Gloucester, MA: Peter Smith, 1964), 233–235, as quoted in William C. Harris, *Lincoln and the Border States: Preserving the Union* (Lawrence: University Press of Kansas, 2011), 19.

8. Harris, *Lincoln and the Border States*, 23, 26.

9. Harrison and Klotter, *A New History of Kentucky*, 187.

10. Ibid., 189.

11. Henry Haviland to Susan Scrogin, April 25, 1861, Scrogin/Haviland Collection, KHS, box 1, folder 6.

12. Susan Scrogin to Henry Haviland, June 5, 1861, Scrogin/Haviland Collection, KHS, box 1, folder 6; Henry Haviland to Susan Scrogin, July 15, 1861, Scrogin/Haviland Collection, KHS, box 1, folder 6. Kentuckians showed their firm divisions in these early days. Henry Haviland reported that in Cynthiana, Kentucky, it was not safe to openly discuss Unionism, while in Cincinnati and Corrington it would be unwise to act openly secessionist. Henry Haviland to Susan Scrogin, April 25, 1861, Scrogin/Haviland Collection, KHS, box 1, folder 6.

13. Journal of Ellen Kenton McGaughey Wallace, September 8, 1861, September 10, 1861, September 25, 1861, Wallace-Starling Diaries and Papers, transcribed by James T. Killebrew, KHS.

14. Harrison and Klotter, *A New History of Kentucky*, 183–194; Marshall, *Creating a Confederate Kentucky*, 16–21.

15. Link, *Roots of Secession*, 218.

16. "The People of Fauquier in Council," November 20, 1860, *Richmond Enquirer*, December 4, 1860, as quoted in Link, *Roots of Secession*, 219.

17. Sheehan-Dean, *Why Confederates Fought*, 23–24; Stephanie McCurry, *Confederate Reckoning: Power and Politics in the Civil War South* (Cambridge, MA: Harvard University Press, 2010), 73.

18. Link, *Roots of Secession*, 227.

19. McCurry, *Masters of Small Worlds*, 258–259, 283; Elizabeth Varon, *We Mean to Be Counted: White Women and Politics in Antebellum Virginia* (Chapel Hill: University of North Carolina Press, 1998), 156.

20. On the other hand, southern men often painted northern men as "city-bred fops and limp-wristed reformers," attacking their masculinity. Bertram Wyatt-Brown argues that, in contrast to the fire-eaters of the South, "*honor* was a term not often used in Garrisonian company." Wyatt-Brown, *The Shaping of Southern Culture: Honor, Grace, and War, 1760s–1880s* (Chapel Hill: University of North Carolina Press, 2001), 178, 181.

21. Greenberg, *Manifest Manhood and Antebellum American Empire*, 11–13; Stewart, "Select Men of Sober and Industrious Habits," 290–293.

22. R. Beverly Fraysee to Waitman T. Willey, June 19, 1866, Willey Papers, WVRHC, box 3.

23. E. C. Bunker to Waitman T. Willey, February 27, 1861, Willey Papers, WVRHC, box 8.

24. Undated letter to *Clarksburg National Guard* in Waitman T. Willey Diary, Willey Papers, WVRHC.

25. Chester D. Hubbard to William Hubbard, November 10, 1860, Hubbard Family Papers, (microfilm, reel 1), WVRHC.

26. Chester D. Hubbard to Waitman T. Willey, April 30, 1861, Willey Papers, WVRHC, box 1.

27. "Coercion," *Wellsburg Herald*, December 21, 1860, as quoted in Link, *Roots of Secession*, 221.

28. George Reese, ed., *Proceedings of the Virginia State Convention of 1861, February 13–May 1* (Richmond: Virginia State Library, 1965), vol. 1, February 28, 1861, 271–291, as quoted in Edward Ayers, *In the Presence of Mine Enemies: War in the Heart of America, 1859–1863* (New York: W. W. Norton, 2003), 121.

29. Chester D. Hubbard to Waitman T. Willey, April 30, 1861, Willey Papers, WVRHC, box 1. The "submissionist" label contained elements of both gender *and* race, as it (and Hubbard's interpretation of it) also implied that Unionists were slave-like.

30. F. H. Pierpont to Waitman T. Willey, March 16, 1859, Willey Papers, WVRHC, box 1.

31. Henry Dering to Waitman T. Willey, March 19, 1861, Willey Papers, WVRHC, box 1.

32. George W. Summers to Waitman T. Willey, June 15, 1862, Willey Papers, WVRHC, box 2. During the 1850 Reform Convention, A. F. Haymond wrote to Waitman T. Willey that the West was "degraded" and would remain so if the East did not agree to share power and aid in their development. A. F. Haymond to Waitman T. Willey, April 28, 1851, Willey Papers, WVRHC, box 1. When pleading with Willey to accept the nomination for lieutenant governor of the state, one man asked him to accept the honor on behalf of his "long neglected" section. L. Berkshire to Waitman T. Willey, February 11, 1859, Willey Papers, WVRHC, box 1.

33. Henry Dering to Waitman T. Willey, March 19, 1861, Willey Papers, WVRHC, box 1.

34. Bertram Wyatt-Brown has argued that, in the South, some secessionist fervor stemmed from feelings of individual worthlessness. In western Virginia, a sense of inadequacy that the leaders had long harbored toward the eastern aristocracy may have instilled in them desires for a secession of their own—to the Union. Wyatt-Brown, *Shaping of Southern Culture*, 188.

35. Otis K. Rice, *West Virginia: A History* (Lexington: University Press of Kentucky, 1985), 116.

36. William P. Willey to Waitman T. Willey, April 29, 1861, Willey Papers, WVRHC, box 1.

37. John J. Davis to Waitman T. Willey and Francis H. Pierpont, April 25, 1861, Willey Papers, WVRHC, box 1; Chester D. Hubbard to Waitman T. Willey, April 30, 1861, Willey Papers, WVRHC, box 1.

38. Richard Orr Curry, *A House Divided: A Study of Statehood Politics and the Copperhead Movement in West Virginia* (Pittsburgh: University of Pittsburgh Press, 1964), 2; Francis H. Pierpont to Julia Pierpont, June 20, 1861, Francis H. Pierpont Papers, WVRHC, box 1.

39. Curry, *A House Divided* 2; Rice, *West Virginia*, 140.

40. "A State of Convenience: The Creation of West Virginia," West Virginia Department of Arts, Culture and History, accessed August 21, 2019, www.wvculture.org/history/statehood/statehood11.html. Of the sixty-one members of the convention, three owned slaves before the war, and I could not determine the slaveholding status of six. Of those I could find in the records, 5.5 percent owned slaves. Of all the members, at least 4.9 percent owned slaves and no more than 14.8 percent.

41. Robert M. Bastress, *The West Virginia State Constitution: A Reference Guide* (Westport, CT: Greenwood, 1995), 10–11. Bastress states that the establishment of the township system based upon the New England model demonstrated a northeastern influence. The delegates also made inroads in establishing a universal education system, something they had not been able to persuade Virginia to do. See also Donna J. Spindel, "Women's Legal Rights in West Virginia, 1863–1984," *West Virginia History* 51 (1992): 29–42.

42. Charles H. Ambler, Frances H. Atwood, and William B. Mathews, eds., *Debates and Proceedings of the First Constitutional Convention of West Virginia (1861–1863)* (Huntington, WV, 1939), 2:51.

43. Lebsock, *Free Women of Petersburg*, 57.

44. Ambler, Atwood, and Mathews, *Debates and Proceedings*, 2:53.

45. McCurry, *Masters of Small Worlds*, 60, 72, 89.

46. Ambler, Atwood, and Mathews, *Debates and Proceedings*, 2:64. Arguments that married women's property acts would alter the relationship between man and wife were at the heart of the law's defeat in some southern states, such as antebellum Georgia. Warbasse, *The Changing Legal Rights of Married Women*, 176.

47. Ambler, Atwood, and Mathews, *Debates and Proceedings*, 2:51, 61–62.

48. Ambler, Atwood, and Mathews, *Debates and Proceedings*, 2:51, 56.

49. Ambler, Atwood, and Mathews, *Debates and Proceedings*, 2:52, 61, 63. Historians such as Suzanne Lebsock have argued that men passed these acts without fully realizing the implications they would have on women's positions in society; this cannot be said of West Virginia. The records of the contentious discussion show that legislators were well aware of the impact of these laws upon women's place in the household and society. Suzanne Lebsock, "Radical Reconstruction and the Property Rights of Southern Women," *Journal of Southern History* 43 (May 1977): 204.

50. Ambler, Atwood, and Mathews, *Debates and Proceedings*, 2:65–66; 3:387.

51. *Code of West Virginia*, chap. 66, sec. 1 (Charleston, 1870).

52. *Code of West Virginia*, chap. 66, sec. 3 (1870); Howe, "Patient Laborers," 137–138.

53. Hoff, *Law, Gender, and Injustice*, 377.

54. Stanley, *From Bondage to Contract*, xi–xiii, 10, 18, 197.

55. Harrison and Klotter, *A New History of Kentucky*, 196–202.

56. Scott, *Southern Lady*, 81–102; Joan Cashin, "'Since the War Broke Out': The Marriage of Kate and William McClure," in *Divided Houses: Gender and the Civil War*, ed. Catherine Clinton and Nina Silber (New York: Oxford University Press, 1992), 200–212; Bardaglio, *Reconstructing the Household*, 129–130.

57. Sheehan-Dean, *Why Confederates Fought*, 3.

58. Estimates vary regarding Kentucky's male military population. Most agree that between twenty-five and forty thousand Kentuckians served in the Confederate military, while between ninety and one hundred thousand fought for the Union. Harrison and Klotter, *A New History of Kentucky*, 195. Kentucky's white male population in 1860 was 474,193, with approximately forty thousand over the age of fifty. This means that about 32 percent of those white Kentucky men below the age of fifty served in either army. In West Virginia, estimates are that forty thousand male citizens served in the military, twenty thousand for the Confederate army and twenty thousand for the Union army. Mark A. Snell, *West Virginia and the Civil War: Mountaineers Are Always Free* (Charleston, SC: History Press, 2011). In 1860, the total white male population of the fifty counties that would eventually form the state was about 176,000. Assuming that a roughly equivalent portion of that population (about 9 percent) was over the age of fifty, about 25 percent of the white male population below the age of fifty served in the military during the war. Historical Census Browser, 2004, University of Virginia, Geospatial and Statistical Data Center, retrieved June 14, 2013, https://mapserver.lib.virginia.edu/. (The Historical Census Browser site has since been permanently closed.) Drew Gilpin Faust estimates that three out of four white men of military age eventually served in the Confederate army. Faust, *Mothers of Invention*, 30.

59. Laura Edwards, *Scarlett Doesn't Live Here Anymore: Southern Women in the Civil War Era* (Urbana: University of Illinois Press, 2000), 66; Marshall, *Creating*

a Confederate Kentucky, 20–21; Gordon B. McKinney, "Women's Role in Civil War Western North Carolina," *North Carolina Historical Review* 69 (Spring 1978): 209–245; Victoria Bynum, *Unruly Women: The Politics of Social and Sexual Control in the Old South* (Chapel Hill: University of North Carolina Press, 1992), 130–150.

60. Faust, *Mothers of Invention*, 53–79; Glymph, *Out of the House of Bondage*, 97–136.

61. Historians have generally been of two opinions about the impact of men's absence and the war on the status of women. Many argue that this provided women the opportunity to embrace new roles and establish some measure of independence. See Scott, *Southern Lady* and Mary Elizabeth Massey, *Bonnet Brigades: American Women and the Civil War* (New York: Knopf, 1966). Others say that the war led women to reinforce their antebellum roles. See Faust, *Mothers of Invention* and George C. Rable, *Civil Wars: Women and the Crisis of Southern Nationalism* (Urbana: University of Illinois Press, 1989).

62. LeeAnn Whites and Alecia P. Long, "Introduction," in *Occupied Women: Gender, Military Occupation, and the American Civil War*, ed. Whites and Long (Baton Rouge: Louisiana State University Press, 2009), 2–3, 6–7. See also Stephen V. Ash, *When the Yankees Came: Conflict and Chaos in the Occupied South* (Chapel Hill: University of North Carolina Press, 1996); Michael Fellman, *Inside War: The Guerrilla Conflict in Missouri during the American Civil War* (New York: Oxford University Press, 1989); and Mark Grimsley, *The Hard Hand of War: Union Military Policy toward Southern Civilians, 1861–1865* (New York: Cambridge University Press, 1995).

63. Fanny Bell to Mildred Fry Bullitt, October 27, 1862, Bullitt Family Papers, FHS.

64. Journal of Ellen Kenton McGaughey Wallace, December 13, 1862, Wallace-Starling Diaries and Papers, transcribed by James T. Killebrew, KHS.

65. Mary Johnstone to Mildred Fry Bullitt, November 10, 1862, Bullitt Family papers, FHS.

66. Hula Winston to Lizzie Jones, April 17, 1864, Winston-Jones Family Papers, FHS, folder 6.

67. Jacqueline Glass Campbell, *When Sherman Marched North from the Sea: Resistance on the Confederate Home Front* (Chapel Hill: University of North Carolina Press, 2003), 44, 52.

68. Journal of Susanna Gordon Waddell, June 28, 1864, folder 3, in the Susanna Gordon Waddell Diary #02383-z, Southern Historical Collection, Chapel Hill, North Carolina (hereafter, SHC).

69. Unknown author to Mollie, February 14, 1862, Robinson Family Papers, WVRHC, box 1, folder 5.

70. Michael Fellman, "Women and Guerrilla Warfare," in *Divided Houses*, ed. Clinton and Silber, 147–148, 155.

71. Journal of Annie Leslie McCarroll Starling, December 12, 1864, December 17, 1864, Wallace-Starling Diaries and Papers, transcribed by James T. Killebrew, KHS.

72. "Recollections of 1864," Sarah Dandridge Cooke Duval Papers, VHS, section b2.

73. Faust, *Mothers of Invention*, 196–219.

74. Catherine Clinton, "'Public Women' and Sexual Politics during the American Civil War," in *Battle Scars: Gender and Sexuality in the American Civil War*, ed. Catherine Clinton and Nina Silber (New York: Oxford University Press, 2006), 64–66.

75. Campbell, *When Sherman Marched North from the Sea*, 14–15.

76. Faust, *Mothers of Invention*, 196–200. For an example of women facing unsanctioned and extramilitary conflict, see John C. Inscoe and Gordon B. McKinney, *The Heart of Confederate Appalachia: Western North Carolina in the Civil War* (Chapel Hill: University of North Carolina Press, 2000), 187–207.

77. F. Gerald Ham, ed. "The Mind of a Copperhead: Letters of John J. Davis on the Secession Crisis and Statehood Politics in Western Virginia 1860–1862," *West Virginia History* 24 (January 1963): 94; Anna Kennedy to John J. Davis, November 30, 1860, Davis Papers, WVRHC, box 4.

78. Henry Haviland to Susan Scrogin, August 4, 1861, Scrogin/Haviland Collection, KHS, box 1, folder 6.

79. Taylor, *Divided Family in Civil War America*, 41–42, 46–47. Taylor documents numerous incidents of women asking their suitors, fiancés, or husbands to leave the military because they did not support the side their partner had chosen.

80. Susan Scrogin to Henry Haviland, December 7, 1861, Scrogin/Haviland Collection, KHS, box 1, folder 6.

81. Taylor, *Divided Family in Civil War America*, 36. The issue of women's divided loyalties and their political ramifications has been most notably explored by Kerber in *No Constitutional Right to Be Ladies*, 3–46.

82. For an excellent article on women's Civil War correspondence in a border state, see LeeAnn Whites, "'Corresponding with the Enemy': Mobilizing the Relational Field of Battle in St. Louis" in *Occupied Women*, ed. Whites and Long, 103–116. See also Streater, "'She-Rebels' on the Supply Line: Gender Conventions in Civil War Kentucky," in *Occupied Women*, ed. Whites and Long, 88–89.

83. From Charles Simrall to Belle Price, September 7, 1864, box 1, folder 7, in the Charles Barrington Simrall Papers #1665, SHC.

84. From Charles Simrall to Belle Price, undated, box 1, folder 6, in the Charles Barrington Simrall Papers #1665, SHC.

85. McCurry, *Confederate Reckoning*, 85–132; Taylor, *Divided Family in Civil War America*, 91–122.

86. Amy Feely Morsman, *The Big House after Slavery: Virginia Plantation Families and Their Postbellum Domestic Experiment* (Charlottesville: University of Virginia Press, 2010), 4.

87. Journal of Mary Boswell Ford, February 2, 1865, Ford Family Papers, FHS.

88. Jacqueline Glass Campbell argues that it was not unusual for southern white women to run plantations in the antebellum period but concurs that they endured unusual and extended confrontations with the Union army on the home

front during the war. Campbell, *When Sherman Marched North from the Sea*, 13–14. For a discussion of deputy husbands in the colonial period, see Laurel Thatcher Ulrich, *Good Wives: Image and Reality in the Lives of Women in Northern New England, 1650–1750* (New York: Vintage, 1990), 35–50.

89. Laura Edwards has argued that most Civil War "deputy husbands" did not expect their changed position to last. Edwards, *Scarlett Doesn't Live Here Anymore*, 77–78, 82.

90. Whites and Long, "Introduction," 2–3.

91. Mary L. Mackall, Stevan F. Meserve, and Anne Mackall Sasscer, eds., *In the Shadow of the Enemy: The Civil War Journal of Ida Powell Dulany* (Knoxville: University of Tennessee Press, 2009), xvii, 31.

92. George Johnson to Ann Johnson, October 20, 1861, George W. Johnson Papers, KHS, box 1, folder 4. He gave her one piece of advice: "Never . . . give up your property to my creditors."

93. Semantha Morgan to John Morgan Jr., October 11, 1878, Atkeson-Morgan Papers, WVRHC.

94. John Morgan Jr. to Semantha Morgan, September 5, 1875, Atkeson-Morgan Papers, WVRHC.

95. Susan Scrogin to Henry Haviland, undated, Scrogin/Haviland Collection, KHS, box 1, folder 10.

96. Robert Powell Page to Martha Turner "Pattie" Hardee, October 21, 1863, October 28, 1863, Robert Powell Page Letters, VHS, folder 1.

97. Carter Harrison to Alice Harrison, May 3, 1861, Harrison Family Papers, VHS, sec. 15.

98. Alice Harrison to Carter Harrison, June 6, 1861; Carter Harrison to Alice Harrison, July 11, 1861. Both found in Harrison Family Papers, VHS, sec. 15.

99. Mrs. Harrison to Alice Harrison, January 27, 1862, Harrison Family Papers, VHS, sec. 10.

100. Unknown author to Helen Robinson, May 20, 1863, Robinson Family Manuscripts, WVRHC, box 1, folder 7.

101. Unknown author to Helen Robinson, December 15, 1861, Robinson Family Manuscripts, WVRHC, box 1, folder 5.

102. Faust, *Mothers of Invention*, 118.

103. From Charles Simrall to Belle Price, June 1864, box 1, folder 6; from Belle Price to Charles Simrall, June 2, 1864. Found in the Charles Barrington Simrall Papers #1665, SHC.

104. Faust, *Mothers of Invention*, 145–152.

105. Robert Powell Page to Martha Turner "Pattie" Hardee, October 29, 1863, Robert Powell Page Letters, VHS, folder 1.

106. From Charles Sydnor to Mary Elizabeth Davis, December 5, 1864, box 1, folder 2; from Charles Sydnor to Mary Elizabeth Davis, February 5, 1865, box 1, folder 3; from Williams W. Drane to Charles Sydnor, March 6, 1865, box 1, folder 3, in the Charles W. Sydnor Letters #02864-z, SHC.

107. Unknown author to Helen Robinson, October 25, 1863, Robinson Family Manuscripts, WVRHC, box 1, folder 9.

108. Drew Gilpin Faust, *This Republic of Suffering: Death and the American Civil War* (New York: Vintage, 2006), 3–6.

109. Sheehan-Dean, *Why Confederates Fought*, 27.

110. George Johnson to Ann Johnson, October 25, 1861, George W. Johnson Papers, KHS, box 1, folder 5.

111. Oscar Styron to Mollie Burroughs, December 29, 1862, Burroughs Family Letters, VHS.

112. From Charles Sydnor to Mary Elizabeth Davis, April 3, 1864, box 1, folder 2, in the Charles W. Sydnor Letters #02864-z, SHC.

113. From Charles Sydnor to Mary Elizabeth Davis, September 26, 1864, box 1, folder 2, in the Charles W. Sydnor Letters #02864-z, SHC.

114. Sheehan-Dean, *Why Confederates Fought*, 4; Berry, *All That Makes a Man*, 171, 182–184.

115. Oscar Styron to Mollie Burroughs, June 20, 1862, Burroughs Family Letters, VHS.

116. George Johnson to Ann Johnson, January 23, 1862, George W. Johnson Papers, KHS, box 1, folder 5.

117. Susan Scrogin to Henry Haviland, December 21, 1863, Scrogin/Haviland Letters, KHS, box 1, folder 8.

118. Semantha Morgan to John Morgan Jr., August 31, 1881, Atkeson-Morgan Papers, WVRHC.

119. Sallie Bullitt to Julia Bullitt, December 19, 1876, Bullitt-Oxmoor Papers, FHS, folder 587.

120. November 15, 1865, George W. Johnson Papers, KHS, box 1, folder 10.

121. From A. P. Farnsley to Mary E. E. Thurman, undated, folder 1, in the A. P. Farnsley Letters #03612-z, SHC.

122. James Carter to Melville Carter, February 16, 1870, Melville Briney Papers, FHS.

123. Faust, *Mothers of Invention*, 140–141.

124. Clinton, "'Public Women,'" 61.

125. From Charles Sydnor to Mollie Davis, April 3, 1864, box 1, folder 2, in the Charles W. Sydnor Letters #02864-z, SHC.

5. Torn Apart

1. *Long, Lewis v. Long, Rosanna* (1866), Ohio County Circuit Court Records, WVRHC, env. 267 b-5.

2. Of 187,000 men from Virginia who served in an army during the Civil War, about 155,000 of them served in the Confederate army. Aaron Sheehan-Dean, *Encyclopedia Virginia* online, http://www.encyclopediavirginia.org/Virginia_Soldiers_Confederate_During_the_Civil_War. From Kentucky, 140,000 served

in the Union and Confederate armies. Harrison and Klotter, *A New History of Kentucky*, 215.

3. The Civil War, considered by many a watershed moment in American history, also served as a critical juncture in domestic legal issues. Hendrik Hartog argues that marriage in the nineteenth century was like private property, untouched by government intervention except for reasons of public good. Therefore, "Government needed strong public reasons to justify entering that private sphere—whether of property or of family." As scholars have shown, the Civil War and the Reconstruction years featured a dramatic rise in the presence and power of the federal government. Trickling down, both state and local governments began to intervene more often in the domestic sphere after the war, possibly explaining the uptick in divorces. Hartog, *Man and Wife in America*, 24. On the growth in the federal government, see Heather Cox Richardson, *West from Appomattox: The Reconstruction of America after the Civil War* (New Haven: Yale University Press, 2007); Faust, *This Republic of Suffering.*

4. *Long, Lewis v. Long, Rosanna* (1866), Ohio County Circuit Court Records, WVRHC, env. 267 b-5.

5. *Ferrell, William v. Ferrell, Rebecca* (1866), Tazewell County Circuit Court Records, LVA, no. 1866-006.

6. *Wimmer, Robert v. Wimmer, Sabra Ann* (1866), Tazewell County Circuit Court Records, LVA, no. 1866-010; *Runyon, Henry v. Runyon, Martha* (1867), Pike County Circuit Court Records, KDLA, no. 2571. Martha Runyon had also, as deponents repeatedly emphasized, gotten "the clap."

7. Edwards, *Gendered Strife and Confusion*, 162–165.

8. Silkenat, *Moments of Despair*, 96, 101–111.

9. *Stroble, Jacob v. Stroble, Ellen* (1865), Ohio County Circuit Court Records, WVRHC, env. 259 b-5.

10. Ibid.

11. Ibid.

12. *White, Archibald v. White, Susan* (1867), Tazewell County Circuit Court Cases, LVA, no. 1867-013.

13. If that had not been enough to convince him of the necessity for divorce, his wife also refused to live with him anymore. *Hutchinson, John R. v. Hutchinson, Mary E.* (1870), Ohio County Circuit Court Records, WVRHC, env. 282 e-1.

14. *Prophater, Wm. v. Prophater, Isabella* (1868), Ohio County Circuit Court Records, WVRHC, env. 276 b-11.

15. *Cecil, William v. Cecil, Emma* (1868), Tazewell County Circuit Court Cases, LVA, no. 1868-007.

16. *Lindemuth, Louis v. Lindemuth, Augusta* (1871), Ohio County Circuit Court Records, WVRHC, env. 289 B-8.

17. *Goudy, Elizabeth O. by her next friend Milleger, James [her father] v. Goudy, James M.* (1868), Ohio County Circuit Court Records, WVRHC, env. 274 e-9.

18. *Heston, Catherine, by her next friend Mulrine, John v. Heston, John* (1867), Ohio County Circuit Court Records, WVRHC, env. 272 b-6.

19. *Hawkins, Eliza v. Hawkins, R. T.* (1869), Franklin County Circuit Court Records, KDLA, no. 1095.

20. *Keefer, Mary—by her next friend Winter, Philip v. Keefer, Xavier* (1868), Ohio County Circuit Court Records, WVRHC, env. 275 b-6.

21. In addition, over 70 percent of eligible white men from Kentucky did not fight in the war. Marshall, *Creating a Confederate Kentucky*, 20.

22. David Silkenat has found a similar trend in Civil War adultery in North Carolina. Silkenat, *Moments of Despair*, 103.

23. Silkenat, *Moments of Despair*, 102.

24. Rothman, *Hands and Hearts*, 157–159.

25. From Charles Simrall to Belle Price, June 1864, box 1, folder 6; Belle Price to Charles Simrall, July 19, 1864, box 1, folder 7; Charles Simrall to Belle Price, August 11, 1864, box 1, folder 7. Found in the Charles Barrington Simrall Papers #1665, SHC.

26. "Oath of Allegiance," October 21, 1862, box 1, folder 4; from Belle Price to Charles Simrall, July 18, 1864, box 1, folder 7; from Charles Simrall to Belle Price, August 11, 1864, box 1, folder 7. All found in the Charles Barrington Simrall Papers #1665, SHC.

27. From Charles Simrall to Belle Price, June 28, 1864, box 1, folder 6; from unknown author to Belle Price, summer 1864, box 1, folder 7; from Charles Simrall to Belle Price, August 11, 1864, box 1, folder 7. All found in the Charles Barrington Simrall Papers #1665, SHC.

28. *Clifford, P. N. v. Clifford, L. A.* (1867), Franklin County Circuit Court Cases, KDLA, no. 1031.

29. Marshall, *Creating a Confederate Kentucky*, 20–23; Harrison and Klotter, *A New History of Kentucky*, 198–205.

30. *Young, Thomas v. Young, Sarah* (1867), Franklin County Circuit Court Cases, KDLA, no. 1039.

31. *Carpenter, Peter v. Carpenter, Mary* (1867), Tazewell County Circuit Court Cases, LVA, no. 1867-017.

32. Faust, *Mothers of Invention*, 147. See also Taylor, *Divided Family in Civil War America*, 49–61. Taylor argues, however, that the community usually frowned upon Union–Confederate alliances, though they did occur.

33. Journal of Annie Leslie McCarroll Starling, December 10, 1861, Wallace-Starling Diaries and Papers, transcribed by James T. Killebrew, KHS.

34. Journal of Annie Leslie McCarroll Starling, December 28, 1861, Wallace-Starling Diaries and Papers, transcribed by James T. Killebrew, KHS.

35. Journal of Annie Leslie McCarroll Starling, May 26, 1864, Wallace-Starling Diaries and Papers, transcribed by James T. Killebrew, KHS.

36. James Bullitt to Mrs. John Henry Chenoweth, October 30, 1862, Bullitt Family Papers, FHS.

37. Benjamin Field Memoir, FHS, 171–174.

38. *Anderson, Fannie E. v. Anderson, James F.* (1870), Franklin County Circuit Court Cases, KDLA, no. 1101.

39. *Ballard, Nancy (a.k.a. Harman) v. Ballard, Jacob* (1867), Tazewell County Circuit Court Cases, LVA, no. 1867-006.

40. Journal of Annie Leslie McCarroll Starling, May 12, 1863, Wallace-Starling Diaries and Papers, transcribed by James T. Killebrew, KHS.

41. Journal of Annie Leslie McCarroll Starling, September 11, 1863, Wallace-Starling Diaries and Papers, transcribed by James T. Killebrew, KHS.

42. E. G. Davison to Helen Robinson, Robinson Family Manuscripts, WVRHC, box 1, folder 6. Opening oneself up to correspondence from strangers had its risks. Davison assured her that he had nothing to do with a "very profein" letter she had recently received from "one of our boys."

43. James Boyd to Helen Robinson, August 7, 1861, Robinson Family Manuscripts, WVRHC, box 1, folder 4; J. Robinson to his mother, August 29, 1861, Robinson Family Manuscripts, WVRHC, box 1, folder 4.

44. W. J. Robinson to his mother, January 31, 1864, Robinson Family Manuscripts, WVRHC, box 1, folder 10.

45. In Ohio County, 46 percent of cases involved the charge of abandonment. Ohio County's most frequent charge was adultery, involved in 54 percent of cases. These numbers include any case in which a petitioner included abandonment as a charge, although not necessarily the only charge. Fauquier County, Warren County, and Tazewell County petitioners accused their partners of abandonment in about half of the cases before the war. Amelia County petitioners used the accusation in both of the prewar divorce cases.

46. Fauquier County petitioners also used the charge more, about 58 percent of the time. Their increase could have been slower because they already had a high number of abandonment charges. However, Warren, Tazewell, and Amelia Counties saw a decrease in the number of abandonment charges, although it was still used in all of them about half the time.

47. Yael A. Sternhell, *Routes of War: The World of Movement in the Confederate South* (Cambridge, MA: Harvard University Press, 2012), 167–179.

48. Edwards, *Gendered Strife and Confusion*, 112–114; Marshall, *Creating a Confederate Identity*, 10.

49. Unsigned letter, January 19, 1865, Winston-Jones Family Papers, FHS, folder 5.

50. *Montgomery, Samuel S. v. Montgomery, Martha* (1866), Franklin County Circuit Court Cases, KDLA, no. 1026; *Boyd, I. B. v. Boyd, T. B.* (1867), Franklin County Circuit Court Cases, KDLA, no. 1040; *Waits, Elizabeth v. Waits, David* (1870), Franklin County Circuit Court Cases, KDLA, no. 1110.

51. *Beamer, Barbary v. Beamer, Jacob* (1869), Franklin County Circuit Court Cases, KDLA, no. 1092.

52. *Zimmerman, Martha M. v. Zimmerman, Leonard N.* (1870), Franklin County Circuit Court Cases, KDLA, no. 1111.

53. *Smithson, Sallie Ann v. Smithson, John M.* (1873), Franklin County Circuit Court Cases, KDLA, no. 1199.

54. *Sayre, B. B. v. Sayre, Catharine* (1868), Franklin County Circuit Court Cases, KDLA, no. 1050; *Morten, Lafayette v. Morten, Belle* (1869), Franklin County Circuit Court Cases, KDLA, no. 1079; *Anderson, Fannie E. v. Anderson, James F.* (1870), Franklin County Circuit Court Cases, KDLA, no. 1101; *Ritchie, Zilphia v. Ritchie, George W.* (1870), Franklin County Circuit Court Cases, KDLA, no. 1119; *Warren, William H. v. Warren, Cynthia E.* (1871), Franklin County Circuit Court Cases, KDLA, no. 1131; *Lynn, Jacob v. Lynn, Nancy Catharine* (1873), Franklin County Circuit Court Cases, KDLA, no. 1186.

55. For an example of this, see *Dillion, Margaret E. v. Dillion, William A.* (1871), Tazewell County Circuit Court Cases, LVA, no. 1871-040.

56. According to Hendrik Hartog, "Because of marital unity, a wife's domicile remained that of her husband, even when she lived hundreds of miles away in a different state." Hartog, *Man and Wife in America*, 106.

57. *Rhyms v. Rhyms*, 70 Kentucky Court of Appeals 316 (1870).

58. *Roberson, Temperance v. Roberson, William* (1868), Warren County Circuit Court Cases, KDLA, no. 3287.

59. After the war, Kentucky citizens had "89,000 fewer horses, 37,000 fewer mules, and 172,000 fewer cattle" than they did at the start of the war. In parts of the state, land values decreased by about one-fourth. Harrison and Klotter, *A New History of Kentucky*, 216.

60. In a discussion of how wartime changes might actually enforce old marital norms, Nancy Cott argues that "the horrors and deprivations of combat, the losses and separations, the maimings and loneliness created longings to return to prewar conventions and resume the familiar customs of home." Cott, *Public Vows*, 78. Edwards argues, "Faced with ruined fields, dilapidated buildings, confiscated stock, an emancipated labor force, and scattered fortunes, few could escape the unsettling sense that they had failed as men." Edwards, *Gendered Strife and Confusion*, 113.

61. According to Laura Edwards, "Not only did the borders of their households shrink but the very basis of [white men's] mastery was called into question." Edwards, *Gendered Strife and Confusion*, 8.

62. Anne Marshall attributes a similar uptick in violence in Kentucky, including intimidation and lynching, to the destabilization of the prewar social and economic system. She includes Frankfort, the county seat of Franklin County, as a location of widespread Ku Klux Klan activity. Wartime violence also left a legacy of bloodshed in the state. Changes in divorce cases reflect a similar trend. Marshall, *Creating a Confederate Kentucky*, 56–58.

63. In addition, a few of these cases extended to the prewar years. As will be shown later, Fauquier and Amelia County residents had the longest marriages at

the time of their divorce filings and waited the longest between a crisis and filing for divorce. This could ultimately skew their statistics and points toward this second explanation: that litigants needed multiple charges to make a case before a more conservative legal system.

64. Schweninger, *Families in Crisis in the Old South*, 48–49.

65. *Walden, Virginia F. v. Walden, John* (1869), Fauquier County Circuit Court Records, LVA, no. 1869-037 and no. 1869-071.

66. *Tunstall, Margaret v. Tunstall, George* (1872), Amelia County Circuit Court Records, LVA, no. 1872-007.

67. James Petrie, *The Marriage Gift* (Philadelphia: Presbyterian Board of Publications, 1864), 7–9. Held by FHS.

68. Ibid., 9, 103.

69. Ibid., 46, 52.

6. Stability in the Face of Great Distress

1. Painting the Confederate cause as one of familial protection drew the sympathy and support of southerners from all walks of life and created fiery support among the women of the South. McCurry, *Masters of Small Worlds*, 293.

2. Bardaglio, *Reconstructing the Household*, xi–xv. See also McCurry, *Masters of Small Worlds*, 219–224.

3. Naturally, this is not to say that white southern households were not contested before the war, rather that this contestation took on new and urgent meaning in light of emancipation. As scholars have shown, black and white southern women challenged the authority of masters and husbands during the antebellum years, in ways both subtle and overt. In this sense, emancipation merely gave these women further opportunity and the means with which to challenge their subordinate status. For an analysis of white women's challenges to male authority in the antebellum era, see Varon, *We Mean to Be Counted.* For a look at both black and white women's struggles on southern plantations, see Fox-Genovese, *Within the Plantation Household*, and Marli Frances Weiner, *Mistresses and Slaves: Plantation Women in South Carolina, 1830–80* (Urbana: University of Illinois Press, 1998). For an analysis of enslaved female resistance, see Stephanie M. H. Camp, *Closer to Freedom: Enslaved Women and Everyday Resistance in the Plantation South* (Chapel Hill: University of North Carolina Press, 2004).

4. Historians have shown that the Confederate loss and the emancipation of four million slaves led to an identity crisis for many southern men as they struggled to define their roles as household heads. White southern women also reevaluated their positions within the household and with respect to the public sphere. Whites, *Civil War as a Crisis in Gender*, 2–5; Faust, *Mothers of Invention*, 250–254; Edwards, *Gendered Strife and Confusion*, 27–30.

5. Lowell H. Harrison, *The Civil War in Kentucky* (Lexington: University Press of Kentucky, 1975), 80.

6. Astor, *Rebels on the Border*, 133–144; Marshall, *Creating a Confederate Kentucky*, 1–3, 55–62.

7. Edwards, *Gendered Strife and Confusion*, 28.

8. Barton, "'Good Cooks and Washers,'" 436–460.

9. Burke, *On Slavery's Border*, 9, 54–60.

10. Jane Turner Censer has argued that many postwar Virginians sought companionate marriages. However, she argues that this depended a good bit upon age, with the youngest generation most easily able to adapt to emancipation and change their marital patterns. Censer, *Reconstruction of White Southern Womanhood*, 32. See also Boswell, *Her Act and Deed*, 4.

11. For more information on the development of companionate marriages in the United States, see Lebsock, *Free Women of Petersburg*, 17; Coontz, *Marriage, a History*, 4–5.

12. James L. Roark, *Masters without Slaves: Southern Planters in the Civil War and Reconstruction* (New York: W. W. Norton, 1977), 157, 203.

13. Silkenat, *Moments of Despair*, 2, 75, 105–106. For two analyses of the impact of Reconstruction constitutional conventions, see Bynum, "Reshaping the Bonds of Womanhood," 320–333, and Lebsock, "Radical Reconstruction and the Property Rights of Southern Women," 195–216.

14. Bardaglio, *Reconstructing the Household*, 135–137. Amy Feely Morsman argues that there was a "subtle shift" from patriarchy to mutuality in postwar Virginia, but it was contingent upon the war and "especially the profound challenges that emancipation wrought." She also makes clear that this change was not without resistance on the part of planters. Additionally, I argue that it happened more gradually than in Kentucky. Morsman, *Big House after Slavery*, 4–6, 8.

15. Both Anne Firor Scott and Jane Turner Censer argue that women's roles expanded in the postwar years. See Scott, *Southern Lady*, 106–107, 118–119, 129–133, and Censer, *Reconstruction of White Southern Womanhood.*

16. Marshall, *Creating a Confederate Kentucky*, 11–13.

17. Eric Foner, *Reconstruction: America's Unfinished Revolution, 1863–1877* (New York: Harper and Row, 1988), 38–39.

18. Astor, *Rebels on the Border*, 123–133. According to Astor, 57 percent of Kentucky's blacks served in the army during the war, with many stationed at home. This only exacerbated postwar racial tension in Kentucky.

19. Marshall, *Creating a Confederate Kentucky*, 34.

20. Astor, *Rebels on the Border*, 122, 149–156.

21. Bardaglio, *Reconstructing the Household*, 118–120.

22. Silkenat, *Moments of Despair*, 104–111.

23. Jones, *An Historical Geography of the Changing Divorce Law*, 37, 40.

24. Silkenat, *Moments of Despair*, 102–103.

25. The eight antebellum divorces were spread over eleven years and the twelve postbellum cases over only nine. The Fauquier County Circuit Court heard 0.7 cases per year in the 1850s and 1.3 cases per year in the late 1860s and early 1870s.

However, these numbers are much lower than the 5.6 cases per year in postbellum Ohio County and the 7.2 cases in postbellum Franklin County (sharp increases from their prewar numbers of 1.2 and 4.25 cases per year, respectively).

26. There was also a notable spike in 1868, three years after the end of the war. West Virginia's state statutes stipulated that residents must wait three years to sue for abandonment; this indicates that many wartime marriages that effectively ended in 1865 did not legally end until 1868. It is curious that Franklin County did not see a similar spike in 1866, when its residents would have been able to sue for divorce on the grounds of abandonment. Perhaps the war was not as big a factor in these divorce cases, but more likely, the flexible statutes allowed petitioners more leeway in what charges to employ and when to file, disguising the war's impact. *Code of West Virginia*, chap. 64, secs. 1–6 (1870); *Code of Virginia*, chap. 109, sec. 14 (1849); Acts of the Legislature of West Virginia, chap. 17 (1867).

27. *Bailey v. Bailey*, 62 Supreme Court of Virginia 43 (1871). Virginia's laws did not formally stipulate how long one must be abandoned before receiving a divorce from bed and board, though the statutes required an absence of five years for a full divorce. Kentucky mandated only one year. *Code of Virginia*, chap. 105, sec. 6 (1873); *Kentucky Revised Statute, Annotated* (unknown, 1867), chap. 47, art. Iii; *Code of Virginia*, chap. 109, sec. 7 (1860); *Carr v. Carr*, 63 Supreme Court of Virginia 168 (1872).

28. *Bailey v. Bailey*, 62 Supreme Court of Virginia 43 (1871); Censer, "'Smiling through her Tears,'" 28; Buckley, *Great Catastrophe of My Life*, 3–4, 8–9.

29. *Bailey v. Bailey*, 62 Supreme Court of Virginia 43 (1871).

30. Whites, *Civil War as a Crisis in Gender*, 222; Suzanne Lebsock, *Virginia Women: 1600–1945* (Richmond: Virginia State Library, 1987), 101. See also Morsman, *Big House after Slavery*, 4, 7–8.

31. *Craig, Mary Jane v. Craig, John* (1871), Fauquier County Circuit Court Records, LVA, no. 1871-024. For a discussion of Indiana as a divorce haven, see Hartog, *Man and Wife in America*, 14.

32. Cott, "Divorce and the Changing Status of Women in Eighteenth-Century Massachusetts," 586–614.

33. *Code of West Virginia*, chap. 64, secs. 1–6 (1870); *Code of Virginia*, chap. 109, sec. 14 (1849); Acts of the Legislature of West Virginia, chap. 17 (1867). The power to prevent remarriage had been a powerful legal tool in antebellum society; in fact, before the American Revolution, one could only obtain the right to remarry in New England. Hartog, *Man and Wife in America*, 64, 70.

34. Hartog, *Man and Wife in America*, 70, 72–73.

35. In fact, Kentucky's acceptance of mutual separation put them ahead of much of the nation. Nancy Cott calls nineteenth-century divorce an "adversarial procedure," which required that one party show the other had explicitly broken their marital contract. Even in the postbellum years, courts frowned upon collusion. Cott, *Public Vows*, 48; *Code of Virginia*, chap. 105, sec. 6 (1873).

36. *Bailey v. Bailey*, 62 Supreme Court of Virginia 43 (1871).

37. *Wilson Reeves v. Elizabeth Reeves,* 3 Kentucky Supreme Court of Appeals 607 (1868). According to Hartog, where both parties were at fault, legal policy "declared that they became thereby 'suitable and proper companions for each other,' locked in permanent matrimony." Hartog, *Man and Wife in America,* 73.

38. *Hensley, ElKanah D. v. Hensley, Orpha* (1867), Franklin County Circuit Court Records, KDLA, no. 1042.

39. *Carr, A. P. v. Carr, W. H.* (1869), Franklin County Circuit Court Records, KDLA, no. 1094.

40. *Crittenden, John J. v. Crittenden, Agnes J.* (1872), Franklin County Circuit Court Records, KDLA, no. 1162.

41. *Trimble, Amanda M. v. Trimble, Ephraim* (1868), Ohio County Circuit Court Records, WVRHC, env. 276, b-5.

42. *Sayre, B. B. v. Sayre, Catherine* (1868), Franklin County Circuit Court Records, KDLA, no. 1050.

43. Chused, *Private Acts in Public Places,* 8.

44. *Lackey, Viola B. v. Lackey, John W.* (1869), Warren County Circuit Court Records, KDLA, no. 3365; *Metzger, Margaret v. Metzger, John* (1869), Warren County Circuit Court Records, KDLA, no. 3437.

45. *Brent, Sarah v. Brent, Joseph* (1867), Fauquier County Circuit Court Records, LVA, no. 1867-031.

46. *Sullivan, Mary E. v. Sullivan, Arthur* (1866), Fauquier County Circuit Court Records, LVA, no. 1866-056.

47. Silkenat, *Moments of Despair,* 116–117.

48. *Turley, Rees v. Turley, Susan* (1866), Tazewell County Circuit Court Records, LVA, no. 188-007.

49. Schweninger, *Families in Crisis in the Old South,* 15–16.

50. *Suddoth, Susannah E. v. Suddoth, William T.* (1866) in Fauquier County Circuit Court Records, LVA, no. 1866-013.

51. Ibid.

52. *Craig, Mary Jane v. Craig, John* (1871), Fauquier County Circuit Court Records, LVA, no. 1871-024.

53. These numbers are only for those cases in which the person filing listed both a date of marriage and a date of crisis (i.e., the year in which their partner left them, committed adultery, or was so cruel and intemperate they were forced to flee). I did not include in the length of marriage the period *after* the crisis but *before* the filing date.

54. These data reflect the date on which a crisis occurred that led the partner either to leave or to decide to seek a divorce and the date on which the actual case was filed.

55. *Sullivan, Mary E. v. Sullivan, Arthur* (1866), Fauquier County Circuit Court Records, LVA, no. 1866-056.

56. Ibid.

57. *Arthur, Hattie v. Arthur, Jesse* (1870), Ohio County Circuit Court Records, WVRHC, env. 284 b-9; *Hamilton, Ann E. v. Hamilton, Smith* (1872), Ohio County Circuit Court Records, WVRHC, env. 293 b-15.

58. Schweninger, *Families in Crisis*, 2–4, 11.

59. *Revised Statutes, Kentucky, vol. 2* (1852), chap. 47, art. iii, sec. i, xi; *Code of Virginia* (1849), title 31, chap. cix, sec. 6–7, 11, 13–14). See Hartog, *Man and Wife in America*, 36, 71.

60. Ohio and Tazewell County residents asked for divorce *a mensa et thoro* about 10 percent of the time.

61. *Bailey v. Bailey* (1868), Franklin County Circuit Court Records, KDLA, no. 1057; *Mack v. Mack* (1868), Franklin County Circuit Court Records, KDLA, no. 1063.

62. Schweninger, *Families in Crisis in the Old South*, 66–67; Boswell, *Her Act and Deed*, 45.

63. Hartog, *Man and Wife in America*, 85; *Cain v. McHarry*, 65 Kentucky Supreme Court of Appeals 263 (1867).

64. *Dillion, Margaret E. v. Dillion, William A.* (1871), Tazewell County Circuit Court Records, LVA, no. 1871-040; *Dowland, W.H. v. Dowland, Susan* (1870), Tazewell County Circuit Court Records, LVA, no. 1870-016; *White, Archibald v. White, Mary* (1871), Tazewell County Circuit Court Records, LVA, no. 1871-034; *Walker, Harvey v. Walker, Frances* (1866), Tazewell County Circuit Court Records, LVA, no. 1866-009.

65. Herbert G. Gutman, *The Black Family in Slavery and Freedom, 1750–1925* (New York: Vintage, 1977), xviii–xxi, 101–104; John W. Blassingame, *The Slave Community: Plantation Life in the Antebellum South* (New York: Oxford University Press, 1979); Larry E. Hudson, *To Have and to Hold: Slave Work and Family Life in Antebellum South Carolina* (Athens: University of Georgia Press, 1997), xx–xxi, 141–144; Stevenson, *Life in Black and White*, 206–208; Deborah Gray White, *Ar'n't I a Woman?: Female Slaves in the Plantation South* (New York: Norton, 1985), 149–152.

66. Laura F. Edwards, "'The Marriage Covenant Is at the Foundation of All Our Rights': The Politics of Slavery Marriages in North Carolina after Emancipation," *Law and History Review* 14 (1996): 81–124.

67. *Craddock, Richard v. Craddock, Malvine a.k.a. Melvine Brown* (1871), Amelia County Circuit Court Records, LVA, no. 1871-005.

68. All five of the postwar Amelia County divorce cases filed by black petitioners resulted in a divorce.

69. *Minge, Samuel v. Minge, Laura* (1872), Amelia County Circuit Court Records, LVA, no. 1872-005.

70. *Mourning v. Mourning* (1866), Franklin County Circuit Court Records, KDLA, no. 1024.

7. Never Happier in Her Life

1. *Trimble, Amanda M. v. Trimble, Ephraim* (1868), Ohio County Circuit Court Records, WVRHC, env. 276 b-5.

2. Arlette Farge finds a similar opening for men and women "stubbornly pursuing their own way" in the fluid world of eighteenth-century Paris, "emerging from the physical promiscuity, the inevitable sharing of fear and want, the difficult separation between public and private life." Farge, *Fragile Lives*, 5–6, 20.

3. Bynum's analysis focuses on how race and class shaped antebellum female behavior in unexpected ways, though her conclusions focus more on the "ways in which power flowed between the private and public spheres of society." I am more interested in how the cultural fusion of border locales shaped female behavior. Bynum, *Unruly Women*, 1–3, 33. Similarly, the essays collected by Michele Gillespie and Susanna Delfino in *Neither Lady nor Slave: Working Women in the Old South* demonstrate the ways in which race, class, and ethnicity came together in unique ways in the lives of working-class women. Their experiences challenge our typical notions of southern womanhood as a dichotomy between slaveholding and slave women. This chapter also explores women outside the traditional narrative, while asking how the blurring of class, racial, and ethnic lines shaped their behavior as wives or toward wives. Gillespie and Delfino, eds., *Neither Lady nor Slave: Working Women in the Old South* (Chapel Hill: University of North Carolina Press, 2002), 3–5.

4. They even shared the same yard. Hettie and Barbara, Ephraim's mother, observed Amanda's alleged behavior even before Ephraim's departure. According to Barbara, Amanda was violent and aggressive with both her husband and his children from another marriage. "She spit in his face," Barbara told the court. She also threatened to kill him and whipped his children. Hettie and Barbara stated that they continually stepped in to feed and clothe the children. *Trimble, Amanda M. v. Trimble, Ephraim* (1868), Ohio County Circuit Court Records, WVRHC, env. 276 b-5.

5. *Trimble, Amanda M. v. Trimble, Ephraim* (1868), Ohio County Circuit Court Records, WVRHC, env. 276 b-5.

6. Ibid.

7. Mary Beth Sievens argues that this contributed to wives' decision to respond to their husbands' divorce petitions in Vermont. Sievens, "'The Wicked Agency of Others': Community, Law, and Marital Conflict in Vermont, 1790–1830," *Journal of the Early Republic* 21, no. 1 (Spring 2001): 26–27.

8. *Trimble, Amanda M. v. Trimble, Ephraim* (1868), Ohio County Circuit Court Records, WVRHC, env. 276 b-5.

9. In such cases, both the women doing the scrutinizing and the women being scrutinized often behaved in unusual ways, with one group enforcing their view of morality and the other defying and redefining it.

10. Farge, *Fragile Lives*, 19–20, 75–77.

11. *Firestone, Benjamin v. Firestone, Elizabeth* (1869), Franklin County Circuit Court Records, KDLA, no. 1074.

12. *Brareton, Enoch v. Brareton, Caroline* (1862), Ohio County Circuit Court Records, WVRHC, env. 233 b-6.

13. This was more likely to happen with women of the poorer classes. Bynum, *Unruly Women*, 89. See also Rothman, *Notorious in the Neighborhood.*

14. *Cecil, William v. Cecil, Emma* (1868), Tazewell County Circuit Court Records, LVA, no. 1868-007.

15. *Hall, Mary v. Hall, Alexander* (1872), Tazewell County Circuit Court Records, LVA, no. 1872-059.

16. *Dillion, Margaret E. v. Dillion, William A.* (1871), Tazewell County Circuit Court Records, LVA, no. 1871-040.

17. Ibid.

18. *Stroble, Jacob v. Stroble, Ellen* (1865), Ohio County Circuit Court Records, WVRHC, env. 259 b-5.

19. *Prophater, Wm. v. Prophater, Isabella* (1868), Ohio County Circuit Court Records, WVRHC, env. 276 b-11.

20. *Clifford, P. N. v. Clifford, L. A.* (1867), Franklin County Circuit Court Records, KDLA, no. 1031.

21. *Martin, William v. Martin, Lydia* (1868), Tazewell County Circuit Court Records, LVA, no. 1868-008.

22. *Turley, Rees v. Turley, Susan* (1866), Tazewell County Circuit Court Records, LVA, no. 1866-007.

23. Beverly Schwartzberg, "'Lots of Them Did That': Desertion, Bigamy, and Marital Fluidity in Late-Nineteenth-Century America," *Journal of Social History* 37, no. 3 (2004): 574.

24. *Boyd, I. B. v. Boyd, T. B.* (1867) in Franklin County Circuit Court Cases, KDLA, no. 1040.

25. *McDonald, Ambrose v. McDonald, Lenarca* (1867) in Franklin County Circuit Court Records, KDLA, no. 1043.

26. *Warren, William H. v. Warren, Cynthia E.* (1871) in Franklin County Circuit Court Records, KDLA, no. 1131.

27. Ibid.

28. Laura Edwards has argued that similar rhetoric in postwar North Carolina reflected the ways in which poor white and black women "drew implicit contrasts between [themselves] and elite white women." While the language of these women in Kentucky certainly reflects a similar non-elite perspective, the usage of the terminology of freedom also introduces a new component, which could have been found in women of all social statuses. Edwards, *Gendered Strife and Confusion*, 145.

29. *Slattery, Elizabeth F. v. Slattery, Thomas* (1869), Franklin County Circuit Court Records, KDLA, no. 1099.

30. Ibid.

31. Ibid.

32. With their fused reverence for frontier independence and honor-bound cavalier culture, Kentuckians could have a mean streak. Anne Marshall has stated that "Kentucky had a reputation as a violent place long before the Civil War." Marshall, *Creating a Confederate Kentucky*, 73.

33. *Armstrong, Eliza Jane v. Armstrong, William B.* (1870), Ohio County Circuit Court Records, WVRHC, env. 284 b-9. Victoria Bynum argues that, in North Carolina, wealthier women were better able to take their husbands to court to protect their property and body. However, Wheeling's court records reflect women of a variety of class backgrounds, but especially working-class women, who employed the legal system to their benefit. Bynum, *Unruly Women*, 33.

34. *Armstrong, Eliza Jane v. Armstrong, William B.* (1870), Ohio County Circuit Court Records, WVRHC, env. 284 b-9.

35. In her study of antebellum New York City, Christine Stansell argues that women used connections with their neighbors to "modify men's abusiveness." Stansell, *City of Women: Sex and Class in New York, 1789–1860* (Urbana: University of Illinois Press, 1987), 81–83. On the other hand, Jeffrey Adler believes that many turn-of-the-century Chicagoans actually became immune to the screams and cries of abused wives, so much so that they often failed to stop murders under way. Adler, *First in Violence, Deepest in Dirt: Homicide in Chicago* (Cambridge: Harvard University Press, 2006), 54–55.

36. *Young, Thomas v. Young, Sarah* (1867), Franklin County Circuit Court Records, KDLA, no. 1039.

37. This also reflects their belief in companionate marriage. Stephanie Coontz has shown how a stronger support for companionate marriage and love-based relationships led to a rise in the divorce rate. Couples began to believe that a loveless marriage was not worth maintaining. Coontz, *Marriage, a History*, 5, 8.

38. Basch argues that "the prevalence of desertion and the growing facility with which it was accomplished as the century unfolded suggest it became ever easier for *men* to find a new companion and start all over again." Basch, "Relief in the Premises," 5, 8, 15. According to Mary Somerville Jones, divorce before the Civil War had been dominated by men. Jones, *An Historical Geography*, 32. David Silkenat has argued that when a "white woman from North Carolina filed for divorce before the Civil War, she was making not only a claim that she wanted to escape from a failed marriage but also a claim against white male authority," but he disagrees with Jones and says that women initiated about two-thirds of the cases in the prewar years. Silkenat, *Moments of Despair*, 76.

39. However, Fauquier County's petitioners were mostly women in both the antebellum and postbellum periods.

40. This assumes that everyone told the truth, which is obviously a rather large assumption in these types of cases. Still, we can assume that kernels of truth lay beneath the inevitable legal manipulation. Women filed thirty-three cases and

men seventeen from 1865 to 1873. For husbands, the charges (in order of popularity) were adultery, abandonment, cruelty, intemperance, and fraud.

41. Conversely, Honor Sachs has argued that men in eighteenth-century Kentucky had a difficult time obtaining divorces for their wives' abandonment because "the legislature's narrative of gender difference simply did not accommodate a wife's active or intentional breach of the marriage contract." Sachs demonstrates, though, that wives were taking an active role in ending their relationships. In Wheeling, wives were ending their relationships, a fact recognized by both the community and the legal system. Sachs, "The Myth of the Abandoned Wife," 8–15.

42. *Trimble, Amanda M. v. Trimble, Ephraim* (1868), Ohio County Circuit Court Records, WVRHC, env. 276 b-5.

43. *Lindemuth, Louis v. Lindemuth, Augusta* (1871), Ohio County Circuit Court Records, WVRHC, env. 289 b-8.

44. *Taylor, Richard v. Taylor, Martha* (1864), *Franklin County Circuit Court Records, KDLA*, no. 987.

45. *Gears, Mary Ann v. Gears, Charles F.* (1869), Franklin County Circuit Court Cases, KDLA, no. 1095.

46. *Leasure, James A. v. Leasure, Elizabeth* (1871), Ohio County Circuit Court Records, WVRHC, env. 290 b-5. According to Bynum, unmarried women who did not fulfill their socially prescribed "pious, dependent" role could become the subject of gossip and speculation by their neighbors. Bynum, *Unruly Women*, 44. Robin Sager found some women similarly willing to use violence in her study of antebellum marital cruelty. Sager, "Marital Cruelty in Antebellum Virginia, Texas, and Wisconsin" (PhD diss., Rice University, 2012).

47. *Scotland, Julia A. v. Scotland, E.W.* (1872), Warren County Circuit Court Records, KDLA, no. 3794; *McNamara, Edward v. McNamara, Kate M.* (1872), Warren County Circuit Court Records, KDLA, no. 3857.

48. *Buchanon, William v. Buchanon, Mary A.* (1867), Tazewell County Circuit Court Records, LVA, no. 1867-003.

49. *Buchanon, William H. v. Buchanon, Mary A.* (1870), Tazewell County Circuit Court Records, LVA, no. 1870-015.

50. Ibid.

51. Ibid.

52. *Champ, Delila v. Champ, John* (1872), Tazewell County Circuit Court Records, LVA, no. 1872-073.

53. Hartog, *Man and Wife in America*, 156. Much of this may seem unsurprising for scholars of northern urban communities, but less work has been done on the economic roles of married women in "small nineteenth-century southern cities." Howe, "Patient Laborers," 123.

54. Barbara Howe found that 25 percent of Wheeling's working women were in the sewing trades, and seamstresses and tailoresses, specifically, were "overwhelmingly *not* the heads of their households." Howe, "Patient Laborers," 131.

55. *Goudy, Elizabeth O. by her next friend Milleger, James [her father] v. Goudy, James M.* (1868), Ohio County Circuit Court Records, WVRHC, env. 274 e-9.

56. Ibid.; Howe, "Patient Laborers," 124.

57. *Heston, Catherine, by her next friend Mulrine, John v. Heston, John* (1867), Ohio County Circuit Court Records, WVRHC, env. 272 b-6.

58. *Baily, Henrietta v. Baily, Gallatin* (1867), Warren County Circuit Court Records, KDLA, no. 3128.

59. Drew Gilpin Faust has argued that "those white southern women who worked did so out of necessity, and their labor carried with it a stigma of debased status and an aura of vague disrespectability." Faust, *Mothers of Invention*, 81. Jane Turner Censer has shown that postwar women did move toward certain occupations, especially teaching, to recover from the financial losses of the war, but the experiences of these non-elite women in the border South are very different. Censer, *Reconstruction of White Southern Womanhood*, 7–8, 153–201.

60. Cott, *Public Vows*, 12; Edwards, *Gendered Strife and Confusion*, 136.

61. *Hebrank, Samuel v. Hebrank, Justina* (1865), Ohio County Circuit Court Records, WVRHC, env. 260 b-7.

62. Laura Edwards argues that in postwar North Carolina, elite white men and women incorporated aspects of northern culture into their households in order to alleviate the loss of status due to emancipation and economic recession. Specifically, women became "paragons of domestic virtue," creating a welcoming environment for their husbands. Men, in return, "supported their families through their own labor" and gave their wives the means to create such a domestic sphere. These tendencies were heightened in the border South, where traces of this northern ideology had been present in the antebellum period as well. In West Virginia, the dual forces of emancipation and prewar cultural evolution pushed men and women toward a Victorian household structure. Edwards, *Gendered Strife and Confusion*, 20, 110.

63. *Hebrank, Samuel v. Hebrank, Justina* (1865), Ohio County Circuit Court Records, WVRHC, env. 260 b-7.

64. *Trimble, Amanda M. v. Trimble, Ephraim* (1868), Ohio County Circuit Court Records, WVRHC, env. 276 b-5.

65. *Harrod, Liney v. Harrod, Holland* (1869), Franklin County Circuit Court Cases, KDLA, no. 1076.

66. *Wimmer, Robert v. Wimmer, Sabra Ann* (1866), Tazewell County Circuit Court Records, LVA, no. 1866-010.

67. *Asberry, Gabriel v. Asberry, Gemimina* (1868), Tazewell County Circuit Court Records, LVA, no. 1868-006.

68. *Williams, Henry v. Williams, Millie* (1871), Tazewell County Circuit Court Records, LVA, no. 1871-051.

Conclusion

1. Semantha Morgan to John Morgan, August 12, 1876, Atkeson-Morgan Papers, WVRHC, Morgantown, WV, box 1.

2. Semantha Morgan to John Morgan, August 19, 1881, August 31, 1881, Atkeson-Morgan Papers, WVRHC, box 1.

3. Marshall, *Creating a Confederate Kentucky*, 16–21, 84. She argues that the Lost Cause, "infused with an assortment of conservative racial, gender, and class values," gave Kentuckians "not only . . . vindication for the past, but . . . a blueprint for shaping the future."

4. Rice, *West Virginia*, 157–169; Charles H. Ambler and Festus P. Summers, *West Virginia: The Mountain State* (Glenwood Cliffs, NJ: Prentice-Hall, 1958); John Alexander Williams, *West Virginia: A Bicentennial History* (New York: W. W. Norton, 1976), 89–94.

5. David Whisnant, *All That Is Native and Fine: The Politics of Culture in an American Region* (Chapel Hill: University of North Carolina Press, 1983), 8–9; Henry D. Shapiro, *Appalachia on Our Minds: The Southern Mountains and Mountaineers in the American Consciousness, 1870–1920* (Chapel Hill: University of North Carolina Press, 1995), 3–31.

6. Wilma A. Dunaway, *Women, Work, and Family in the Antebellum Mountain South* (New York: Cambridge University Press, 2008).

7. Vance, *Hillbilly Elegy: Memoir of a Family and Culture in Crisis* (New York: HarperCollins, 2016); Elizabeth Catte, *What You Are Getting Wrong about Appalachia* (Cleveland, OH: Belt, 2018), 10–15.

Bibliography

Primary Sources

Government Documents

Ambler, Charles H., Frances H. Atwood, and William B. Mathews, eds. *Debates and Proceedings of the First Constitutional Convention of West Virginia (1861–1863).* Huntington, WV, 1939.

Census of the United States, 1800, 1850, 1860.

Charleston, WV. *Code of West Virginia.* 1870.

Charleston, WV. *Code of West Virginia.* 1884.

Decisions of the Kentucky Court of Appeals in *Kentucky Law Reporter* and *Kentucky State Reports.*

Kentucky. *Journal of the House of Representatives of the Commonwealth of Kentucky.* 1849–1850.

Kentucky. *Journal of the House of Representatives of the Commonwealth of Kentucky.* 1851–1852.

Kentucky. *Revised Statutes of Kentucky.* 1852.

Kentucky. *Revised Statutes of Kentucky.* 1867.

Lewis, Virgil A., ed. *How West Virginia Was Made; Proceedings of the First Convention of the People of Northwestern Virginia at Wheeling, May 13, 14 and 15, 1861, and the Journal of the Second Convention of the People of Northwestern Virginia at Wheeling, Which Assembled June 11th 1861.* Charleston, WV, 1909.

Louisiana. *Civil Code of the State of Louisiana.* 1853.

Reports of Cases Decided in the Supreme Court of Appeals of West Virginia, vol. 1–12. Reprint, Morgantown, KY: Acme, 1906.

Richmond, VA. *Code of Virginia.* 1849.

Richmond, VA. *Code of Virginia.* 1860.

Richmond, VA. *Code of Virginia.* 1873.

Virginia. *Acts of the General Assembly of Virginia.* 1862.

Virginia. *Acts of the General Assembly of Virginia.* 1865.

Virginia. *Ordinances and Acts of the Restored Government of Virginia.* 1866.

Virginia. *Proceedings and Debates of the Virginia State Convention 1829–1830.* Richmond: Samuel Shepherd & Co., 1830.

Virginia. *Statutes at Large of Virginia, From October Session 1792 to December Session 1806.* Richmond: Samuel Shepherd & Co., 1835.

West Virginia. *Acts of the Legislature of West Virginia.* 1861–1867.

West Virginia. *Journal of the Constitutional Convention, Assembled at Charleston, West Virginia, January 16, 1872.* Charleston: H. S. Walker, 1872.

West Virginia. *Revised Statutes of West Virginia.* 1878.

Manuscripts and Archives

Filson Historical Society, Louisville, KY
- Edward A. Bennett Papers
- Bodley Family Papers
- Melville Briney Papers
- Bullitt Family Papers
- Bullitt-Chenoweth Family Papers
- Bullitt-Oxmoor Papers
- Albana C. Carson Papers
- Phoebe Wood Coburn Daugherty Papers
- Benjamin Field Memoir
- Ford Family Papers
- Green Family Papers
- Helm Family Papers
- Barnabas Lee Papers
- William Thomas McElroy Papers
- Moxley-Offutt Family Papers
- Mary Woolridge Voris Papers
- Wall-Machir Papers
- Wall and Machir Families
- A. C. Williams Letters
- Winston-Jones Family Papers

Kentucky Department of Libraries and Archives, Frankfort
- Records of the Circuit Court of Franklin County
  - Case Files 1840–1873
- Records of the Circuit Court of Pike County
  - Case Files 1867
- Records of the Circuit Court of Warren County
  - Case Files 1850–1873

Kentucky Historical Society, Frankfort
- George W. Johnson Papers
- George Robertson Manuscript
- Scrogin-Haviland Letters
- Wallace-Starling Diaries and Papers

Library of Virginia, Richmond
- Records of the Circuit Court of Amelia County
  - Case Files 1850–1873
- Records of the Circuit Court of Fauquier County

Case Files 1850–1873
Records of the Circuit Court of Tazewell County
Case Files 1850–1873
Southern Historical Collection, Louis Round Wilson Special Collections Library, University of North Carolina, Chapel Hill
A. P. Farnsley Letters
Charles Barrington Simrall Papers
Charles W. Sydnor Letters
Susanna Gordon Waddell Diary
Virginia Historical Society, Richmond
Burroughs Family Letters
Sarah Dandridge Cooke Duval Papers
Harrison Family Papers
Louthan Family Papers
Robert Powell Page Letters
Taliaferro Family Papers
West Virginia and Regional History Center, West Virginia University Libraries, Morgantown
Atkeson-Morgan Family Papers
John J. Davis Papers
Hubbard Family Papers
Francis H. Pierpont Papers
Records of the Circuit Court of Ohio County
Case Files 1850–1873
Robinson Family Manuscripts
Peter Van Winkle Papers
Waitman T. Willey Papers

Newspapers

Louisville Courier-Journal
Wheeling Intelligencer

Published Primary Documents

Bean, James. *The Christian Minister's Affectionate Advice to a Married Couple.* New York: American Tract Society, 1840.

Bishop, Joel. *Commentaries on the Law of Marriage and Divorce and Evidence in Matrimonial Suits.* 2 vols. Boston, 1873.

Blackstone, William. *Commentaries on the Laws of England.* Edited by W. G. Hammond. San Francisco, 1898.

Collins, Lewis. *Collins' Historical Sketches of Kentucky: History of Kentucky, Volume 2.* Covington, KY: Collins & Co., 1882.

The Etiquette of Courtship and Matrimony: With a Complete Guide to the Forms of a Wedding. London: George Routledge & Sons, 1852.

Fedric, Francis. *Slave Life in Virginia and Kentucky; or, Fifty Years of Slavery in the Southern States of America.* London: Wertheim, Macintosh, and Hunt, 1863.

Ham, F. Gerald, ed. "The Mind of a Copperhead: Letters of John J. Davis on the Secession Crisis and Statehood Politics in Western Virginia 1860–1862." *West Virginia History* 24 (January 1963): 416–433.

Leonard, Cynthia Miller, ed. *The General Assembly of Virginia, July 30, 1619–January 11, 1978: A Bicentennial Register of Members.* Richmond: Virginia State Library, 1978.

Mackall, Mary L., Stevan F. Meserve, and Anne Mackall Sasscer, eds. *In the Shadow of the Enemy: The Civil War Journal of Ida Powell Dulany.* Knoxville: University of Tennessee Press, 2009.

Morehead, Charles. *An Address Delivered on the Second Anniversary of Van Doren's Collegiate Institute for Young Ladies, In the City of Lexington, Kentucky, on the Last Thursday in July, 1833.* Lexington, KY: Wm. M. Todd and Thos. T. Skillman, 1833.

Petrie, James. *The Marriage Gift.* Philadelphia: Presbyterian Board of Publication, 1864.

Reeve, Tapping. *The Law of Baron and Femme, of Parent and Child, Guardian and Ward, Master and Servant, and of the Powers of the Courts of Chancery; with an Essay on the Terms Heir, Heirs, Heirs of the Body.* Albany: William Gould, 1862.

Robertson, George. *An Outline of the Life of George Robertson, Written by Himself.* Lexington, KY: Transylvania Printing & Publishing Co., 1876.

Stanton, Elizabeth Cady. "The Need of Liberal Divorce Laws." *North American Review* 139 (September 1884): 242–243.

Wise, Daniel. *Bridal Greetings: A Marriage Gift, in Which the Mutual Duties of Husband and Wife are Familiarly Illustrated and Enforced.* New York: Carlton & Phillips, 1856.

Secondary Sources

Books

Adler, Jeffrey. *First in Violence, Deepest in Dirt: Homicide in Chicago.* Cambridge: Harvard University Press, 2006.

Ambler, Charles H. *The Makers of West Virginia and Their Work.* Huntington, WV: Gentry Brothers, 1942.

Ambler, Charles H., and Festus P. Summers. *West Virginia: The Mountain State.* Glenwood Cliffs, NJ: Prentice-Hall, 1958.

Anderson, Benedict R. *Imagined Communities: Reflections on the Origin and Spread of Nationalism.* London: Verso, 1991.

Anzilotti, Cara. *In the Affairs of the World: Women, Patriarchy, and Power in Colonial South Carolina.* Westport, CT: Greenwood, 2002.

Ash, Stephen V. *When the Yankees Came: Conflict and Chaos in the Occupied South.* Chapel Hill: University of North Carolina Press, 1996.

Astor, Aaron. *Rebels on the Border: Civil War, Emancipation, and the Reconstruction of Kentucky and Missouri.* Baton Rouge: Louisiana State University Press, 2012.

Atkinson, George W., and Alvaro F. Gibbens. *Prominent Men of West Virginia: Biographical Sketches of Representative Men in Every Honorable Vocation, including Politics, the Law, Theology, Medicine, Education, Finance, Journalism, Trade, Commerce and Agriculture.* Wheeling, WV: W.L. Callin, 1890.

Ayers, Edward. *In the Presence of Mine Enemies: War in the Heart of America, 1859–1863.* New York: W. W. Norton, 2003.

Bardaglio, Peter W. *Reconstructing the Household: Families, Sex, and the Law in the Nineteenth-Century South.* Chapel Hill: University of North Carolina Press, 1995.

Basch, Norma. *Framing American Divorce: From the Revolutionary Generation to the Victorians.* Berkeley: University of California Press, 1999.

———. *In the Eyes of the Law: Women, Marriage, and Property in Nineteenth-Century New York.* Ithaca: Cornell University Press, 1982.

Bastress, Robert M. *The West Virginia State Constitution: A Reference Guide.* Westport, CT: Greenwood, 1995.

Beard, Mary Ritter. *Women as a Force in History.* New York: Macmillan, 1946.

Berlin, Ira. *Many Thousands Gone: The First Two Centuries of Slavery in North America.* Cambridge, MA: Harvard University Press, 1998.

Berry, Mary Frances. *The Pig Farmer's Daughter and Other Tales of American Justice: Episodes of Racism and Sexism in the Courts from 1865 to the Present.* New York: Knopf, 1999.

Berry, Stephen. *All That Makes a Man: Love and Ambition in the Civil War South.* Chapel Hill: University of North Carolina Press, 1992.

———. *House of Abraham: Lincoln and the Todds, A Family Divided by War.* New York: Houghton Mifflin, 2007.

Blair, William. *Virginia's Private War: Feeding Body and Soul in the Confederacy, 1861–1865.* New York: Oxford University Press, 1998.

Blassingame, John W. *The Slave Community: Plantation Life in the Antebellum South.* New York: Oxford University Press, 1979.

Boswell, Angela. *Her Act and Deed: Women's Lives in a Rural Southern County, 1837–1873.* College Station: Texas A&M University Press, 2001.

Boydston, Jeanne. *Home and Work: Housework, Wages, and the Ideology of Labor in the Early Republic.* New York: Oxford University Press, 1990.

Brown, Kathi Ann, Walter Nicklin, and John T. Toler. *250 Years in Fauquier County: A Virginia Story.* Fairfax, VA: George Mason University Press, 2008.

Bruce, Dickson D. *Violence and Culture in the Antebellum South.* Austin: University of Texas Press, 1979.

Buckley, Thomas E. *The Great Catastrophe of My Life: Divorce in the Old Dominion.* Chapel Hill: University of North Carolina Press, 2001.

Burke, Diane Mutti. *On Slavery's Border: Missouri's Small-Slaveholding Households, 1815–1865.* Athens: University of Georgia Press, 2010.

Bynum, Victoria. *Unruly Women: The Politics of Social and Sexual Control in the Old South.* Chapel Hill: University of North Carolina Press, 1992.

Camp, Stephanie M. H. *Closer to Freedom: Enslaved Women and Everyday Resistance in the Plantation South.* Chapel Hill: University of North Carolina Press, 2004.

Campbell, Jacqueline Glass. *When Sherman Marched North from the Sea: Resistance on the Confederate Home Front.* Chapel Hill: University of North Carolina Press, 2003.

Carlson, A. Cheree. *The Crimes of Womanhood: Defining Femininity in a Court of Law.* Urbana: University of Illinois Press, 2009.

Catte, Elizabeth. *What You Are Getting Wrong about Appalachia.* Cleveland, OH: Belt, 2018.

Censer, Jane Turner. *The Reconstruction of White Southern Womanhood, 1865–1895.* Baton Rouge: Louisiana State University Press, 2003.

Chused, Richard H. *Private Acts in Public Places: A Social History of Divorce in the Formative Era of American Family Law.* Philadelphia: University of Pennsylvania Press, 1994.

Clinton, Catherine. *Plantation Mistress: Woman's World in the Old South.* New York: Pantheon, 1982.

Clinton, Catherine, and Nina Silber, eds. *Divided Houses: Gender and the Civil War.* New York: Oxford University Press, 1992.

Coontz, Stephanie. *Marriage, a History: From Obedience to Intimacy, or How Love Conquered Marriage.* New York: Viking, 2005.

Cott, Nancy. *The Bonds of Womanhood: "Woman's Sphere" in New England, 1780–1835.* New Haven: Yale University Press, 1977.

———. *Public Vows: A History of Marriage and the Nation.* Cambridge, MA: Harvard University Press, 2000.

Curry, Richard Orr. *A House Divided: A Study of Statehood Politics and the Copperhead Movement in West Virginia.* Pittsburgh: University of Pittsburgh Press, 1964.

Dayton, Cornelia Hughes. *Women before the Bar: Gender, Law, and Society in Connecticut, 1639–1789.* Chapel Hill: University of North Carolina Press, 1995.

Delfino, Susanna, and Michele Gillespie, eds. *Neither Lady nor Slave: Working Women in the Old South.* Chapel Hill: University of North Carolina Press, 2002.

Dunaway, Wilma A. *The First American Frontier: Transition to Capitalism in Southern Appalachia, 1700–1860.* Chapel Hill: University of North Carolina Press, 1996.

———. *Women, Work, and Family in the Antebellum Mountain South.* New York: Cambridge University Press, 2008.

Edwards, Laura. *Gendered Strife and Confusion: The Political Culture of Reconstruction*. Urbana: University of Illinois Press, 1997.

———. *The People and Their Peace: Legal Culture and the Transformation of Inequality in the Post-Revolutionary South*. Chapel Hill: University of North Carolina Press, 2009.

———. *Scarlett Doesn't Live Here Anymore: Southern Women in the Civil War Era*. Urbana: University of Illinois Press, 2000.

Engel, Barbara Alpern. *Breaking the Ties That Bound: The Politics of Marital Strife in Late Imperial Russia*. Ithaca, NY: Cornell University Press, 2011.

Farge, Arlette. *Fragile Lives: Violence, Power and Solidarity in Eighteenth-Century Paris*. Cambridge, MA: Harvard University Press, 1993.

Farnham, Christie Anne. *The Education of the Southern Belle: Higher Education and Student Socialization in the Antebellum South*. New York: New York University Press, 1994.

Faust, Drew Gilpin. *Mothers of Invention: Women of the Slaveholding South in the American Civil War*. Chapel Hill: University of North Carolina Press, 1996.

———. *This Republic of Suffering: Death and the American Civil War*. New York: Vintage, 2006.

Fellman, Michael. *Inside War: The Guerrilla Conflict in Missouri during the American Civil War*. New York: Oxford University Press, 1989.

Fields, Barbara Jeanne. *Slavery and Freedom on the Middle Ground: Maryland during the Nineteenth Century*. New Haven: Yale University Press, 1985.

Fischer, David Hackett, and James C. Kelly. *Bound Away: Virginia and the Westward Movement*. Charlottesville: University of Virginia Press, 2000.

Foner, Eric. *Free Soil, Free Labor, Free Men: The Ideology of the Republican Party before the Civil War*. New York: Oxford University Press, 1971.

———. *Reconstruction: America's Unfinished Revolution, 1863–1877*. New York: Harper and Row, 1988.

Fones-Wolf, Kenneth, and Ronald L. Lewis. *Transnational West Virginia: Ethnic Communities and Economic Change, 1840–1940*. Morgantown, WV: West Virginia University Press, 2003.

Ford, Bridget. *Bonds of Union: Religion, Race, and Politics in a Civil War Borderland*. Chapel Hill: University of North Carolina Press, 2016.

Fox-Genovese, Elizabeth. *Within the Plantation Household: Black and White Women of the Old South*. Chapel Hill: University of North Carolina Press, 1988.

Freehling, William W. *The South vs. the South: How Anti-Confederate Southerners Shaped the Course of the Civil War*. Oxford: Oxford University Press, 2001.

Friend, Craig Thompson, and Anya Jabour. *Family Values in the Old South*. Gainesville: University of Florida Press, 2010.

Glymph, Thavolia. *Out of the House of Bondage: The Transformation of the Plantation Household*. New York: Cambridge University Press, 2008.

Greenberg, Amy. *Manifest Manhood and Antebellum American Empire*. New York: Cambridge University Press, 2005.

Grimsley, Mark. *The Hard Hand of War: Union Military Policy toward Southern Civilians, 1861–1865*. New York: Cambridge University Press, 1995.

Griswold, Robert L. *Family and Divorce in California, 1850–1890: Victorian Illusions and Everyday Realities*. Albany: State University of New York Press, 1982.

Grossberg, Michael. *Governing the Hearth: Law and the Family in Nineteenth-Century America*. Chapel Hill: University of North Carolina Press, 1985.

———. *A Judgment for Solomon: The d'Hauteville Case and Legal Experience in Antebellum America*. New York: Cambridge University Press, 1996.

Gutman, Herbert G. *The Black Family in Slavery and Freedom, 1750–1925*. New York: Vintage, 1977.

Hadfield, Kathleen Halverson, ed. *Historical Notes on Amelia County, Virginia*. Amelia, VA: Amelia County Historical Committee, 1982.

Harris, William C. *Lincoln and the Border States: Preserving the Union*. Lawrence: University Press of Kansas, 2011.

Harrison, Lowell H. *The Civil War in Kentucky*. Lexington: University Press of Kentucky, 1975.

Harrison, Lowell H., and James C. Klotter. *A New History of Kentucky*. Lexington: University of Kentucky Press, 1997.

Hartog, Hendrik. *Man and Wife in America: A History*. Cambridge: Harvard University Press, 2000.

Hemphill, C. Dallett. *Bowing to Necessities: A History of Manners, 1620–1860*. New York: Oxford University Press, 2002.

Hodes, Martha. *White Women, Black Men: Illicit Sex in the Nineteenth-Century South*. New Haven: Yale University Press, 1997.

Hoff, Joan. *Law, Gender, and Injustice: A Legal History of U.S. Women*. New York: New York University Press, 1991.

Hudson, Larry E. *To Have and to Hold: Slave Work and Family Life in Antebellum South Carolina*. Athens: University of Georgia Press, 1997.

Hunter, Tera. *Bound in Wedlock: Slave and Free Black Marriage in the Nineteenth Century*. Cambridge, MA: Harvard University Press, 2017.

Hyde, Sarah L. *Schooling in the Antebellum South: The Rise of Public and Private Education in Louisiana, Mississippi, and Alabama*. Baton Rouge: Louisiana State University Press, 2016.

Inscoe, John C., and Gordon B. McKinney. *The Heart of Confederate Appalachia: Western North Carolina in the Civil War*. Chapel Hill: University of North Carolina Press, 2000.

Johansen, Shawn. *Family Men: Middle-Class Fatherhood in Early Industrializing America*. New York: Routledge, 2001.

Jones, Mary Somerville. *An Historical Geography of the Changing Divorce Law in the United States*. New York: Garland, 1987.

Kelley, Mary. *Learning to Stand and Speak: Women, Education, and Public Life in America's Republic*. Chapel Hill: University of North Carolina Press, 2006.

Kerber, Linda K. *No Constitutional Right to Be Ladies: Women and the Obligations of Citizenship*. New York: Hill and Wang, 1998.

———. *Women of the Republic: Intellect and Ideology in Revolutionary America*. Chapel Hill: University of North Carolina Press, 1980.

Lebsock, Suzanne. *The Free Women of Petersburg: Status and Culture in a Southern Town, 1784–1860*. New York: W. W. Norton, 1984.

———. *Virginia Women: 1600–1945*. Richmond: Virginia State Library, 1987.

Levitt, Sarah A. *From Catherine Beecher to Martha Stewart: A Cultural History of Domestic Advice*. Chapel Hill: University of North Carolina Press, 2002.

Lewis, Jan. *The Pursuit of Happiness: Family and Values in Jefferson's Virginia*. Cambridge: Cambridge University Press, 1983.

Link, William A. *Roots of Secession: Slavery and Politics in Antebellum Virginia*. Chapel Hill: University of North Carolina Press, 2003.

Marshall, Anne. *Creating a Confederate Kentucky: The Lost Cause and Civil War Memory in a Border State*. Chapel Hill: University of North Carolina Press, 2010.

Massey, Mary Elizabeth. *Bonnet Brigades: American Women and the Civil War*. New York: Knopf, 1966.

McCurry, Stephanie. *Confederate Reckoning: Power and Politics in the Civil War South*. Cambridge, MA: Harvard University Press, 2010.

———. *Masters of Small Worlds: Yeoman Households, Gender Relations, and the Political Culture of the Antebellum South Carolina Low Country*. New York: Oxford University Press, 1995.

Michaelsen, Scott, and David E. Johnson. *Border Theory: The Limits of Cultural Politics*. Minneapolis: University of Minnesota Press, 1997.

Morsman, Amy Feely. *The Big House after Slavery: Virginia Plantation Families and Their Postbellum Domestic Experiment*. Charlottesville: University of Virginia Press, 2010.

Pascoe, Peggy. *What Comes Naturally: Miscegenation Law and the Making of Race in America*. New York: Oxford University Press, 2010.

Phillips, Christopher. *The Rivers Ran Backward: The Civil War and the Remaking of the American Middle Border*. New York: Oxford University Press, 2016.

Pitts, Yvonne. *Family, Law, and Inheritance in America: A Social and Legal History of Nineteenth-Century Kentucky*. New York: Cambridge University Press, 2013.

Rable, George C. *Civil Wars: Women and the Crisis of Southern Nationalism*. Urbana: University of Illinois Press, 1989.

Resendez, Andres. *Changing National Identities at the Frontier: Texas and New Mexico, 1800–1850*. New York: Cambridge University Press, 2006.

Rice, Otis K. *West Virginia: A History*. Lexington: University Press of Kentucky, 1985.

Richardson, Heather Cox. *West from Appomattox: The Reconstruction of America after the Civil War*. New Haven: Yale University Press, 2007.

Roark, James L. *Masters without Slaves: Southern Planters in the Civil War and Reconstruction*. New York: W. W. Norton, 1977.

Rothman, Ellen K. *Hands and Hearts: A History of Courtship in America.* Cambridge, MA: Harvard University Press, 1987.

Rothman, Joshua D. *Notorious in the Neighborhood: Sex and Families across the Color Line in Virginia, 1787–1861.* Chapel Hill: University of North Carolina Press, 2003.

Rotundo, E. Anthony. *American Manhood: Transformations in Masculinity from the Revolution to the Modern Era.* New York: Basic, 1993.

Ryan, Mary. *Cradle of the Middle Class: The Family in Oneida County, New York, 1790–1865.* Cambridge: Cambridge University Press, 1981.

———. *The Empire of the Mother: American Writing about Domesticity, 1830–1860.* New York: Routledge, 1985.

Sager, Robin. *Marital Cruelty in Antebellum America.* Baton Rouge: Louisiana State University Press, 2016.

Sahlins, Peter. *Boundaries: The Making of France and Spain in the Pyrenees.* Berkeley: University of California Press, 1989.

Salafia, Matthew. *Slavery's Borderlands: Freedom and Bondage along the Ohio River.* Philadelphia: University of Pennsylvania Press, 2013.

Salmon, Marylynn. *Women and the Law of Property in Early America.* Chapel Hill: University of North Carolina Press, 1986.

Schweninger, Loren. *Families in Crisis in the Old South: Divorce, Slavery, and the Law.* Chapel Hill: University of North Carolina Press, 2012.

Scott, Anne Firor. *The Southern Lady: From Pedestal to Politics, 1830–1930.* Chicago: University of Chicago Press, 1970.

Shapiro, Henry D. *Appalachia on Our Minds: The Southern Mountains and Mountaineers in the American Consciousness, 1870–1920.* Chapel Hill: University of North Carolina Press, 1995.

Sheehan-Dean, Aaron. *Why Confederates Fought: Family and Nation in Civil War Virginia.* Chapel Hill: University of North Carolina Press, 2007.

Silber, Nina. *Gender and the Sectional Conflict.* Chapel Hill: University of North Carolina Press, 2008.

Silkenat, David. *Moments of Despair: Suicide, Divorce and Debt in Civil War Era North Carolina.* Chapel Hill: University of North Carolina Press, 2011.

Sklar, Kathryn. *Catherine Beecher: A Study in American Domesticity.* New Haven: Yale University Press, 1973.

Snell, Mark A. *West Virginia and the Civil War: Mountaineers Are Always Free.* Charleston, SC: History Press, 2011.

Stanley, Amy Dru. *From Bondage to Contract: Wage, Labor, Marriage, and the Market in the Age of Slave Emancipation.* Cambridge: Cambridge University Press, 1998.

Stansell, Christine. *City of Women: Sex and Class in New York, 1789–1860.* Urbana: University of Illinois Press, 1987.

Sternhell, Yael A. *Routes of War: The World of Movement in the Confederate South.* Cambridge, MA: Harvard University Press, 2012.

Stevenson, Brenda. *Life in Black and White: Family and Community in the Slave South.* New York: Oxford University Press, 1997.

Stone, Lawrence. *The Family, Sex and Marriage in England, 1500–1800.* New York: Harper and Row, 1979.

Strasser, Susan. *Never Done: A History of American Housework.* New York: Pantheon, 1982.

Takagi, Midori. *"Rearing Wolves to Our Own Destruction": Slavery in Richmond, Virginia, 1782–1865.* Charlottesville: University of Virginia Press, 1999.

Taylor, Amy Murrell. *The Divided Family in Civil War America.* Chapel Hill: University of North Carolina Press, 2005.

Tosh, John. *A Man's Place: Masculinity and the Middle-Class Home in Victorian England.* New Haven: Yale University Press, 1999.

Ulrich, Laurel Thatcher. *Good Wives: Image and Reality in the Lives of Women in Northern New England, 1650–1750.* New York: Vintage, 1990.

Vance, J. D. *Hillbilly Elegy: A Memoir of a Family and Culture in Crisis.* New York: HarperCollins, 2016.

Varon, Elizabeth. *We Mean to be Counted: White Women and Politics in Antebellum Virginia.* Chapel Hill: University of North Carolina Press, 1998.

Warbasse, Elizabeth Bowles. *The Changing Legal Rights of Married Women: 1800–1861.* New York: Garland, 1987.

Weiner, Marli Frances. *Mistresses and Slaves: Plantation Women in South Carolina, 1830–80.* Urbana: University of Illinois Press, 1998.

Wells, Jonathan Daniel. *The Origins of the Southern Middle Class: 1800–1861.* Chapel Hill: University of North Carolina Press, 2004.

Whisnant, David. *All That is Native and Fine: The Politics of Culture in an American Region.* Chapel Hill: University of North Carolina Press, 1983.

White, Deborah Gray. *Ar'n't I a Woman?: Female Slaves in the Plantation South.* New York: Norton, 1985.

Whites, LeeAnn. *The Civil War as Crisis in Gender: Augusta, Georgia, 1860–1890.* Athens: University of Georgia Press, 1995.

Whites, LeeAnn, and Alecia P. Long, eds. *Occupied Women: Gender, Military Occupation, and the American Civil War.* Baton Rouge: Louisiana State University Press, 2009.

Willey, William P. *An Inside View of the Formation of the State of West Virginia.* Wheeling, WV: The News Pub. Co., 1901.

Williams, John Alexander. *West Virginia: A Bicentennial History.* New York: W. W. Norton, 1976.

Wires, Richard. *The Divorce Issue and Reform in Nineteenth-Century Indiana.* Muncie, IN: Ball State University, 1967.

Wyatt-Brown, Bertram. *The Shaping of Southern Culture: Honor, Grace, and War, 1760s–1880s.* Chapel Hill: University of North Carolina Press, 2001.

———. *Southern Honor: Ethics and Behavior in the Old South.* New York: Oxford University Press, 1982.

Articles

Barton, Keith C. "'Good Cooks and Washers': Slave Hiring, Domestic Labor, and the Market in Bourbon County, Kentucky." *Journal of American History* 84, no. 2 (September 1997): 436–460.

Basch, Norma. "Relief in the Premises: Divorce as a Woman's Remedy in New York and Indiana, 1815–1870." *Law and History Review* 8, no. 1 (Spring 1990): 1–24.

Buckley, Thomas E. "'Placed in the Power of Violence': The Divorce Petition of Evelina Gregory Roane, 1824." *Virginia Magazine of History and Biography* 100, no. 1 (January 1992): 29–78.

Bynum, Victoria. "Reshaping the Bonds of Womanhood: Divorce in Reconstruction North Carolina," in *Divided Houses: Gender and the Civil War*, edited by Catherine Clinton and Nina Silber, 320–333. New York: Oxford University Press, 1992.

Cashin, Joan. "'Since the War Broke Out': The Marriage of Kate and William McClure," in *Divided Houses: Gender and the Civil War*, edited by Catherine Clinton and Nina Silber. New York: Oxford University Press, 1992.

Censer, Jane Turner. "'Smiling through her Tears': Ante-Bellum Southern Women and Divorce." *American Journal of Legal History* 25 (January 1982): 114–134.

Clinton, Catherine. "'Public Women' and Sexual Politics during the American Civil War," in *Battle Scars: Gender and Sexuality in the American Civil War*, edited by Catherine Clinton and Nina Silber, 61–77. New York: Oxford University Press, 2006.

Cole, Stephanie. "Servants and Slaves in Louisville: Race, Ethnicity, and Household Labor in an Antebellum Border City." *Ohio Valley History* 11, no. 1 (Spring 2011): 3–25.

Cott, Nancy F. "Divorce and the Changing Status of Women in Eighteenth-Century Massachusetts." *William and Mary Quarterly* 33 (1976): 586–614.

Davis, Rebecca L. "'Not Marriage at All, but Simple Harlotry': The Companionate Marriage Controversy." *Journal of American History* 94, no. 4 (2008): 1137–1163.

Edwards, Laura F. "'The Marriage Covenant Is at the Foundation of All Our Rights': The Politics of Slavery Marriages in North Carolina after Emancipation." *Law and History Review* 14 (1996): 81–124.

———. "The Politics of Marriage and Households in North Carolina during Reconstruction," in *Jumpin' Jim Crow: Southern Politics from Civil War to Civil Rights*, edited by Jane Dailey, Glenda Elizabeth Gilmore, and Bryant Simon, 7–27. Princeton: Princeton University Press, 2000.

Ely, James W., Jr., and David J. Bodenhamer. "Regionalism and the Legal History of the South," in *Ambivalent Legacy: A Legal History of the South*, edited by David J. Bodenhamer and James W. Ely Jr., 3–49. Jackson: University Press of Mississippi, 1984.

Fellman, Michael. "Women and Guerrilla Warfare," in *Divided Houses: Gender and the Civil War*, edited by Catherine Clinton and Nina Silber, 147–165. New York: Oxford University Press, 1992.

Fones-Wolf, Ken. "Caught between Revolutions: Wheeling Germans in the Civil War Era," in *Transnational West Virginia: Ethnic Communities and Economic Change, 1840–1940*, edited by Ken Fones-Wolf and Ronald L. Lewis, 19–40. Morgantown: West Virginia University Press, 2003.

Friedman, Lawrence M. "Rights of Passage: Divorce Law in Historical Perspective." *Oregon Law Review* 63 (1984): 649–669.

Goodheart, Lawrence B., Neil Hanks, and Elizabeth Johnson. "'An Act for the Relief of Females . . .': Divorce and the Changing Legal Status of Women in Tennessee, 1796–1860, Part 1," *Tennessee Historical Quarterly* 44, no. 3 (Fall 1985): 318–339.

Griswold, Robert L. "Divorce and the Legal Redefinition of Victorian Manhood," in *Meanings for Manhood: Construction of Masculinity in Victorian America*, edited by Mark Carnes and Clyde Griffin, 205–211. Chicago: University of Chicago Press, 1990.

Howe, Barbara J. "Patient Laborers: Women at Work in the Formal Economy of West(ern) Virginia," in *Neither Lady nor Slave: Working Women in the Old South*, edited by Susanna Delfino and Michele Gillespie, 121–151. Chapel Hill: University of North Carolina Press, 2002.

Kerber, Linda K. "Separate Spheres, Female Worlds, Woman's Place: The Rhetoric of Women's History." *Journal of American History* 75 (June 1988): 9–39.

Lebsock, Suzanne. "Radical Reconstruction and the Property Rights of Southern Women." *Journal of Southern History* 43 (May 1977): 195–216.

Mann, Ralph. "Diversity in the Antebellum Appalachian South: Four Farm Communities in Tazewell County, Virginia," in *Appalachia in the Making: The Mountain South in the Nineteenth Century*, edited by Mary Beth Pudup, Dwight B. Billings, and Altina L. Waller, 132–162. Chapel Hill: University of North Carolina Press, 1995.

McKinney, Gordon B. "Women's Role in Civil War Western North Carolina." *North Carolina Historical Review* 69 (Spring 1978): 209–245.

Morgan, Philip D., and Michael L. Nicholls. "Slaves in Piedmont Virginia, 1720–1790." *William and Mary Quarterly* 46, no. 2 (April 1989): 211–251.

Riley, Glenda. "Legislative Divorce in Virginia, 1803–1850." *Journal of the Early Republic* 11, no. 1 (Spring 1991): 51–67.

Rothman, Joshua. "'To Be Freed from Thate Curs and Let at Liberty': Interracial Adultery and Divorce in Antebellum Virginia." *Virginia Magazine of History and Biography* 106 (Autumn 1998): 443–481.

Sachs, Honor. "The Myth of the Abandoned Wife: Married Women's Agency and the Legal Narrative of Gender in Eighteenth-Century Kentucky." *Ohio Valley History* 3, no. 4 (2003): 3–20.

Schwartzberg, Beverly. "'Lots of Them Did That': Desertion, Bigamy, and Marital Fluidity in Late-Nineteenth-Century America." *Journal of Social History* 37, no. 3 (2004): 573–600.

Shammas, Carole. "Re-Assessing the Married Women's Property Acts." *Journal of Women's History* 6, no. 1 (Spring 1994): 9–30.

Sievens, Mary Beth. "'The Wicked Agency of Others': Community, Law, and Marital Conflict in Vermont, 1790–1830." *Journal of the Early Republic* 21, no. 1 (Spring 2001): 19.

Smith-Rosenberg, Carroll. "The Female World of Love and Ritual: Relations between Women in Nineteenth-Century America." *Signs* 1, no. 1 (Autumn 1975): 1–29.

Spindel, Donna J. "Women's Legal Rights in West Virginia, 1863–1984." *West Virginia History* 51 (1992): 29–42.

Stewart, Bruce E. "Select Men of Sober and Industrious Habits: Alcohol Reform and Social Conflict in Antebellum Appalachia." *Journal of Southern History* 73, no. 2 (May 2007): 289–322.

Streater, Kristen L. "'She-Rebels' on the Supply Line: Gender Conventions in Civil War Kentucky" in *Occupied Women: Gender, Military Occupation, and the American Civil War*, edited by LeeAnn Whites and Alecia P. Long. Baton Rouge: Louisiana State University Press, 2009.

Welter, Barbara. "The Cult of True Womanhood: 1820–1860." *American Quarterly* 18, no. 2, part 1 (Summer 1966): 151–174.

Whites, LeeAnn. "'Corresponding with the Enemy': Mobilizing the Relational Field of Battle in St. Louis," in *Occupied Women: Gender, Military Occupation, and the American Civil War*, edited by LeeAnn Whites and Alecia P. Long, 103–116. Baton Rouge: Louisiana State University Press, 2009.

Whites, LeeAnn, and Alecia P. Long. "Introduction," in *Occupied Women: Gender, Military Occupation, and the American Civil War*, edited by LeeAnn Whites and Alecia P. Long, 1–13. Baton Rouge: Louisiana State University Press, 2009.

Websites

Historical Census Browser. University of Virginia, Geospatial and Statistical Data Center. Retrieved June 14, 2013. http://mapserver.lib.virginia.edu/collections/stats/histcensus/index.html.

Library of Virginia Chancery Court Records Index. Accessed February 2, 2017. http://www.virginiamemory.com/collections/chancery/.

Martin, McKenzie. "Shake Rag." Kentucky Historical Society (website). Accessed January 31, 2019. https://explorekyhistory.ky.gov/items/show/380.

"A State of Convenience: The Creation of West Virginia." West Virginia Department of Arts, Culture and History. Accessed August 21, 2018. www.wvculture.org/history/statehood/statehood11.html.

Theses/Dissertations

Ray, Amanda. "The Impact of Statehood and Republican Politics on Women's Legal Rights in West Virginia, 1863–1872." Master's thesis, West Virginia University, 2001.

Sager, Robin. "Marital Cruelty in Antebellum Virginia, Texas, and Wisconsin." PhD diss., Rice University, 2012.

Streater, Kristen Leonore. "She-Rebels on the Border: Gender and Politics in Civil War Kentucky." PhD diss., University of Kentucky, 2001.

Index

New Directions in Southern History

Series editors
Michele Gillespie, Wake Forest University
William A. Link, University of Florida

The Lost State of Franklin: America's First Secession
Kevin T. Barksdale

The Civil War Guerrilla: Unfolding the Black Flag in History, Memory, and Myth
edited by Joseph M. Beilein Jr. and Matthew C. Hulbert

Bluecoats and Tar Heels: Soldiers and Civilians in Reconstruction North Carolina
Mark L. Bradley

Becoming Bourgeois: Merchant Culture in the South, 1820–1865
Frank J. Byrne

Willis Duke Weatherford: Race, Religion, and Reform in the American South
Andrew McNeill Canady

Cowboy Conservatism: Texas and the Rise of the Modern Right
Sean P. Cunningham

Confederate Citadel: Richmond and Its People at War
Mary A. DeCredico

A Tour of Reconstruction: Travel Letters of 1875
Anna Dickinson (J. Matthew Gallman, ed.)

Raising Racists: The Socialization of White Children in the Jim Crow South
Kristina DuRocher

Rethinking the Civil War Era: Directions for Research
Paul D. Escott

Marriage on the Border: Love, Mutuality, and Divorce in the Upper South during the Civil War
Allison Dorothy Fredette

Lum and Abner: Rural America and the Golden Age of Radio
Randal L. Hall

Mountains on the Market: Industry, the Environment, and the South
Randal L. Hall

The New Southern University: Academic Freedom and Liberalism at UNC
Charles J. Holden

Entangled by White Supremacy: Reform in World War I–era South Carolina
Janet G. Hudson

Bloody Breathitt: Politics and Violence in the Appalachian South
T. R. C. Hutton

Cultivating Race: The Expansion of Slavery in Georgia, 1750–1860
Watson W. Jennison

De Bow's Review: *The Antebellum Vision of a New South*
John F. Kvach

Remembering The Battle of the Crater: War as Murder
Kevin M. Levin

My Brother Slaves: Friendship, Masculinity, and Resistance in the Antebellum South
Sergio A. Lussana

The Political Career of W. Kerr Scott: The Squire from Haw River
Julian Pleasants

The View from the Ground: Experiences of Civil War Soldiers
edited by Aaron Sheehan-Dean

Reconstructing Appalachia: The Civil War's Aftermath
edited by Andrew L. Slap

A Rape in the Early Republic: Gender and Legal Culture in an 1806 Virginia Trial
Alexander Smyth, edited by Randal L. Hall

Blood in the Hills: A History of Violence in Appalachia
edited by Bruce E. Stewart

Moonshiners and Prohibitionists: The Battle over Alcohol in Southern Appalachia
Bruce E. Stewart

The U.S. South and Europe: Transatlantic Relations in the Nineteenth and Twentieth Centuries
edited by Cornelis A. van Minnen and Manfred Berg

Southern Farmers and Their Stories: Memory and Meaning in Oral History
Melissa Walker

Law and Society in the South: A History of North Carolina Court Cases
John W. Wertheimer

Family or Freedom: People of Color in the Antebellum South
Emily West